THE RACIALISATION OF DISORDER IN TWENTIETH CENTURY BRITAIN

to Anna and Derry, with much love

The Racialisation of Disorder in Twentieth Century Britain

MICHAEL ROWE
University of Leicester

Ashgate
Aldershot • Brookfield USA • Singapore • Sydney

Published by
Ashgate Publishing Limited
Gower House
Croft Road
Aldershot
Hants GU11 3HR
England

Ashgate Publishing Company
Old Post Road
Brookfield
Vermont 05036
USA

Reprinted 1999

Ashgate website:http://www.ashgate.com

British Library Cataloguing in Publication Data
Rowe, Michael
The racialisation of disorder in twentieth century Britain.
- (Research in ethnic relations)
1. Social problems - Great Britain - History - 20th century
2. Ethnic groups - Great Britain - History - 20th century
3. Great Britain - Social conditions - 20th century 4. Great Britain - Race relations
I. Title
305.8'00941

Library of Congress Catalog Card Number: 98-71405

ISBN 18014 528 5

Printed in Great Britain by
Antony Rowe Ltd, Chippeham, Wiltshire

Contents

List of figures

List of tables

Acknowledgements

The list of people who deserve thanks for this study is too extensive to be catalogued on this single page. What follows is one aspect of this work that I will readily admit is incomplete and in need of further development.

The staff and students of the Scarman Centre for the Study of Public Order at Leicester University have provided a stimulating and lively atmosphere, in which it has been rewarding to work. In particular I would like to register my thanks to Adrian Beck, Professor John Benyon, Dr Bola Dauda, Adam Edwards, Jon Garland, Dr Mike King, Dr Surajit Mukhopadhyay, and all the other past and present staff who have contributed towards such a supportive environment.

A number of institutions have been visited in the preparation of this book, and the staff working in them have provided vital assistance. In particular the staff of the Public Records Office at Kew, the British National Newspaper Library at Colindale, the Bruce Castle Museum archives in Tottenham, and the University of Leicester Library, have searched for documents and supplied items that have been central to the completion of this work. Jeremy Clay, of the Leicester Mercury, and the staff of the resources centre at the Centre for Research on Ethnic Relations, at Warwick University provided archive material which was of great use. I would also like to express my gratitude to those people who gave generously of their time and granted me interviews which provided a rich source of material for this work.

Special thanks are due to my Mum and Dad, Liz and Ken Rowe, who have always managed to come up with the necessary support to keep me going and who have, at times, shown greater faith in this project than I could manage. I owe an enormous debt to Anna McClure, who has been a constant source of strength and has cajoled me back to my desk and kept my head above water with her humour and enthusiasm.

Michael Rowe
Leicester

Introduction: Law, Disorder and the Nation

Many commentators and politicians reacted to the urban riots of the early and mid-1980s as though such events were unprecedented in British history. The Commissioner of the Metropolitan Police, Sir Kenneth Newman, reportedly remarked that the Tottenham disorders of 1985 were 'alien to our streets' (Benyon and Solomos, 1987: 8), a turn of phrase which might be considered as either especially unfortunate or particularly revealing when one considers that the popular press portrayed the disorders as clashes between black youths and the police. The *Sun* newspaper (6 July 1981) was not untypical of the general press reaction when it exclaimed 'To think this is England'. Politicians of all parties, police officers of various ranks and clergymen from many denominations often expressed the view that what had occurred was an aberration from the law-abiding and peaceful normality of the English nation (Pearson, 1983; Benyon, 1984). The *Daily Express* said:

> People are bound to ask what is happening to our country ... Having been one of the most law-abiding countries in the world — a byword for stability, order, and decency — are we changing into something else?[1]

Such incidents gave some backbench MPs and tabloid leader-writers an opportunity for remarks which distanced their constituents or readers from any culpability for the events, by portraying them as 'outside of decent society', and so reassuring them that they were unusual and irrational, and thus inexplicable and without reason. Such reactions also served to present the disorders as marginal and 'alien' rather than something which has occurred, albeit periodically, throughout British history, sometimes in order to gain the very democratic rights which are held to be threatened by urban unrest (see Morton, 1938; Thompson, 1968; Benyon, 1993). For example, in the nineteenth century, violent unrest sometimes accompanied the Chartists' campaign for the basic democratic right of voting (Pearson, 1983, chapter 7). When Margaret Thatcher famously remarked that 'the British character has done so much for democracy, for law, and done so much throughout the world',[2] she overlooked the fact that many of the democratic achievements she claimed to value so highly were won in spite of, rather than because of, the law of the day.

Whatever the factual inaccuracies of this conception of English history and national identity it was commonly cited in the aftermath of many disorders in the 1980s, as discussed in more detail in Chapter Five. It is shown in the conclusion that this assertion was inextricably linked to the racialisation of the unrest, which is a key consideration in this study. A central argument of this study is that the widespread denial of the social, economic and political causes of the disorders of the 1980s — a denial central to the conservative response to unrest (see Benyon, 1984) — involved the inculpation of the black community in Britain. The fact that substantial numbers of white people were involved in the disorders is in itself sufficient to discredit such explanations. Another problem with this prevailing construction of the disorders by the media and senior politicians is that it relies upon unsustainable assumptions about 'race' and reifies a social construct into a 'real fact'. This analytic point is further developed in the literature review in Chapter One, and forms an important aspect of the book as a whole. Five related themes are identified in the analysis of the disorders considered in this work, and together they represent the contribution that this study makes to wider debates about disorder in twentieth-century Britain. The first of these themes is that the racialisation of unrest, identified in several contexts in this study, is closely linked to attempts to explain public disorder in terms of the personal characteristics of participants, and thus denies, or at least minimises, their socio-economic roots.

Another contribution of this work is to uncover something of the historical precedents for the process of racialisation evident in the 1980s. Whilst the events at Broadwater Farm in north London in October 1985 are described and analysed in Chapter Five, the other three case studies which are examined took place in earlier periods. The events in Liverpool in 1919, London and elsewhere in the mid-1930s, and Nottingham and Notting Hill in 1958-59, are described in some detail and the reactions to them are analysed in chapters two, three, and four of this book. A study of each of these instances of disorder indicates that explanations of urban unrest in terms of the 'racial' characteristics of those involved was a common feature and there was nothing wholly new in the political, policing and media reactions to the disorder in the 1980s. The racialisation problematic that is developed in this text, and explained more thoroughly in Chapter One, forms the theoretical basis of this work. It emphasises that the social construction of 'race' occurs as a process over time, and a key aim of the study is to examine some of the historical precedents for more recent events. The second theme of this study is thus that the historical precedents for the racialisation of disorder evident in the 1980s need to be considered more fully, and this work aims to contribute to such an examination.

A further dimension of the study concerns the popular conception of British identity and political development. Underlying the complex web of arguments which followed incidents of public disorder in the 1980s was a particular conception of British national identity and political culture. It was often suggested, or at least implied, that traditions of law, order, tolerance, fairness and democracy were the prevailing characteristics of British history. Within this framework, the events on the streets of Bristol, London, Liverpool, Manchester, as well as the relatively forgotten disorders in St Albans, High Wycombe, Leicester, and Cirencester, amongst others,[3] were regarded as dangerous aberrations from British traditions. The development of national identity can be explained in a variety of ways, for example by the construction and teaching of a common national history through formal state education (Gill *et al*, 1992; Gillborn, 1995). A third theme of this book is to explore the nature of arguments that have sought to racialise public disorder by suggesting that such incidents are deviations from the fundamental national character.

Following on from this, the perceived threats to national identity posed by disorder may be particularly acute. There are two reasons for this, both of which relate to the role and symbolic importance of the law to both the state and, by implication, to the 'nation' itself. First, the law is one of the principal ways that the state operates and articulates a common interest. Hence, any sustained threat to the role of law can be considered as a threat to notions of national sovereignty embodied in parliamentary democracy, at least on an ideological and perhaps a practical level. Secondly, the law and the legal system are perceived as a symbolic form of the nation. One key aspect of this is the link between the formal codes of the legal system and the monarchy. Not only does the monarch give formal assent to all Acts of Parliament, but the legal system also operates through a *Crown* Prosecution Service and order is often discussed in terms of the *Queen's* peace. It is dimensions such as these that led Gilroy (1987: 74) to remark that 'the subject of the law is also the subject of the nation' and to argue that observance of the law represents a symbolic adherence to the national community. It can thus be argued that serious and sustained illegal activity constitutes a break with the community of the nation. However, instances of mass law-breaking in the form of disorder are often represented as a much greater threat to the nation than individual criminal acts — although large numbers of such acts may be conflated into images of threats to the whole community as for example, in the crime prevention campaign developed in the late 1980s which portrayed car thieves as hyenas, preying on an unwitting host community. The fourth theme explored in this work is related to the third, and considers an often-cited feature of British national character — respect for the law. Once this idea is established in political debate then it becomes axiomatic that urban unrest is 'un-British', and so explanations rooted in analysis of broader social, economic or political factors are regarded as untenable,

Incidents of public disorder have a specific discursive power in terms of the 'imagined community' of the nation when compared to other forms of criminal behaviour (Anderson, 1991). There are various reasons for this, some of which relate to the actual nature of much public disorder. Although other forms of crime may cumulatively affect a greater number of people, and have greater financial implications, urban unrest is a peculiarly public event. Not only does it occur relatively rarely — although not as rarely as is often claimed — but it is dramatic and invariably involves direct confrontation with the state in the guise of the police. Few other forms of crime *occur* so visibly in the public domain, often in the full gaze of the media which can obtain dramatic stories and pictures for newspapers and television. Given that incidents of public disorder pose a perceived threat to the sovereignty of the state, such events become all the more newsworthy and dramatic. A fifth theme which runs through this study examines the role of the media in reporting unrest, and some tentative explanations are offered in order to place this coverage in the broader social context of each period.

A number of related themes have been identified which, when taken together, constitute the main contribution of this work. First, the process of racialising disorder in the 1980s was closely related to a particular understanding of English national identity. The central dimensions of this view of national character are the rule of law, orderliness, tolerance, and parliamentary democracy. It will be shown that these arguments have been frequently mustered in response to previous incidents of disorder this century. This ties in with the second theme of this study, which is that the historical precedents of the racialisation of disorder need to be fully considered in order better to appreciate more recent developments. This study aims to contribute to such an examination. A third theme is an exploration of arguments that have sought historically to racialise unrest by suggesting that such events are incompatible with the fundamental national character. Closely related to this is the fourth theme, which is that an important dimension of British national character is often held to be obedience to the law. Contentious though it may be, once this idea is established it becomes relatively easy to argue that public disorder is incompatible with national traditions, and so alternative explanations of unrest rooted in analysis of British social or political problems can be marginalised. An important dimension of public debates regarding disorder is the nature of the media coverage such incidents receive. Consequently, the fifth theme of this study is a consideration of the media portrayal of incidents of unrest, and this is offered in terms of the broader context in each case. These themes are closely interrelated and their nature and development are explored in the chapters that follow.

These themes run through the analysis of each of the case studies considered here and generate its main contribution to debates about public disorder in Britain. This is that the racialisation of urban unrest in the 1980s, which drew upon historically established as well as more locally specific ideas about 'race', was an integral feature of many responses to the disorders and was closely linked with conservative perspectives on such events. Explanations which posited that the personal or cultural proclivities of the participants were the primary cause were a common feature of press and political responses to the riots, and a central aspect of this argument revolved around images of black youths pitched in violent confrontations with the police. It is argued in this study that, even if it could be demonstrated that a significant majority of those who participated in the unrest was black, the disorders were racialised in as much as the ethnicity of those involved assumed a causal role. In other words, reference to 'race riots', 'black mobs' or 'hundreds of West Indian youths', which appeared in media reports of disorder in the 1980s and are detailed elsewhere in this study, served not just as a description but were invested with explanatory power as a complex series of events was reduced to a single factor: the 'race' of those attacking police lines. It is argued in the conclusion to this study that the racialisation of the disorders was integral to the denial of alternative explanations for the unrest which referred instead to social, political and economic factors.

An important theoretical contribution made by this study arises from the critical realist racialisation problematic that is developed in order to explore more fully the incidents of unrest which are analysed. Whilst the racialisation of disorder was clearly evident in the 1980s, it is argued in this study that the historical precedents for this process played a vital constitutive role in more recent media and political representations. In other words, the interpretations highlighted in this introduction and in Chapter Five formed the predominant framework of explanation in the 1980s because they were historically resonant and revisited racialised discourse that had been established over many decades. By recognising that racialised ideas in any context are informed by an unpredictable conflation of locally specific themes with well-established images and stereotypes this book seeks to provide a coherent and inclusive account of such processes. The critical realist racialisation problematic is considered in more detail later in this introduction and towards the end of Chapter One.

The rest of this introduction is devoted to further consideration of the political and ideological climate within which racialisation of explanations of public disorder in the 1980s occurred, and also to a discussion of the methodology used in undertaking the study. It is suggested here, and in the literature review that forms the next Chapter, that whilst the racialisation of unrest in the 1980s must be understood in the broader context of Thatcherism, the process was a development of earlier approaches to public disorder. One aim of this work is that by charting some of the historical antecedents of the racialisation evident in the 1980s it will be possible to understand in more depth the arguments which were advanced for the recent unrest.

Public disorder in the 1980s: 'hell-bent on confrontation'

Although the disorder that occurred in Brixton in April 1981 may be more widely remembered, the urban unrest which took place in the St Paul's district of Bristol in April 1980 marked the beginning of the inner-city disorders which occurred in the 1980s. The events in Bristol were less intense than many of those that followed and lasted for a matter of hours whereas those in Brixton continued intermittently for several days. They were also less dramatic than the riots in many cities in the United States during the 1960s to which they were sometimes compared (Thomas, 1987). The number of arrests in Bristol amounted to hundreds and not the thousands arrested during the riots in the United States. It is informative to examine the discourse surrounding the disorders in St Paul's because they were perhaps the first distinctly urban confrontation for many years, as opposed to the 'industrial' or 'political' disorders of the 1970s.

Disorder occurred in Bristol on the 2 April 1980 and lasted for seven or eight hours. Unrest began after a police raid on a cafe escalated into street disturbances and only ended after the police had withdrawn from the area — a development which led to allegations from some politicians and in the media that the district had become a 'no-go' area. Joshua and Wallace (1983) explored the details and the causes of the events at some length and suggested that the reactions to the disorder could be characterised in two ways. First, there were those reactions that highlighted urban deprivation and unemployment and, second, there were others that concentrated on 'race', law, and order. The refusal of the Home Secretary to conduct a public inquiry into the underlying causes whilst announcing a review of the policing issues reflected a wider tendency to understand the events primarily in terms of lawlessness and criminality. Fryer (1984: 398) suggested that the unrest at Bristol became 'a symbol of resistance'. The disturbances also became a benchmark in the sense that they represented an early stage in the racialisation of public disorder that continued throughout the decade.

The press coverage of these disorders tended to focus on the perceived ethnicity of those involved. The *Daily Telegraph*[4] ran the headline 19 POLICE HURT IN BLACK RIOT, whilst the *Sun*[5] described 'police injured in a pitched battle with black youth'. The *Daily Mail*[6] ran the following under the headline RIOT MOB STONE POLICE:

> A riot-torn immigrant area of Bristol was virtually a no-go area to police last night. Mobs of black youths roamed the streets after nearly eight hours of violence.

Although the disturbances do seem to have involved many black youths, other newspapers and commentators referred to the participation of white people as well. It is, of course, notoriously difficult to determine the composition of those involved in street disorders. One, imperfect, indication can be gleaned from the arrest figures. Following the St Paul's unrest 132 people were arrested (Joshua and Wallace, 1983: 142). Of those the majority, 88, was black but one-third was white. Many of the newspaper headlines and stories presented an inaccurate impression of who was involved.

The arrest figures may not reflect the composition of all those who took part and therefore must be treated with some caution. However, they are evidence that the portrayal in much of the media of the disorders as a concerted assault principally or wholly by black people on the forces of law and order was erroneous. Even if it is accepted that a significant majority of those involved was black, many of the press images of a 'black riot' were partial and selective. Press stories and headlines inevitably simplify and partially represent real events (van Dijk, 1991), however, it remains to be explained why much of the press and television chose to portray the disorders to their readers and viewers in terms of one major variable: *that the rioters were black*. Other incidents of disorder, for example, much 'football hooliganism' of the 1970s, or the disorders surrounding the anti-poll tax campaigns of the late 1980s and 1990s, or the disorders in various British cities in the early 1990s, involved, predominantly, white people. Such events were not explained in terms of the ethnicity of the participants, and so it seems important to ask why this racialised portrayal was prevalent in the case of the Bristol disorders of 1980.

Racialised discourse was also employed by many newspapers in features and editorials. The *Daily Telegraph* included many of the spectres of the neo-liberal vision of society during this period in the following editorial:

> Lacking parental care many (black youths) ran wild. Incited by race-relations witch-finders and left-wing teachers and social workers to blame British society for their own short-comings, lacking the work ethic and perseverance, lost in a society itself demoralised by socialism, they all too easily sink into a criminal subculture.[7]

This 'argument' implicitly rejects explanations involving racism and discrimination or those which highlight structural social changes as a contribution to urban unrest in many British cities (Hytner, 1981; Scarman, 1981; Gifford, 1985; Silverman, 1985). Effectively, it blames black people for the disorders and suggests that their supposed cultural predilections and behaviour were responsible. This discourse reflects the 'new racism' identified by Barker (1981), although the actual 'newness' of this strain can be questioned since cultural arguments have long been combined with biological themes in British racism (see Rich, 1990). It also reflects an emphasis that was echoed in other debates during this period, for example those around 'race' and 'family values' (Lawrence, 1982).

The identification of much if not all of the black population as beyond the cultures and values of mainstream (white) society was a central feature of the reaction to the disorders. Such a conception served to equate disorder with the presence of certain minority ethnic groups, rather than specific activities of certain individuals, open to explanation in other terms. This amplification of the activities of individuals to the level of attributes of an entire community can be readily seen in an article written by the Conservative MP Sir Ronald Bell in the *Sunday Express* of 6 April 1980. In the Commons debate of 3 April 1980, on the St Paul's disorders, Enoch Powell MP had asked Home Secretary William Whitelaw whether he had been taken unawares by the events. Whitelaw claimed to have been surprised, a reaction not shared by Bell:

> But was Mr Whitelaw really surprised? If so he showed less than his usual shrewdness. Had not Conservative spokesmen often warned ... of the dangers to the community in high Commonwealth immigration? The police were attacked not because they were the Bristol police ... but because they were the people charged with applying the ordinary law of the land to everybody, and they did not exempt the West Indian community of St Paul's.

The suggestion that an ethnically diverse society is inherently incompatible with an effectively functioning legal system was made most clearly by Lord Denning, then Master of the Rolls, in his 1982 book *What Next in the Law?* Denning argued that juries should not be selected randomly because:

> The English are no longer a homogeneous race. They are white and black, coloured and brown. They no longer share the same standards of conduct. Some of them come from countries were bribe and graft are accepted as an integral part of life: and where stealing is a virtue as long as you are not caught.[8]

Shortly after this quote appeared in *The Times*, the *Guardian* reported[9] that Denning cited a trial of 12 black people on charges of riotous assembly as an example of a 'packed' jury where black jurors would not convict black defendants. The two black jurors in the case (where none of the defendants were found guilty) threatened to sue, and Denning withdrew the book, apologised, and announced that his retirement was to be brought forward.

In many respects, such reactions to the disorders at Bristol were indicative of the racialisation that was also to follow events later in the decade at Brixton, Toxteth, Handsworth, and Broadwater Farm. Although alternative explanations were offered in places, they did not usually appear in mainstream tabloid newspapers or in the comments of government ministers. Their interpretation was that the disorder was caused primarily by the problems of policing a multiracial society, as though such problems are inevitable. Such a focus suggested not only intractability but also that the fundamental issue was the presence of the ethnic minority communities themselves. Sir Ronald Bell's assessment, that the police were simply trying to apply the 'law of the land' to an unappreciative community, misunderstood the nature of the complaints about the policing of the locality, which revolved around treatment of members of the black population. These views also serve as an example of the type of argument that followed many of the later disorders which suggested that policing black communities was essentially problematic. After the disorders at Broadwater Farm in 1985, for example, the Commissioner of the Metropolitan Police, Sir Kenneth Newman, was reported as saying that 'in a *volatile ethnic area* what you need is policing that is emphatic'.[10] Apart from the difficulties associated with ascribing an ethnicity to a physical location, such a comment also reduces the problems of policing certain areas to one central feature: ethnicity.

As discussed further in Chapter One, many writers (Hall *et al*, 1978; Centre for Contemporary Cultural Studies (CCCS), 1982; Gilroy, 1987) assessed the process of racialising disorder in the 1970s and 1980s in terms of the broader political and ideological changes associated with the New Right. They suggested that the predominant arguments and interpretations were integral elements of an ideological shift in British politics, the roots of which could be traced back to the economic and political crisis of the early 1970s. Although there were important differences of detail, these writers adopted a neo-Marxist 'relative autonomy' framework which based explanation upon economic relations but recognised a certain degree of independence for ideological dimensions, such as 'race' and racism. These ideas are discussed in more detail in Chapter One.

These accounts of developments of neo-liberal ideology during the 1970s began with an examination of the economic 'crisis' held to have transformed the western capitalist bloc during the late 1960s and early 1970s. The arguments about this transformation cannot be outlined in detail here, but a crucial factor arising was that the prevailing postwar conception of the state was fundamentally challenged. Keynesian welfarism, predicated upon a high taxation and high spending role for the state, which had characterised the period from 1945, became untenable in the face of rising unemployment and inflation. The neo-liberal response to the crisis involved an ideological reconceptualisation of the function of the state, a central feature of which was the creation of a stronger state, but one with a narrower role. An important element of this neo-liberal redefinition of the state role was the macroeconomic switch of emphasis from demand management to supply side policies, which in turn meant that unemployment was no longer regarded as the primary problem for governments to tackle (Gamble, 1990).

Solomos *et al*, (1982) suggested that the withdrawal of the shelter offered by consensual welfarist governments required ideological justification. They argued (1982: 23) that a key feature of the ideological work necessary to engineer consent for these changes involved redefining the nature of the problems facing the nation:

> The idea that 'the nation' is diseased and slowly destroying itself is not new; it has been a recurrent theme in British political discourse. What was new in the sixties was that the threat came to be conceptualised as the 'enemy within' rather than a model of coercion from without.

The racialised discourse discussed in this introduction is an integral part of this wider process. As the quotation from the *Daily Telegraph* cited on page 15 indicates, black people were not the only objects of this New Right strategy. Trade unionists and peace protesters were also identified as antithetical to the national interest, but nonetheless Solomos *et al*, (1982: 11) maintained that 'race has increasingly become one of the means through which hegemonic relations are secured in a period of structural crisis management'.

One way in which this was applied to the black residents of inner-city Britain was by relying on discourse which suggested that they were beyond the community of the nation — beyond the social contract, because they had broken it by their inability to conform to the traditional English virtue of obedience to the law. Of course, this traditional virtue was itself mythical, but a widespread amnesia in respect of Britain's riotous history allowed it to pass largely unchallenged.

However, these neo-Marxist explanations tend to overlook the evidence which shows that disorder has often been racialised in other eras, which indicates that this process cannot be understood simply as a result of an 'organic crisis' of the 1970s. Although the particular context of the politics of Thatcherism is crucial to a full understanding of responses to urban disorder in 1980s Britain, the process of racialisation cannot be explained *solely* in terms of the specific circumstances of a particular era. As argued more fully in Chapter One, the case studies analysed in this work indicate that racialisation draws upon pre-existing themes. Thus, the racialisation of the disturbances at Broadwater Farm, in North London, in October 1985, cannot be explained solely in terms of the ideological or hegemonic needs of the Thatcherite project. Whilst that specific context is important to an understanding of this case study it is not all-encompassing. Although this racialised discourse was resonant in the particular climate of the day, a more historically grounded interpretation is needed. Indeed, the racialised discourse evident during the 1980s was powerful principally because of this historical entrenchment of the themes and assumptions it utilised. The strong connection between the themes of 'race', nation, and gender that can be seen in response to the events in St Paul's, Bristol, or at Broadwater Farm occurred because the discourse was well established in British history and society.

None of the academic accounts of the role of ideas about 'race' and urban unrest deny that the historical context in which racialised debates have been generated in this country are irrelevant or unimportant in explaining more recent events. Indeed, they often allude to factors such as the legacy of the British empire in their discussions of Thatcherism's battle for hegemony, which relied heavily on notions of British national identity. However, the framework adopted here is designed to move the historical aspects of the racialisation of disorder from the margins to the centre of analysis. A key theoretical point advanced in this text is that ideas about 'race' in any one context, such as the aftermath of urban unrest, are formed in the light of prevailing racialised discourse which has arisen over a relatively lengthy period. Whilst pre-established ideas are crucial to the manner in which particular events are racialised it is recognised in this work that the specific local context is also important. One contribution that this study makes is to consider the relation between both of these dimensions in the debates that followed the incidents of unrest.

Consequently, this study explores in more detail how the disorders at Broadwater Farm were racialised and how this process can be understood in terms of the broader context of the period. Moreover, by examining three previous events the analysis can be complemented by a study of some of the historical precedents for more recent incidents. In conclusion, it is intended that the nature of the articulation between racialised understandings of disorder and the imagined community of the British nation in the twentieth century can be more fully understood.

Methodology

In exploring the relationship between the racialisation of disorder and conceptions of British nationhood this study adopts a case study approach. The empirical material that has been collected relates to four specific instances of disorder which occurred in Britain this century. These are:

- *Liverpool, 1919*: the physical attacks on black seamen by whites during the summer of 1919 occurred in many areas, including Cardiff, Tyneside, and London, but those in Liverpool are examined in particular detail;
- *London, 1930s*: the disturbances, both small and large scale, which surrounded the activities of the BUF in many localities during the mid-1930s are examined, focusing in particular on the East End of London;
- *Nottingham and London, 1958–59*: the anti-black violence in Nottingham and Notting Hill, London, which took place at various times during 1958–59;
- *London, 1985*: the disorders at Broadwater Farm, in Tottenham, north London, in October 1985.

There are similarities between each of the events, but all of them have distinctive features. Whilst the incidents in Liverpool in 1919 consisted of attacks on a population of migrant labourers who were perceived as causing social problems, the violence in the 1930s was of a more obviously political nature and involved questions about the position of Jews in British society. The disorders in Nottingham and Notting Hill in the late 1950s consisted of sporadic clashes between white people and some of the recently-arrived migrants from the Caribbean, whereas the unrest at Broadwater Farm consisted of a relatively brief but intense clash between local people and the police.

Of course, the four case studies do not represent 'typical' incidents of civil disturbance, and cannot offer universally applicable lessons about outbreaks of urban unrest. The nature of public disorder, with the complexity of factors found in each particular case, means that any attempt to provide a definitive catalogue of events is doomed to fail. These case studies have been chosen partly because of the differences between them and the fruitful insights that can be gained from the comparison of apparently contrasting events. The rationale for selecting these particular case studies is discussed in greater detail below.

The main method of case-study research has been to isolate a group of similar situations in the hope that some more generally applicable features can be discerned. Hamel *et al* (1993) outlined the development of the case-study method in the work of the Chicago School in the first decades of the twentieth century and argued that the initial influence of this approach was eventually undermined by the quantitative emphasis of social scientists based at Columbia University, New York. The central criticism of qualitative case study methods was that there was a need for an empirically-based, value-free, approach, which, it was claimed, could only be achieved using rigorously scientific techniques, such as surveys and statistical analysis. Hamel *et al* (1993: 20) explained that:

> Case studies were also rejected because of the lack of assurance that any sociological explanation spawned by them would be sufficiently general. In other words, how could one particular case explain a problem in general terms? Even more important, how could such generality be achieved in the absence of evidence that the case study is truly representative?

Yin (1994) argued that this concern with the representativeness of case-study research was misplaced. He accepted that this was an important test for quantitative methods. For example, a public opinion survey is only considered valid if the sample of respondents represents the whole community in terms of certain key criteria, such as age, gender, or socio-economic background. This, Yin (1994: 36) suggested, could be considered as the requirement for *statistical* reliability and was quite inappropriate for case-study research where, in contrast, the demand was for *analytical* generalisation whereby 'the investigator is striving to generalise a particular set of results to some broader theory'. In this study the broader theory developed, which is considered in the light of the cases selected, is the critical realist racialisation problematic, the role and nature of which is discussed in more detail below, and in Chapter One.

This study seeks to explore the contrasting as well as complementary features of the cases in order to understand more about the processes of racialisation. As previously stated, the notion that a definitive selection of incidents of unrest could be studied in order to reveal generalisable insights into the causality or nature of public disorder *per se* is fundamentally flawed. In short, such an attempt would be founded on the mistaken belief that it is possible to define what constitutes 'public disorder' and then compile an exhaustive catalogue of events, places, and dates. Given that this is not possible, the study endeavours to learn more about the way in which racialised discourse has been used to explain specific outbreaks of disorder and the broader social and political implications of this discourse. A particular theoretical framework, the racialisation problematic, has been developed here to enable cases to be selected and to allow analytical points to be generated from the studies of particular events. This framework could be applied to different incidents, and could be refined and developed in their light, but it is not imagined that identical results would be found. This reflects an important point made by Schofield (1993: 202):

> The goal is *not* to produce a standardised set of results that any other careful researcher in the same situation or studying the same issues would have produced. Rather, it is to produce a coherent and illuminating description of, and perspective on, a situation that is based on, and consistent with, detailed study of that situation. Qualitative researchers have to question seriously the *internal* validity of their work if other researchers reading their field notes feel the evidence does not support the way in which they have depicted the situation. However, they do not expect other researchers in a similar or even the same situation to replicate their findings in the sense of independently coming up with a precisely similar conceptualisation. As long as the other researchers' conclusions are not inconsistent with the original account, differences in the reports would not generally raise serious questions related to validity or generalisability [emphasis in original].

The methodology adopted for this study has been derived from Yin's (1994) model of case study research, which prioritises the role of theory in the design and selection of cases and provides a framework for their analysis. This is outlined diagramatically in Figure 1. The critical realist racialisation problematic developed here thus provides the rationale for the choice of incidents explored in the empirical chapters of this work. Four particular features constitute the racialisation problematic. The following propositions are considered in more detail towards the end of Chapter One:

- ideas about 'race' in any one period cannot be divorced from the specific context in question. They are always contingent and never fixed or pre-ordained, but may be used to understand or interpret real material events;

- nonetheless, racialised debates also draw upon prevailing historical discourse which interacts with the specific contexts;
- racialisation is an inconsistent, contradictory, and multi-directional process. It holds mutually incompatible beliefs at once and relies upon diverse myths and stereotypes in regard of different groups. It does not necessarily involve direct reference to genetics, biology, or culture;
- racialised discourse articulates with other themes, of which gendered debates and ideas about 'law and order' are obvious examples.

As Figure 1 illustrates, the theoretical starting point provides the framework for the entire study. It has been used to select particular cases in the following ways. As the first feature of the racialisation problematic suggests, ideas about 'race' have been used to make sense of real events. This clearly applies in each incidence of disorder which has been studied. In three of them (1919, 1958–59, and 1985) racialised explanations were explicitly apparent in press reports, statements from certain politicians, and the responses of some police officers. In short, all of these events were represented in some sense as 'race riots', a term that is applied to such a diversity of forms of unrest that it becomes virtually meaningless, except as a simplistic label which provides a readily understandable interpretation (that 'racial differences' were the cause) of otherwise complicated incidents.

The other case selected (BUF-related disorder in the 1930s) was not overtly labelled in public debates as a 'race riot'. However, in terms of the third criterion in the definition of racialisation above, ideas about 'race' were still evident, albeit implicitly in many cases, in responses to the violence. For example, the debate about the presence and role of Jews in Britain was not presented explicitly in racialised terms. As is discussed more fully in Chapter Three, however, some have argued that the presence of Jews in certain areas explained the events. Even though references to 'race' as an empirical fact rooted in biology or culture may not have been made, these arguments were nonetheless racialised, as the third characteristic above suggests. This reflects the theoretical point made by many authors (Hall *et al*, 1978; Keith, 1993; Cole, 1996) that racialised understandings can be made without direct reference to the explicit nomenclature of 'race' — for example, without discussing biology, genetics, or pigmentation.

Figure 1: The Case Study Method

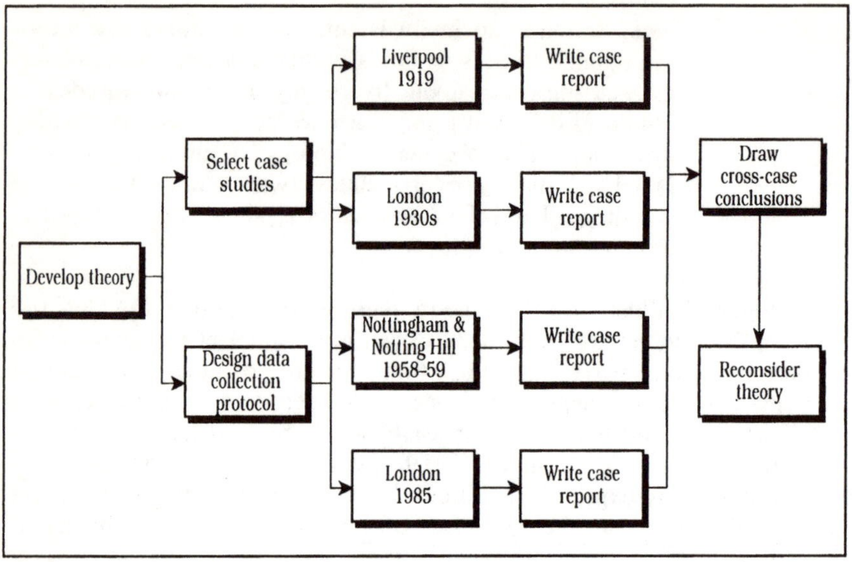

Source: adapted from Yin (1994: 49)

There is another key way in which the racialisation problematic has informed the selection of the particular cases examined in this account. The criteria outlined above refer to the processual and contingent nature of racialised ideas, a point which reflects the argument that 'race' is a socially-produced concept that develops over time in a diverse and context-specific manner (Miles, 1989; Solomos, 1993; Small, 1994). The case studies have been selected with these points in mind. The time span covered by the examples studied is 66 years, and the four sets of events are arranged more or less evenly across this period. Something of the varied forms that racialised discourse take can also be uncovered, in particular the differences between representations of the Jewish community in 1930s Britain and those of groups in the other incidents of disorder.

The notion that racialised discourse is contingent upon wider factors is closely related to another important conceptual point that has informed the selection of case studies for this work. It is partly because of the importance of the specific context in which such ideas develop that there is considerable connection between racialised debates and other concepts. By including varied case studies, rather than a set of similar incidents, it is intended that the relationship between racialised debates and other socially significant concepts can be uncovered. Thus, the relevance of gendered discourse, notions of sexuality, images of national identity, and rhetoric of law and order in British society, with ideas about 'race' may be uncovered using the four case studies in this work.

A variety of methods has been used to gather empirical data relating to the case studies. Primarily these have involved content analysis of various primary documentary sources, such as official records, police reports, newspaper articles, and personal memoirs. Secondary analysis of historical records of the various periods, academic literature, and biographies of key persons has also been undertaken, as have a number of interviews with individuals directly involved in the disturbances. For various, largely practical, reasons it has not been possible to use identical research methods for each case study. The most obvious example has been that analysis of official public documents has been undertaken for the case studies of 1919, 1936, and 1958–59, but this source is not yet available in respect of the more recent events of 1985, under the Thirty Year Rule.

Structure of the book

In addition to illustrating the relation between the theoretical foundation of this book and the case studies selected, Figure 1.1 also outlines the structure of this study, which can be considered in three main parts. First, Chapter One undertakes an examination of the theoretical debates which underpin the racialisation problematic devised for this study. It is explained that this approach has emerged from debates within a neo-Marxist tradition and related postmodernist critiques of an essentialist approach to 'race'. These debates have led to an emphasis on the importance of contingent and specific relations in determining the precise nature of racialisation in any context. Whilst this point is accepted, it is argued that not everything can be reduced to the particular and it is a key objective of this work to chart how racialised discourse has unfolded in four specific instances. Although the local in time and space is important, the broader development of ideas about 'race', transcending any particular circumstances, also determines how specific events are understood. Chapter One ends by identifying four essential themes which run through each case study, forming the basis for the ultimate conclusion to the book.

Chapters Two to Five form the second main section of the book and outline the four case studies. Each instance of public disorder that is examined enables the racialisation problematic to be applied. In each of the four chapters, a basic outline of events, and their background and context, is provided and a critical discussion of the key themes is offered. Although some comparative points between the case studies are made, the bulk of the comparative discussion is undertaken in the concluding chapter, which is the third section of the study. In this final chapter the material is organised around two central themes — the racialisation of public disorder and the nature of political debates about law and order in Britain. It is argued that both features are interrelated and revolve around a particular conception of British national identity which claims that disorder is anathema. In the final part of the conclusion the four key themes regarding racialisation are reconsidered in the light of the evidence produced by the case studies, as Figure 1 illustrates.

In view of the historical amnesia often apparent in responses to the urban unrest in various British cities in the early and mid-1980s, this work provides a further examination of several events which debunk this view. A wide variety of disorders feature in British history, but it is clear that ethnic and religious minorities have often been subjected to violence (Pearson, 1983; Panayi, 1993). Episodes such as the massacre of Jewish people in twelfth century England, anti-Catholic violence in the late eighteenth century, and disorder targeted at Irish migrants during the Victorian era are just a few instances drawn from Britain's history of racist violence (Cohen, 1994; Hibbert, 1989; Holmes, 1991). This study provides important evidence relating to some more recent examples of disorder and explores points of similarity and difference between them. In addition to contributing towards the history of unrest in Britain, this study recognises the importance of placing debates about disorder in the social, economic, and political context in which they occur.

Notes

1 *Daily Express*, 6 July 1981.
2 *Daily Mail*, 31 January 1978, 1.
3 For a fuller account of places which experienced unrest see Benyon, 1984; Keith, 1993.
4 *Daily Telegraph*, 3 April 1980.
5 *Sun*, 3 April 1980.
6 *Daily Mail*, 3 April 1980.
7 *Daily Telegraph*, 7 April 1980.
8 Quoted in *The Times*, 22 May 1982.
9 *Guardian*, 23 May 1982.
10 Quoted in the *Daily Telegraph*, 7 October 1985 (emphasis added).

1 Marxism, Postmodernism, and the Racialisation Problematic

Introduction

The introduction referred to some academic analyses which endeavoured to identify the relation between ideas about 'race' and broader debates concerning law and order in Britain during the 1970s and 1980s, and did so in terms of the wider ideological and political project of the New Right. This Chapter reviews the relevant literature and explores the theoretical positions behind these arguments. Given that most of these debates were within the Marxist tradition, the discussion in this Chapter begins by exploring the theoretical assumptions behind this broad approach. A large part of the Chapter is dedicated to this, partly because of its importance to debates about 'race' and racism, as well as the social sciences more generally, and partly because of the diversity of the Marxist approach. Three main strands, identified by Solomos (1986), are critically discussed — the 'classical tradition', the migrant labour model, and the relative-autonomy approach. The Chapter also evaluates 'postmodern' critiques of Marxism in general and, by inference, the assumptions made about the nature of 'race' in a capitalist society. However, whilst postmodernist positions make some interesting criticisms of Marxism, they also raise other difficulties. One possible way of moving beyond this debate is the critical realist approach to 'race' developed in this book, which utilises a 'racialisation problematic'. The Chapter outlines this approach and considers its relation to the specific case studies which are explored in subsequent chapters.

Marxism, neo-Marxism and 'race'

In order to consider the theoretical debates which impinge on the empirical discussions in the chapters which follow, neo-Marxism offers an appropriate starting point. A full discussion of theories of 'race' and racism is not possible here and others have charted their development in much greater detail (Banton, 1967; Rex and Mason, 1986; Banton,

1987; Goldberg, 1990; Solomos, 1993a). Banton (1967) outlined the emergence of sociological interest in race and ethnicity in the United States in the 1920s and showed that investigation of these subjects was closely bound up with the analysis of urban development associated with Robert Park and the Chicago School. Rex (1970; 1986) suggested that consideration of these features of social life were continued in the immediate postwar period by work developed by UNESCO that was designed to investigate the scientific status of race. When these studies reported that genetic or biological factors bore no relation to political or social differences between different groups,[1] UNESCO commissioned a panel of sociologists to consider the social contexts in which racism flourished (Rex 1986). It was this approach that characterised studies of racial and ethnic relations in Britain during the 1950s and 1960s, some of which are considered in more detail in the discussion of the 1958–59 disorders outlined in Chapter Four of this text. These studies, often characterised as a liberal 'sociology of race relations' (Miles, 1984; Banton, 1991; Solomos and Back, 1996), tended to adopt a social boundaries approach and considered the nature and basis of contacts between those of different races in various areas of social life, such as employment and housing.

A fundamental criticism of this school is that the ontological status of the concept of race has often been neglected (Solomos and Back, 1996). Banton (1967: chapter one) rejects the argument that the lack of genetic evidence to support the concept should deter sociologists from researching the field of 'race relations'. He argues that the repudiation, in biological and genetic terms, of the idea of race does not mean that sociology should disregard attitudes towards it on the grounds that they are at odds with scientific evidence (1967: 4):

> Beliefs about the nature of race — whether true or false — still have considerable social significance, and, when a category is labelled in the popular mind by racial terminology rather than by religious or class criteria, certain predictable consequences ensue.

For Banton then, the fact that many people ascribe validity to the concept of race is sufficient to justify taking it seriously and examining the social contexts in which it becomes an important basis for action. The main theoretical criticism of the work on 'race relations', conducted by researchers such as Glass (1960), Banton (1967), and Rex and Tomlinson (1979), is that they accept the ontological reality of 'race' as a means of categorising human beings. The 'race relations' school focuses on illuminating those conditions where the different 'races' come into conflict and suggests means whereby this may be alleviated. The central advantage of Marxist approaches is that they problematise the concept of 'race' and seek to explain it critically in a socio-economic context. For those who adopt the 'sociology of race relations' approach, the fact that individuals believe in the existence of races is enough to give the concept credibility, even though it may be acknowledged that it has no biological or genetic basis. Their critics adopt a more rigorous approach, as exemplified by Miles (1984a: 232) who goes so far as to reject even the use of the word 'race':

> The idea of 'race' has profound meanings in the everyday world, but these have no scientific credibility and I can therefore find no reason why those who write in the Marxist tradition should wish to legitimate an ideological notion by elevating it to a central analytical position.

The lack of scientific credibility for the term 'race' is one reason why the concept of racialisation, developed in this study, is preferable and some of the 'profound meanings' Miles suggests are associated with it are examined in the chapters that follow.

Choosing to begin this discussion with debates informed by a Marxist analytical framework is not, then, simply a random intervention into the history of these ideas. In addition to the theoretical advantages already highlighted, they have been selected as a point of departure because of their importance to political and academic activity surrounding racism and disorder in Britain during the 1970s and 1980s. As was highlighted in the Introduction, a major feature of the deliberations that followed the events which occurred at Broadwater Farm in October 1985, described in Chapter Five, was their relation to the ideological and political project of Thatcherite neo-liberalism. This link is considered in more detail later in this Chapter, where it is suggested that although it makes some important contributions to understandings of 'race' and racism problems with this approach remain and a less deterministic conception is preferable.

Having explained why Marxism has been chosen as the starting point for discussion it is necessary to echo the caution made by Solomos (1986) when he remarks that significant differences exist between the texts loosely corralled behind the umbrella of Marxism. Despite their differences, the three strands identified earlier share a common focus on rooting explanations of 'race' and racism in a broader analysis of economic, social and political relations. The migrant labour model is the prime exemplar of their shared rejection of the 'race relations problematic' which dominated studies in this field in the 1950s and 1960s, which is discussed further in Chapter Four in relation to the disturbances in Nottingham and Notting Hill in 1958–59. This Chapter moves on to examine the three varieties of Marxist approaches to 'race' and racism previously mentioned.

The classical Marxist approach

As previously indicated, the kinds of arguments which explained the politics of 'race', law and order in the 1970s and 1980s in terms of the broader context of Thatcherism can be located within a Marxist framework. Writers such as Hall *et al*, (1978), CCCS (1982), and Gilroy (1987) adapt and refine economically-reductionist analysis of 'race' and racism in accordance with crucial developments within Marxist theory which came to prominence in the late 1960s and early 1970s (Solomos, 1986). Put simply, the main argument of this 'western Marxism' was the insistence that ideological spheres had a certain dynamic of their own and that they should be treated seriously on their own terms and not just as a second-order epiphenomenon of the economy. In order to consider in more detail the conceptual break that such developments made possible in relation to Marxist approaches to the issue of 'race', it is useful first to examine the classical Marxist approach, found most notably in the influential work of Cox (1948).

Cox argued that notions of 'race' and the practice of racism could only be understood by reference to the economic 'base' of capitalist societies. Fundamentally, Cox suggested, racism exists in order to justify the super-exploitation of one group, such as a colonial proletariat, by another, such as colonial capitalists. This argument relies on the notion that the superstructural forms in a capitalist society, such as political debate, culture, and social relations, are determined by the demands of the economic base, that is capital. For Cox, 'racial identities' and the prejudices which accompany them were inherently subjective and could thus be contrasted with objective class relations. He argued (1948: 336) that 'race relations are proletarian-bourgeois relations and hence political-class relations' and he contrasted them with other, pre-capitalist, forms of social relations such as caste or religious affiliations.

A number of problems can be identified with Cox's approach. First, his notion that racism arose from the need of the European bourgeois to provide ideological justification for their proletarianization of colonial peoples can be criticised on historical grounds. As Miles (1993: 33) argues: 'what distinguished the establishment of agricultural commodity production in the Caribbean ...was the *absence* of proletarianization'. In other words, Cox was wrong to identify the relations which it is claimed gave rise to racism as those between the owners of the means of production and those who commodify their labour and sell it in the market. Instead, such relations were typically those of slavery, which whilst exploitative did not correspond to the Marxist model of surplus value.

Quite apart from the empirical detail of Cox's argument, a number of conceptual problems also arise. Crucially, this approach to 'race' and racism has been subjected to the more general criticisms levelled at the economic reductionism of the 'base-superstructure' model. The reduction of 'race' to a subjective by-product of objective class relations ignores the multifaceted construction of 'race' which occurs at various social sites, rather than just the economic. From a postmodern perspective, Goldberg (1993: 26-27) makes a similar argument when he suggests that:

> Racial definition and discourse ... have from their outset followed an independent set of logics, related to and intersecting with economic, political, legal, and cultural considerations, to be sure, but with assumptions, concerns, projects, and goals that can properly be identified as their own.

The role of the state in the social formation of 'race', for example, nationally through immigration legislation (Layton Henry, 1984), or locally (Ball and Solomos, 1990), is one manner in which the 'superstructure' plays a crucial constitutive part. The economic determinism found in Cox's approach, which gives such formative power only to the 'base' of capital relations, overlooks such dimensions.

Another difficulty with the attribution of racism to economic relations is that the complexity and even contradictory nature of various different *racisms* cannot be reduced to a causal relationship of this kind. 'Race' and racism are not coherent unitary concepts that can be understood as attributable to some other foundation, as though they were just a surface manifestation of deep-seated forces. Cox's conception does not allow for the discursive power of 'race' to constitute and reconstitute itself as a different concept in varying circumstances. Thus, the divergent forms of racism, such as anti-Semitism in Victorian London, racism directed at aborigines in Australia, or native Americans in the USA, or Ugandan Asians in early 1970s Britain, cannot tenably be reduced to a single explanatory factor. The diversity of racist discourse is a central theme of the case studies detailed in the chapters which follow. As Gabriel and Ben-Tovim argue (1978: 132, emphasis in original):

> the complex, changing and at times contradictory nature of racial ideologies *defy* a straightforward reduction to certain forms of production relations.

Gilroy (1990) extends this argument by suggesting that the nature of 'racism' is disparate and so cannot be explained by a single theory and is always contingent and context-specific. Whilst this contingency is acknowledged and examined in the case studies in this work it is also argued that structural features provide similarities between different forms of racism and that not everything can be reduced to the specific. The racialisation problematic delineated toward the end of this Chapter provides the means to consider the interplay between specific and more general sites in the formation of 'race'.

A further difficulty arising from Cox's conception is that there is no recognition of the part that individuals play in construing 'race', perhaps even as a form of resistance to oppressive ideologies (see, for example, Werbner, 1988). Perhaps the most obvious example of this is the rise of the 'Black Power' movement in the United States in the 1960s which invoked notions of 'racial identity' and destiny, for example, through the much older notion of Afro-centrism. Of course, it is unfair to blame Cox for not anticipating theoretical and political developments that occurred twenty years after his book was first published. The relation between 'race' and class is a central concern of the migrant labour model, which similarly suggests that the class position of minority ethnic groups is emphasised above other factors. It has the advantage, however, of recognising that 'race' is an inherently problematic concept and of concentrating on the process of racialisation as the focus of analysis.

The migrant labour model

The debates within liberal sociology of 'race relations' have been fundamentally criticised by the migrant labour model as developed by Phizacklea and Miles (1980) and Miles (1982). This position rejects the approach which suggests that the object of interest is the nature of 'race relations', and also argues that many Marxist writers, such as Cox, rely upon the same premise as liberal sociological explanations in that they both give analytical credence to the concept of 'race'. The only distinction between them is that they use different terms of reference to explain the aetiology of racism (see Miles, 1984a). Phizacklea and Miles (1980) argue that Marxist writers must be prepared to give analytical priority to the role of productive forces in their attempts to explain broader social phenomenon. Writers who insist on the relative autonomy of 'race' are mistaken in that the granting of such autonomy reifies an ideological construction into an ontological fact.

The migrant labour model argues that it is not enough to accept that 'race' has a real and constitutive role in society simply because individuals hold it to be a real phenomenon. Rather, what should be explained is the process and development of this constructed notion. Miles (1984a: 218) criticises both the liberal sociologists and the work of the CCCS on the grounds that they 'attribute the ideological notion of "race" with descriptive and explanatory importance. "Race", for both groups of writers, is a real political phenomenon'.

Miles also suggests that one of the disadvantages of arguments that prioritise the importance of 'race', is that they inevitably marginalize, or even exclude altogether, the role of class. Thus Sivanandan (1982), for example, suggests that the experience of racism is not only the most important defining influence on the lives of black people in Britain, but also that it serves to unite them. This, he argues, makes the black population especially prone to revolutionary fervour and dynamism. Miles (1984a) claims that Sivanandan raises the black population to the position of the vanguard of the proletariat, a point which reflects Hall's (1992: 254) concern about the creation of an unidimensional 'essential black subject', a concern also discussed by Brah (1992). It is clear that other factors also influence the lived experience of black people. Miles suggests (1982 and 1984a, for example) that their class position — most likely working class or unemployed — is also a vital and powerful constituent which should be regarded as primary. Thus, he argues that the history of, first, black immigration into Britain and, secondly, the continuing disadvantage of the black population can be explained by the labour requirements of the economy. He stresses 'the differential location of "black" agents to different sites in production relations and the determinate effects that this has upon political practices' (1984a: 225-6).

A further criticism of this romanticised view of the black population centres around the notion that the common experience of racism serves to unite the black population, which would otherwise be divided by class, gender, and other variables, like any other community. This imparting of solidarity to an otherwise divided group may be an example of wishful thinking and certainly ignores the position of black entrepreneurs, for example, who 'exploit' their workforce, who might be black. Miles (1984a) argues that it is contradictory for an expressed Marxist to argue that black capitalists will feel solidarity for black members of the working class before they feel solidarity with other, white, members of their own class. The conception of a unitary black community also ignores the position of black women who occupy a distinct position within a more general 'politic of dominance' (hooks, 1989: 175).

The implication that Miles draws from this need to avoid reifying 'race' is that the proper object of analysis should be the processes by which social life becomes 'racialised'. The ideological construction of 'race' over time is the key issue, rather than the immutable belief in 'race' which influences day-to-day reality. In this respect the migrant labour model offers a useful development from the earlier theories. By recognising that 'race' is a process rather than an outcome, this argument stresses that ideas about 'race' are essentially contestable, and are fluid rather than fixed. Given this, though, it is hard to understand the continued insistence on the fundamentality of class to social relations. It seems that Miles is trying to have it both ways. His recognition that 'race' is expressed through spheres other than the economic, including the social and the political, is welcome, as is the argument that it is a process rather than a fixed entity. Yet, he still apparently seeks to prioritise the predominant influence of the economic dimension. He still argues from a position that holds class relations to be the determinant of others.

Further examination of Miles' (1984a) criticism of Sivanandan's assertion that race is the most important issue around which the black population coalesces illustrates this point. Whilst Miles' argument that class is also a key factor in the social position and identity of the black population is valid, it is hard to explain why he does not mention the role of other variables. Clearly, he is suggesting that class is the key to the conundrum. Yet, other factors have also been highlighted in attempts to diffuse the notion of a homogeneous black population. The emergence of a distinctly black feminist movement has served to emphasise the role of sexism and gender relations and the 'articulation of multiple oppressions' (Brewer, 1993: 13).[2] More contentiously, perhaps, Gilroy (1993) has stressed the influence of the 'black Atlantic' on the identity of black people in Britain. He uses this geographical metaphor to describe the United States-Caribbean-African-European axis around which black culture is formed. This enables him to explain, for example, the influence of the film *Malcolm X* on the young black population in Britain, or the political effects of South African apartheid on black people — an influence referred to in Chapter Five. Of course, class is not removed from any of these factors either. It is mistaken, however, to conceive of the theoretical argument in terms of an either/or dichotomy between 'race' and class. The nature of human agency and identity is a great deal more fractured and contestable than a simple bi-polar conceptualisation between 'race' and class. The critical realist racialisation problematic developed later in this Chapter provides a framework in which these various factors can be examined.

The nature of the relationship between class and 'race', base and superstructure, is a central feature of the relative-autonomy model. This appears at first to provide a useful way of reconciling the differential influence of class and racism on social life. However, ultimately the model does not provide a way through this particular maze, as discussed in the next section.

The relative autonomy model

Although Gilroy (1987: 18) suggests that 'some of the most anachronistic strands in Marxian thought have lived on like residual dinosaurs in the lost valley of "race relations" analysis', there has been some movement out of the Jurassic Park by those writers influenced by the developments in Marxist theory which occurred in the late 1960s. The problems associated with the economic reductionism discussed earlier are, to some extent, overcome by those who assert that 'race' is not determined directly by the economic base but, rather, that is has a certain logic and role of its own. Most often it is suggested that 'race' has an ideological role in capitalist societies and is not just a straightforward function of capital. One advantage of this approach is that it can more easily tolerate the contradictory and partial nature of many *racisms*. What is more it does not become overburdened with concerns about the 'objective' nature of class compared to the 'subjectivity' of 'race'.

This emphasis on relative-autonomy is usually traced back to the work of those associated with the Centre for Contemporary Cultural Studies at Birmingham University during the 1970s. The most influential texts in this debate were both written by authors associated with this Centre. The publication of *Policing the Crisis* (Hall *et al*) in 1978 and *The Empire Strikes Back* (CCCS, 1982) saw a new emphasis on the notion that 'race' was able to operate independently, at least to some extent, of fundamental economic structures and take on a role of its own in political and social life.

Both books utilise the Gramscian notion of hegemony in order to explain why 'race' became such a powerful and emotionally charged concept in Britain during the 1970s. Their approach relies upon the idea that the structure of dominance and subordination within economic relations cannot be sustained without a corresponding dominance in social, political and cultural spheres. As well as creating the conditions for the recreation of economic relations, the state must also win the hegemonic 'battle of ideas' in order to persuade people that existing inequitable structural relations are not only justifiable but also inevitable, and thus unavoidable. The relative-autonomy school claim that the late 1960s and early 1970s witnessed a period of economic crisis for advanced capitalist economies and that this crisis was reflected and reproduced in political and social relations. This is not to suggest that the former led inexorably to the latter, however. The model emphasises a degree of autonomy for such 'superstructural' features and recognises that they can serve to influence material reality as well as being influenced by it.

The role of 'race' in the response to the crisis stems from the efforts of the New Right to recreate a sense of nationhood and British identity that would serve to reimpose a new social and political order to justify the economic restructuring and reordering of the state that was needed in the light of changing global capitalism. Hall *et al*, (1978) explore the moral panic which occurred in relation to the crime of 'mugging' in the early years of the 1970s. They show that the panic did not occur as a straightforward response to an increase in this type of crime and suggest that the issue can be understood as a metaphor for structural transformations in society, changes which they suggest amounted to a fundamental crisis. They are not claiming that economic problems led directly to the racialisation of 'mugging' but rather that (1978: 333):

> race has come to provide the objective correlative of the crisis — the arena in which complex fears, tensions and anxieties, generated by the impact of the totality of the crisis as a whole on the whole society, can be most conveniently and explicitly projected and, as the euphemistic phrase runs, 'worked through'.

In a similar vein, Solomos *et al*, (CCCS, 1982: 11) argue that 'race has increasingly become one of the means through which hegemonic relations are secured in a period of structural crisis management'.

The relative-autonomy model of 'race' advances our understanding in that it locates the production of ideology in terms of the specific features and demands of particular historical periods. In other words, it overcomes the ahistorical reduction of 'race' to the economic base that was a feature of earlier Marxist thought in this area. By stressing the specificity of 'race' to social relations in a broader sense, allowance can be made for the partial and contradictory nature of the concept. Differences between various forms of racism can thus be explained by the different contexts in which they appear. The nature of the hegemonic struggle over ideology can be considered as profoundly different in South Africa in the 1970s compared to the southern United States in the 1950s, for example, and this approach can accommodate the various forms of racism which existed in these situations without trying to 'reduce' them to some essential unidimensional form. The 'relative-autonomy' of 'race' from the capital base permits a host of forms of racism. Furthermore, the rejection of economic determinism means that the effect of ideology on economic relations can also be recognised and not confined to the status of a merely subjective epiphenomenon. In other words, the effect ideas about 'race' can have upon material reality can be accommodated by the relative-autonomy model.

However, whilst developing our understanding in the above respects, the relative-autonomy model has been criticised on a number of levels. First, it has been argued by Gabriel and Ben-Tovim (1978) that this model is still ultimately reductionist since it relates the ideological importance of 'race' in the late 1970s and 1980s back to the changing nature of British capitalism which was occasioned by the global recession of the early 1970s. This can be seen in the quote from Solomos *et al*, (CCCS: 1982, 11), cited above, which related the ideology back to 'structural' features of society. Gabriel and Ben-Tovim point out that the notion of 'relative-autonomy' is oxymoronic and, hence, ultimately meaningless. As Solomos (1986) explained, Gabriel and Ben-Tovim argued that the continuing, albeit implicit and loose, reliance on an economic conception of racism is unhelpful in that it effectively precludes anti-racist activity independent of a wider class struggle. They argue that 'race' and racism should be conceived as entirely autonomous from the economic system and considered as a purely ideological matter. The problem arising from their alternative position is that there is a danger of resorting to an ahistorical conceptualisation divorced from broader social, not just economic, relations. This problem is also encountered in respect of the postmodern approach to 'race', discussed in the next section.

Other difficulties can also be identified in the model advanced by Hall *et al*, (1978) and the CCCS (1982). The model does not pay sufficient attention to the methods by which 'race' is deployed and understood in society. There is a danger in that the relative-autonomy model suggests that 'race' in the 1970s was manufactured by ideological producers of the New Right and then consumed by the public at large. Broader conceptions of power in society are important. It is assumed that the battle for hegemony involves a macro-level debate of the powerful which produces a particular 'victory' for public consumption. As Jenkins (1994: 199) suggests, the role of the individual in society is also important in the production and constitution of identities:

> identity is located within a two-way social process, an interaction between 'ego' and 'other', inside and outside. It is in the meeting of internal and external definition that identity, whether social or personal, is created.

Whilst the proponents of the relative-autonomy model do explicitly recognise the relation of ideology to the actual experience of the individual — in respect of the moral panic relating to 'mugging', for example — this factor tends to be marginalised by the weight of their analysis which concentrates on more macro-level developments.

A related issue is that whilst it can be agreed that 'race' played a particular role during the period, the arguments expressed cannot explain why 'race' was able to fulfil this role at that particular moment in history. There is an implicit danger that it will appear as if 'race' somehow appeared in a specific form from nowhere in the 1970s which marginalises the developmental aspect of the concept over time. This relates to the previous problem identified in that it is precisely the history of racialisation of British politics over decades or centuries that makes the concept particularly resonant in any era. Unravelling this history is a key aspect of this book and it permits a coherent account of more recent examples of the racialisation of disorder. This history enabled 'race' to play such a powerful ideological role in the 1970s. Again this legacy is often cited in passing, usually by reference to Britain's imperial past, but the development of ideas of 'race' over time tends to be marginalised by the concentration on recent developments. Of course, a contemporary focus is understandable in many respects, but an overwhelming concentration on recent events and issues tends to reduce the history of racialisation to a secondary level. In fact, the longevity of ideas relating to 'race' is a major constituent of contemporary understanding and debate. A major advantage of the racialisation problematic developed here is that it emphasises the processual nature of ideas about 'race', which do not tend to be fully appreciated by the Marxist approaches.

Solomos (1986) offers an alternative framework as a means of furthering the debate. He outlines (1986: 104) a conceptual model based on three premises:

> (a) there is no problem of 'race relations' which can be thought of separately from the structural (economic, political and ideological) features of capitalist society; (b) there can be no general Marxist theory of racism, since each historical situation needs to be analysed in its own specificity; and (c) 'racial' and 'ethnic' divisions cannot be reduced to or seen as completely determined by the structural contradictions of capitalist societies.

In may respects these points reflect the more general disillusionment with Marxism's quest for a grand narrative and anticipates the intellectual shift that some members of the CCCS school have taken into postmodernist analysis which rejects essentialism of any kind. Here, though, Solomos still suggested that the 'structural features of capitalist society' play some kind of formative role in respect of racism, although the precise nature of this role is not clarified. Indeed, Solomos suggests that it can never be defined in an all-encompassing manner, but is instead always contingent upon the particular conditions of the moment. The chapters which follow reflect this latter point and explore the specific circumstances in which disorder has been racialised in twentieth century Britain.

It should be apparent from this discussion that the quest for a definitive theory of racism as a singular concept is ultimately doomed. The particular local circumstances of manifestations of racism render such a search chimerical. It is only by accepting this that it is possible to account for the contradictory and contested nature of different *racisms*. However, some degree of essentialism is inevitable, for otherwise, it is not possible even to begin to discuss incidents of 'racism'. By labelling certain events, actions, or beliefs as 'racist' there is an inevitable suggestion that such manifestations hold something in common with others that are similarly defined. Otherwise everything and nothing could be considered 'racist'. Whilst this degree of essentialism need not constitute a 'general (Marxist) theory' as Solomos suggests, nor can it be abandoned so that any event becomes no more than a local, phenomenon existing in isolation from any other. It is this reduction of events to the purely local level and the corresponding inability to make links between different instances of racism that Vieux (1994) argues has prevented anti-racists from providing a coherent opposition to neo-liberals in the United States, a point considered further at the end of the next section. It is the nature of the relationship between the local and the processual development of the concept that is being considered in the case studies in this book.

A number of points have been made about the varieties of Marxist theory that have been outlined, and the main points will be reviewed by way of conclusion to this section. A central advantage identified in the Marxist approach is the examination of 'race' in its socio-economic context and the emphasis on the importance of more fundamental power relations. However, the structural approach adopted by some Marxist accounts is also problematic and suffers from an over-arching determinism which pays insufficient attention to the specificity and diversity of racism. Although crude economic reductionism needs to be avoided, the Marxist approaches are preferable to the liberal sociology of race relations which preceded them in that they place racism in its context and avoid the assumption that it is a natural feature of human psychology or culture.

The migrant labour model is critical of the traditional Marxist approach on the grounds that it reflects the analytical credence given to the concept of 'race' by the liberal sociology of 'race relations'. Instead it argues that class-based analysis of the labour market provides the key to understanding the position of black people in British society and the racism to which they are subjected. It has been suggested in this section that the migrant labour model's emphasis on examining ways in which migrant labour is racialised as a process over time offers a useful framework of analysis but that this model relies upon economic reductionism, a general feature of Marxist analysis criticised in this Chapter.

Charges of economic reductionism have been recognised by writers who place themselves within the Marxist tradition who have sought to develop a 'relative autonomy' model. This position draws upon Gramscian Marxism and suggests that spheres other than the economic should be afforded a formative role. In other words, the relative autonomy approach posits that the state needs to secure political and social relations, as well as economic conditions, in order to maintain capitalist society. A key advantage of this analysis is that it directs attention towards specific social, economic and political contexts in which ideas about 'race' are generated and so avoids the problem of ahistorical reductionism.

The postmodern challenge

The essence of postmodernism's critique of the (neo) Marxist analysis of 'race' stems from a scepticism towards 'grand narratives' which seek universal explanations of the social world. An early proponent, Lyotard (1984, xxiv), claimed that the essence of postmodernism was 'incredulity towards meta-narratives'. Whilst this may represent an oversimplification of a diverse — and on occasions impenetrable — set of arguments, it is clear that epistemological uncertainty is a central principle. As Callinicos (1989) points out, postmodernism often identifies Marxism as chief amongst the grand narratives representing the height of the Enlightenment rationalism, which is regarded as untenable. In other words, the postmodern critique of the association of 'race' with more fundamental economic relations, which is a feature of the orthodox, migrant labour and, albeit in a weaker vein, the relative-autonomy models, stems from the more general concern with the economic reductionism central to Marxist grand theory. In this section, something of this general epistemological criticism is outlined and related specifically to the study of 'race'. It is suggested that whilst the postmodern position offers some useful reminders about the dangers of reifying 'race' it also raises other problems. Finally, it is argued that a realist position that adopts the racialisation problematic offers a way of moving beyond the problems associated variously with Marxism and postmodernism.

In trying to discuss a range of heterogeneous positions that can be loosely united beneath the term 'postmodern' a number of authors have considered them in terms of their shared critique of modernity (Bauman, 1988; Callinicos, 1989; Boyne and Rattansi, 1990; Lyon, 1994). The starting point quickly becomes the definition of the key characteristics of modernity and, relatedly, the role of intellectuals and their relation to material practices carried out in its name. Bauman (1988: 220) described the typical conception of modernity:

> The grounds for certainty and self-confidence could not be stronger. Human reality indeed seemed subject to unshakeable laws and stronger ('progressive') values looked set to supersede or eradicate the weaker ('retrograde', ignorant, superstitious) ones. It was this historically given certainty, grounded in the unchallenged superiority of forces aimed at universal domination which had been articulated, from the perspective of the intellectual mode, as universality of the standards of truth, judgement and taste. The strategy such articulation legitimated was to supply the forces, bent on universal and active domination, with designs dictated by universal science, ethics and aesthetics.

In many respects postmodernism can be regarded as the intellectual mirror of the grand conception, replacing certainty with contingency, universalism with relativism, and domination with pluralism. Seidman (1994: 119) argued that postmodernism involved rejection of the idea that social theory could provide a blueprint for progress and liberation:

> to revitalise sociological theory requires that we renounce scientism — that is the increasingly absurd attempt to speak Truth, to be an epistemologically privileged discourse. We must relinquish our quest for foundations or the search for one correct or grounded set of premises, conceptual strategy, and explanation.

Giddens (1990) suggested that the epistemological doubt that is central to postmodernist analysis actually stems from the 'reflexivity' at the heart the modernist project. He claimed (1990: 38) that 'the reflexivity of modern social life consists in the fact that social practices are constantly examined and reformed in the light of incoming information about those very practices, thus constitutively altering their character'. A key feature of this process, Giddens argued, has been the application of reflexivity to reason itself, an application that has drawn scientific claims to rationality into doubt. Although Giddens argued that the modernist root of reflexivity precludes the adoption of the label 'postmodern' he did recognise an epistemological problem shared by many who do maintain that a distinctively different paradigm is required (1990: 39):

> Probably we are only now, in the late twentieth century, beginning to realise in a full sense how deeply unsettling this outlook is. For when the claims of reason replaced those of tradition, they appeared to offer a sense of certitude greater than that provided by pre-existing dogma. But this idea only appears persuasive so long as we do not see that the reflexivity of modernity actually subverts reason, at any rate where reason is understood as the gaining of certain knowledge. Modernity is constituted in and through reflexively applied knowledge, but the equation of knowledge with certitude has turned out to be misconceived. We are abroad in a world which is thoroughly constituted through reflexively applied knowledge, but where at the same time we can never be sure that any given element of that knowledge will not be revised.[3]

The mistake of Marxism, postmodernists argue, is that it assumes an objectivity to the world which can be discovered by rigorous intellectual enquiry and used as an explanandum for all social, political, cultural, and ideological forms. In the context of the Marxist conception of 'race' this point is similar in effect to that made by the relative-autonomy model. Postmodernity goes further, though, in that it does not just refute the direct link between 'race' and economic relations it actually challenges the ontological status of the concepts. By throwing doubt on to the modernist belief in rationalism and certainty, postmodernism questions the ability of researchers to arrive at any final understanding of the world they inhabit. Indeed postmodernism holds that the two cannot be considered as though they were separate fields where researchers are somehow objective and divorced from the social situation in which they are rooted. Rosaldo (1994: 171) argued that the classical scientific demand for objectivity is misplaced and that the notion that researchers can adopt 'God's eye view' is naive:

> in my view, social analysts can rarely, if ever, become detached observers. There is no Archimedean point from which to remove oneself from the mutual conditioning of social relations and human knowledge. Cultures and their "positioned subjects" are laced with power, and power is in turn shaped by cultural forms. Like form and feeling, culture and power are inextricably intertwined. In discussing forms of social knowledge, both of analysts and of human actors, one must consider their social positions. What are the complexities of the speaker's social identity? What life experiences have shaped it? Does the person speak from a position of relative dominance of relative subordination?

This said, the postmodernist emphasis on all knowledge being subjective, local, and contingent becomes apparent. Lyon (1984: 11-12) described this attribute of postmodernism:

> The very possibility of acquiring knowledge or of giving an account of the world is called into question. Whereas one could observe how the structure of knowledge reflected the structure of the society that produced it — think of Weber's studies of bureaucratic rationality in modernising Germany — the postmodern denies such structure in either knowledge or society. Farewell to 'knowledge' as once construed; welcome instead to circulating, pliable discourses.

The insistence that social enquiry can seek no more than partial and contestable understandings — which are not, it should be added, intrinsically superior to any other belief system (Lyotard, 1993) — has important implications for the study of 'race'. The contestation that 'race' can only be understood in its local context, isolated from any fundamental causality, which could never be known, is variously considered as a problematic weakness for anti-racist agendas or, alternatively, as offering a pluralist opportunity for previously marginalised groups to enter cultural, social and educational arenas (Malik, 1996: 261-265). This dichotomy was described by Lather (1991, in Cole and Hill, 1995: 169) as the difference between the 'postmodernism of reaction', deemed to be cynical and nihilistic, and the 'postmodernism of resistance', regarded as participatory and pluralist. These competing perspectives have unfolded amongst feminist academics, as well as in other fields, some of whom (for example, Lovibond, 1990, discussed further below) regard postmodernism as a dangerous and divisive doctrine which overemphasises the differences between women's experience, where in fact there are similarities and potential for unity. Others, however, endorse the 'resistance' school, and suggest that the postmodern celebration of difference allows for marginalised peoples, such as minority ethnic groups and women, to engage in the 'new cultural politics of difference', which West (1993, 203-4) described:

> Distinctive features of the new cultural politics of difference are to trash the monolithic and homogeneous in the name of diversity, multiplicity, and heterogeneity; to reject the abstract, general, and universal in the light of the concrete, specific, and particular; and to historicize, contextualize, and pluralize by highlighting the contingent, provisional, variable, tentative, shifting, and changing.

Whilst this ambivalence about the political implications of postmodernism cannot be resolved here, it does suggest a serious problem at the heart of responses to racism. Although postmodernism does encourage the recognition of the partiality, contradiction, and uneven nature of racisms, in doing this it raises other, practical and analytical, difficulties in its denial of grand narratives. Even though it may be agreed that racism cannot simply be explained in terms of meta-narratives — be they biologically or economically based — it is equally true that there are themes which transcend particular sites of racism. As Fraser and Nicholson (1988: 378) point out:

> There is no place in Lyotard's universe for critiques of pervasive axes of stratification, for critiques of broad-based relations of dominance and subordination along lines like gender, race, and class.

The case studies explored in this text indicate this point clearly — the nature of the racist discourse surrounding public disorder are different in each case but are not entirely distinct, and not all can be reduced to local contingent relations. They share some overlapping features whilst exhibiting others which are not replicated in the other instances under review. If different case studies had been examined there would have been, no doubt, other areas of overlap and diverse aspects of each case would have been distinct.

The postmodern insistence that social inquiry turns away from searching for universal truths, whilst making an important epistemological point, runs the risk of reducing all to specific local contexts. This throws up philosophical difficulties in that the convergence of racist discourse across different spatial and temporal cases, as demonstrated in the four chapters which follow, suggests some degree of essentialism is vital to a full understanding. On a more practical level, the pluralism and contingency celebrated by some postmodernists also provides political problems. As has been mentioned, this has been a feature of debates within feminism about reactions to postmodernity. Lovibond's (1990: 172) argument that the celebration of diversity and pluralism is problematic because it ignores the convergence of women's experience of sexism applies equally to those whose identity is partly formed in the face of racism. The postmodernism of resistance is also politically naive in ignoring the reality of social stratification, and the impact of macro-level forces upon individuals lives is unlikely to be challenged. As Lovibond (1990: 172) observed: 'who will do what to whom under the new pluralism is depressingly predictable'. The view that differences between groups in society are the result of a pluralistically chosen identity are misplaced, as Malik (1996: 252) suggested:

> If this were true ... then racism would not be a problem. If we could choose identities like we choose our clothes every morning, if we could erect social boundaries from a cultural Lego pack, then racial hostility would be no different from disagreements between lovers of Mozart and those who prefer Charlie Parker, or between supporters of different

> football clubs. In other words there would be no social content to racial differences, simply prejudice borne out of a plurality of tastes or outlooks.

Similar points can be made in relation to postmodernism and anti-racism. The heart of the concern may be expressed in the notion that, while postmodernists are stressing the specificity and contingency of the concept, racism itself tends to the opposite direction: by relying upon the aggregation of individuals together, on making negative and dangerous generalisations about 'foreigners', and on proposing permanent fixed identities. It may be the case that the racist beliefs and practices which follow from these New Right/'New Racist' (Barker, 1981) positions are ontologically wrong but, as Cole and Hill argue (1995: 167):

> postmodern analysis, with its stress on segmentation, differentiation, collective disempowerment, and its telos of individual desire, serves well the purpose of justifying and adumbrating marketised Radical Right projects.

As mentioned earlier a similar criticism of postmodernism's inability to provide coherent political platforms is made in the US context by Vieux (1994), when he suggests that the neo-liberal movement centring around the Reagan and Bush presidencies in the 1980s went largely unchallenged by a left 'opposition' diverted into a postmodern cul-de-sac. Vieux (1994: 28) argues that scapegoating minority ethnic groups was a central feature of the neo-liberal project and that, in postmodernism, 'one can hardly imagine an antagonist of neo-liberal theory less equipped to do battle with its ideas, in either theoretical or practical form'.

This section has provided an outline of postmodern critiques of Marxism in general, and in particular of the various neo-Marxist perspectives on 'race' that were identified earlier in this study. It has been suggested that the central philosophical feature of postmodernism is an epistemological uncertainty which holds that explanations of the social world can never be more than partial and temporary. When these conditions are applied to the study of 'race' and racism it is apparent that, whilst they offer some salutary reminders about the dangers of generalisation, other conceptual and political difficulties are raised. The chief advantage of the postmodern approach is that it encourages the analysis of racialised relations in their specific local context, and so direct attention towards the plurality of *racisms* rather than a singular *racism*. As is shown in the chapters which follow racialised discourse varies from context to context and can not be satisfactorily considered as a unified coherent process. However, the postmodern perspectives delineated also suffer from fundamental limitations. As many feminist writers have identified in the context of studies of gender and sexism, not all aspects of social life can be explained only in terms of particular discreet circumstances. The case studies examined in this book demonstrate that, whilst there are outstanding differences in the way racialised discourse applies in any instance, there are also important similarities and parallels. Postmodernism is ill-equipped to deal with the structural macro-level dimensions of racism, either conceptually or politically.

Reconceptualising 'race': a critically realist racialisation problematic

This study offers a reconceptualisation of the construction of 'race' which attempts to overcome the problems with the other approaches discussed in this Chapter. The framework advanced here attempts to surmount the prevailing concern with the relationship between 'race' and class. Without denying any link between the two, it will be suggested that the concern with the influence of class on the process of 'race' has led to two serious problems. The first of these is that there has been a preoccupation with developing the theoretical status of the concept of 'race' which has meant that the reality of racialised constructions in particular circumstances has been relegated to a secondary position behind the theory. The second problem is that the influence of other factors, apart from class, has also been relatively overlooked. The influence of the political, the ideological, and the social is examined in the case studies that are considered in the following chapters.

Analysis of the two broad theoretical camps of Marxism and postmodernism reveals an interesting tension between them. The limitations of reductionist explanations of 'race' within Marxism are directly mirrored by the equally problematic inability of postmodernism to discuss 'race' in anything other than discreet isolated circumstances. Both these debates can inform an approach predicated upon a critical realist method (Sayer, 1992). Both Marxism and postmodernism are based upon an assumption that a distinction can be drawn between the objective reality of the world and our knowledge of it. Marxism, to put it simply, assumes that there is a real form to the world which is fixed and can be uncovered. In terms of social science and the particular debate addressed here, it is assumed that concepts such as class, economic exploitation, and production relations have an independent status: they are real and discoverable. The Marxist approach suffers from an over-arching determinism which holds that once a theoretical framework is in place to explain fundamental structures it is possible to 'read off' subsequent superstructural forms, including racism.

The postmodern challenge suffers from the opposite limitation. Whilst the critique of universalism and determinism is in many ways appealing, its explanatory power is seriously weakened. It may be that scientific enquiry cannot discover immutable truths about the nature of the social world, but this need not mean that everything is reduced to mere speculation in an environment where nothing can become more than one narrative account amongst many. Goldberg (1993: 212) characterised the respective weaknesses of both grand theoretical and postmodern theories of 'race' and racism and highlighted their political limitations:

> Universalisms offer the virtues of principles generally acknowledging the injustices of broadly constructed racist expressions. However, they hide in the claims to universal values the inherent limitations of their lack of specificity and they deny the value of culturally construed particularities inconsistent with the putatively universal principle ... Particularisms, by contrast, recognise the virtues of communities, traditions and specific cultural values, but they may find themselves incapable of offering any principled restriction of exclusivist expressions mounted in their name.

The racialisation problematic developed in this study draws upon the critical realist position advanced by Sayer (1992). Figure 2.1 provides an illustration of the theoretical structure applied to the four case studies, and it is explained in more detail later in this section. Sayer (1992: 5-6) identifies some key tenets of critical realism which suggest that the distinction between knowledge and empirical reality is less clear-cut than the debate between Marxism and postmodernism assumes. Whilst this approach concedes a certain reality to independent empirical fact it maintains that an understanding of social phenomena is concept-dependent and thus socially based. In practice social scientists do not increase knowledge simply by continued observation and recording of empirical facts. Sayer (1992: 31) illustrates this by pointing out that researchers could observe for years individuals swapping small metal discs and printed pieces of paper but not understand what was occurring without some, socially produced, concepts of money, price, and transaction.

The racialisation problematic developed here builds upon this philosophical position. It offers a framework which acknowledges the reality of social circumstances which have enabled ideas about 'race' to proliferate. In doing so, however — and this is a crucial point — a critical stance towards the concept of 'race' itself is adopted. This is reflected in the emphasis central to this framework, but very different from the liberal sociology of race relations, which is on the ideas and stereotypes that have developed about 'race' in the particular context of a former imperial society. As Small (1994: 33) has argued, the use of the term racialisation '... redirects our primary concern from "race", "race relations" and black people to "racisms", "racialised relations", and whites'.

Drawing from these points, four related features constitute the racialisation problematic formulated in this text. As outlined in the introduction and elaborated upon here, these are that:

- ideas about 'race' in any one period cannot be divorced from the specific context in question. One implication of this is that, contrary to Marxist accounts, the nature of racialised discourse cannot be accurately predicted on the basis of a pre-existing theory. Instead the dynamics of a particular context inform the way in which ideas about 'race' appear. Cognisance of the local spatial and temporal dimensions of racialised understandings of particular events enables the contradictory and multifaceted nature of racism, which forms part of the third feature, to be recognised;
- racialised debates also draw upon prevailing historical discourse which interact with the specific contexts. Although the 'salience of the particular' (Keith, 1993: 12) is recognised in this approach, not everything can be reduced to the local and the constitutive role of more general racialised discourse must also be considered. The importance of analysing structural and ideological features of racialised thought reflects the criticism of postmodernism outlined above, which was that it was unable to recognise broader macro-level social features that impinge upon otherwise diverse local phenomena. The critical realist approach developed in this study allows analysis which synthesises local and more general features of racialised discourse;
- racialisation is an inconsistent, contradictory, and multidirectional process. Different stereotypes and themes are directed at diverse groups and internally contradictory arguments can be identified. It may be that racialised discourse does not always involve overtly negative evaluation of those involved but, ultimately, the deployment of stereotypes, even where they are apparently 'positive', distorts reality and has damaging potential consequences.[4] Furthermore, racialised discourse may not explicitly refer to biological, genetic or cultural themes and may be advanced in an apparently 'colour-blind' manner. This is apparent in some of the reactions to the Broadwater Farm disorders analysed in Chapter Five, which were often inherently racialised but were presented in

apparently neutral 'colour-blind' terms of debates about inner-city decline, family breakdown, or 'problem youth';

- racialised discourse articulate with other themes, in this work the correspondence between racialised ideas and those relating to gender and sexuality are often highlighted. To some extent this feature follows on from the first outlined, in that the specific context in which racialised understandings are generated will partly determine which other concepts are drawn upon. This process of articulation also reflects the assertion that racialised ideas are complex and diverse.

The racialisation problematic which forms the framework of this book develops the work of 'a number of writers [who] have attempted to use these concepts to analyse the process by which race has been socially and politically constructed in specific historical, political and institutional contexts' (Solomos, 1993: 31). The insistence that this process of boundary formation and identity creation develops over time is of central importance, as the history of this process has a constitutive effect on its actual deployment in any particular period.

It should not be assumed from the first point above that racialised ideas are themselves real or true: the fact that they are built around a belief in the existence of distinct cultural or biological groups means that they cannot be. A common example of racialised thought in the case studies in this study revolves around the notion that the presence of a certain group, for example, the migrants from the Caribbean who settled in Nottingham during the mid-1950s, had a detrimental impact upon the employment opportunities and living conditions of indigenous communities. Now, these judgements — which contributed to very real violent confrontations — could be considered as a mixture of truth and falsehood, fact and supposition, and the racialisation problematic allows us to understand this more clearly. First, the material circumstances in which the white population lived were demonstrably poor. For example, a survey referred to in Chapter Four (Coates and Silburn, 1967) suggested that the St Ann's district of Nottingham where disturbances occurred in 1958 did suffer higher levels of deprivation than other areas. The unofficial inquiry into the events at Broadwater Farm in 1985 also revealed social and economic deprivation (Gifford, 1986). Having reviewed research which measured, counted, and recorded some empirical facts it is clear that there was some reality to the context in which the disorders took place.

However, what also has to be recognised is that the racialised beliefs that held various migrant groups to be responsible for the strained material circumstances were either not true or unverifiable. If an earlier example is considered again, it can be shown, for instance, that migrants from the Caribbean arriving in London during the 1950s were not responsible for the unemployment and housing problems of those areas, as discussed further in Chapter Four. This aspect of the racialised understanding, can be shown to be false, by reference to empirical sources. Other aspects of the racialised discourse are not open to verification in this way, but are a matter of belief, culture, and ideology. A key aspect of the complaints made against the black sailors in Liverpool was that they posed a 'threat to the morality' of white women of the city. As is analysed in more detail in Chapter Two, this was a confused and contradictory complaint, which cannot be tested against fact, since it is essentially a matter of judgement — what does 'threat to morality' mean? Such arguments have been a familiar feature of racialised debates in British society, a fact borne out by their recurrence in the aftermath of the disorders in 1958–59, discussed in Chapter Four. This emphasis on the continuities in racialised ideas over time reflects another advantage of this conceptual approach. As Small (1994: 33) suggests, the racialisation problematic refers to '... a process of attribution which has been unfolding over time, and which continues to unfold'.

The open-ended nature of explanations arrived at via the critical realist model advocated in this study offer a more pragmatic and effective opportunity to counter racism. Goldberg (1993: 214) argued that efficacy in challenging racism should be the key test of theoretical formulations surrounding racialisation and suggested this requires that:

> Those actively committed to resisting racisms cannot define their resistance or transformative projects in terms of abstract, transcendental ideals, atemporal universals or fixed social foundations ... Rather, the emancipatory ideals and the means to their institution must be considered provisional and revisable, situated in the transformative and transgressive possibilities of the sociohistorical contexts in which social subjects generally find themselves struggling individually and collectively.

Figure 2 illustrates some of the key points about the racialisation problematic developed here and its relation to the case studies. The approach adopts the method outlined by Gilbert (1993: 23) whereby, in keeping with critical realism, conceptual tools are problematised and used to examine particular social phenomena. Gilbert (1993: 22-25) suggests that theory can be considered in two analytically distinct ways: as theory by induction, and as theory by deduction. The former occurs when the researcher observes a range of cases, searching for similarities, differences, and patterns, and uses this empirical information to generate

Figure 2: The Critical Realist Racialisation Problematic

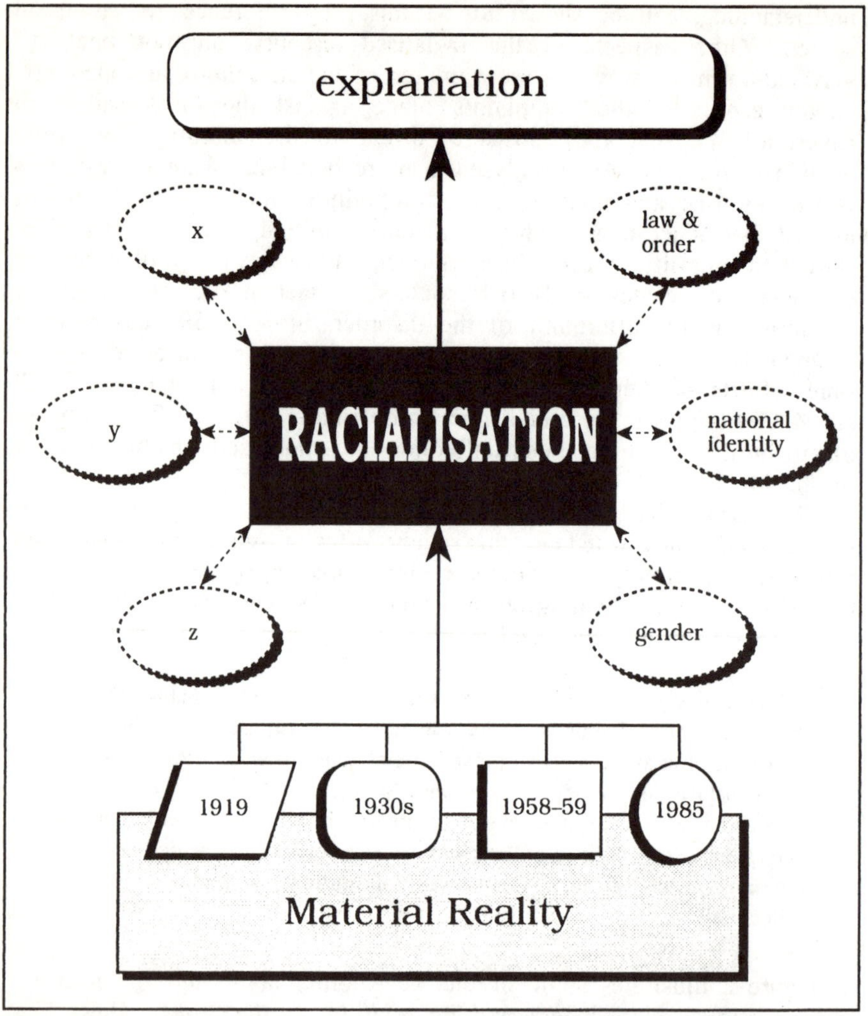

theoretical models. The deductive method foregrounds the importance of theory *a priori* to empirical enquiry — it uses a prevailing theoretical model and applies it to the particular case in hand. Of course, in the practice of research both methods become intertwined: as particular cases throw up data, existing theory is refined before being subsequently reapplied. In this examination, however, the deductive approach is emphasised in the discussion of the case studies as the racialisation problematic is being applied to a new set of situations. By foregrounding the theoretical paradigm, the problematic nature of the concept of 'race', and its status as a social structure, is highlighted.

Having outlined the method which lies behind Figure 2, it is appropriate to discuss the relations between the components in more detail. In the lower part of the diagram are the four case studies discussed in the following chapters. They are grounded in material reality: the socio-economic and political context — housing and unemployment problems, local and national politics, and so on — in which each event occurred. The shapes which figuratively represent each of them are different, indicating that the spatial and temporal character of each was distinct to that case, and that the actual chain of events was also specific to it. It should also be observed that the events are not entirely subsumed within material reality, but that they are also socially constructed and mediated. On a macro-level this might mean that the events assume some broad symbolic role within wider debates — for example, it is argued in Chapter Four that the events of 1958–59 became harbingers of perceived social transformation. At a micro-level, this social construction of disorder may take place around the interactions of key local players or the significance of certain locations to emergent events. Keith (1993) makes a similar point about the importance of symbolic 'frontlines' in the riots of 1981 in London, and it is argued in Chapter Five that locally-produced expectations of disorder were an important factor in the case of the 1985 unrest at Broadwater Farm.

Just as the case studies cannot be completely reduced to material reality, they do not constitute the entire sphere that could be studied using this framework. Obviously, it is important to recognise that other events at other times in different places could have been legitimately selected. According to Gilbert's (1993) notion of 'theory by induction', a different choice of case studies would provide a different account of the process of racialisation. However, selectivity is an inevitable task of the researcher and the rationale by which these particular cases have been chosen has already been outlined in the discussion of methodology in the Introduction.

The racialisation problematic that is being used to examine these part-material part-constructed events is a heuristic device, allowing for a wide range of micro- and macro-level analysis to be synthesised in order to gain a greater explanation of how ideas about 'race' in British society have developed over time and have closely connected with themes of law and order. This is represented in Figure 2 by the various concepts which are linked to the 'racialisation problematic' shaded box. The broken lines which link them represent both the two way nature of this articulation and the epistemological difficulty of considering them apart. For example, even though gender inhabits a different categorical space in this diagram, when individual instances are considered — such as the role of sexual relations in the case of Liverpool in 1919 — it is often impossible to distinguish the dividing point between the two. Those concepts which feature particularly strongly in dialogue with racialised discourse in this study are identified in the diagram. The presence of 'x', 'y', and 'z' indicates that the catalogue of possible concepts involved is large.

Having used the racialisation problematic to examine these particular events, and considered the broader themes with which it has articulated, some broader explanation of the nature of 'race' and law and order is then possible. However, it is not suggested that such an explanation would be valid when applied to all cases. It is worth reiterating that the selection of different initial cases would, no doubt, produce results with more or less distinct findings. In that sense, the postmodern critique of Marxist determinism and the quest for the grand narrative has been recognised, and Gilroy's (1990) assertion that no general theory of 'race' is achievable is acknowledged. The advantage of this approach, though, is that the opposite trap is also avoided, as the co-importance of material reality and socially-created discourse to a full understanding is also acknowledged. The analysis produced can be relied upon with some certainty in terms of the events considered, but its provisional nature is also recognised. The broken line which surrounds the 'explanation' box in the diagram is intended to represent the ultimate transience of the analysis offered and its openness to development and reformulation in the light of future research studies. Following the need to eschew generalist explanations of 'race' and racism, this study reflects Goldberg's (1993: 41) caution that:

> ... architectural safeguards against the theoretical imperative to closure must be built into [the] framework so that it will be open to identifying and theorising continuities or new additions to transforming racialised discourse, as well as discontinuities and aberrant expressions.

Summary and conclusion

One purpose of this Chapter has been to offer a review of theories of 'race' that draw upon a Marxist tradition. It is suggested that all of these share an unhelpful preoccupation that has meant there has been a concern to locate the status of 'race' within a social theory that prioritises the role of class. Whilst there are, as Solomos (1986) argues, differences within this tradition which means that it is not possible to talk of a 'Marxist tradition' in any fully coherent sense, it has been shown that all of those authors discussed share the basic premise that 'race' is somehow dependent upon more fundamental class relations. Instead, a less deterministic position should be afforded to class relations and, relatedly, greater attention should be paid to the reality of particular social settings and the role of other influences. The relationship between conceptions of 'race' and nationalism, culture, gender relations, and the broader political environment is explored further in Chapter Six.

The issue of determinism has been a major feature of the broad critique made of Marxism by those within the postmodern tradition. It has been argued in this Chapter that the resultant emphasis on the localised, specific, and temporary status of knowledge, about racism or anything else, reflects an important feature of the racialisation problematic which is advanced in this book. However, there are significant ontological and political problems with this approach. In the former category is the issue of how it can be possible to talk about structural macro-level dimensions of racism if any reification is eschewed. Second, and in common with many feminists, it has been shown that the political reach of anti-racism becomes much restricted by a position which emphasises difference and flux. As Goldberg (1993: 216) argued, by taking 'race' pragmatically it is possible to:

> ... recognise and respond to racisms' renewals and to articulate broad principles of renewable and revisable social relations committed to resisting the emergence and refinement of racist thinking and practice.

Explanations from authors such as Hall *et al*, (1978) and the CCCS (1982) of the construction of 'race' during the 1970s have been discussed and criticised. To claim that 'race' became a feature of British political discourse as part of the New Right's position in a 'battle of hegemony' during the early 1970s betrays a simplistic understanding of the concept. It is not suggested that 'race' did not occupy a crucial place during this era, or even that this was something which had not occurred to the same extent during the 1950s and 1960s. Such notions of 'race', culture and nationhood were not, however, particular to this era. They were not deployed in any straightforward sense in response to a more fundamental structural change. Rather 'race' played an important part in the ideological struggles of the period precisely because of its historical resonance. If this is overlooked then explanatory power is reduced. It can still be demonstrated that 'race' was an important constituent of politics during this time. However, it is only possible to understand why and how this was the case by examining the term both as a process and as a concept employed in particular contexts. It has been shown that the racialisation problematic allows such insights to emerge.

However, this disavowal of a deterministic conception of 'race' does not mean that broader links cannot be made between these different times and places. In other words, the postmodernist insistence on the local and the specific is also confusing and unhelpful. The advantage of the racialisation problematic advocated here is that it allows for the consideration of the relations between the structural and the contingent, the macro- and micro-level, the reality of social relations and the impact of discourse and ideology.

For this reason, the 'race-class' debate that has occupied neo-Marxist writers for the last two decades or so misunderstands the reality of the concept of 'race'. It is unhelpful to reify 'race' into a macro-level concept and seek an ultimate meaning for it. Identity is in part contingent on context. This does not mean that 'race' can never exist at a more general level or that it is purely a matter of abstract discourse — the construction of black youth as criminal, for example, does influence the criminal justice system and it would be arrogant to suggest that somehow this is not a real experience for many people. Ultimately, however, such general constructions depend upon the existence of a particular context. Essentially 'race' exists in at least two places at once. In a particular context which may not be transferable to any other, and as part of a process of 'race' which has its own momentum and influence.

The implication for the manner in which 'race' is conceptualised may be that it is necessary to avoid searching for a definitive location of the concept. Rather, it needs to be considered in the discreet and specific areas in which it is produced. This does not mean that 'race' does not have any independent identity applicable across time and place but rather that it is always mediated through specific experiences and contexts. One purpose of the following chapters is to illustrate exactly how this has occurred in four particular 'law and order' situations. It is argued in the conclusion that one key feature which spans all the case studies is the strong articulation between racialised ideas and themes of law and order in British society.

The events outlined in the four case studies which have been selected cannot be understood as either entirely based in material reality, nor as entirely a matter of ideology or free-floating discourse. The advantage of the critical realist racialisation problematic is that it enables a consideration of the interplay of all of these factors in and between specific cases without becoming unduly concerned to establish their ontological status.

The analytic complexity that the racialisation problematic allows is reflected in the multilayered and multifaceted nature of the discussion which follows. One central hypothesis will be tested therein. This is that the understanding of 'race' in any situation is contingent upon two distinct, but related, sets of relations. One is the specific locale in which the situation occurs, and the specific nature of the event which can be considered, analytically at least, as separate from other situations and relations. Often this will be precisely the kind of local material realities — such as housing conditions or particular crime problems — already mentioned. By considering discreet instances of public disorder it is hoped that the problem of reification that Keith (1993) alerts us to, whereby the nuances of specific events are lost in the quest for a more general understanding of wider processes, will be avoided. The case studies that follow will examine how racialised ideas informed the reaction of various parties to instances of disorder that occurred in 1919, 1936, 1958 and 1985.

The other set of relations that will be considered reflect the assertion that it is the *process* of racialisation which should be considered. The relatively fixed nature of the Marxist analysis of 'race' was remarked upon earlier and this approach overcomes this problem. In other words, it is suggested that the history of racialised ideas has a bearing on the way in which 'race' is understood and acted upon in any given circumstance. It is also shown, that this process of constructing racialised discourse does not occur in a uniform or linear fashion. Rather, their ideological development is always grounded in specific local relations which will not always correspond or articulate with those that went before. Racialisation does not occur as a response to the needs of the economic base, although this does have some role to play, nor does it reflect biological or cultural reality, although the belief in such a reality is also influential. Instead, the concept of 'race' is continually shifting and sifted through particular conditions and influences. This insistence on the role of 'race' as a process means that Miles' (1993) assertion that some degree of essentialism has to be present, even if only implicitly, is not forgotten. However, the search for a grand narrative which can explain 'race' in all manifestations is avoided.

The relationship between these two aspects of the construction of 'race' is examined in the conclusion to this work. The connections between the process of racialisation which cuts across and influences the various case studies and the specific understandings of 'race' which are particular to each incident are explored. Each case study is influenced by the conceptions of 'race' that have gone before and, in turn, influences those that follow. However, this does not occur in a deterministic fashion, but is always ultimately contingent upon particular contexts.

Notes

1 Rex (1970: 3–4) outlines six key findings of the UNESCO report on the biological status of race: (i) that human populations represent a continuum and that the genetic diversity within groups is as great as that between them; (ii) that observable human characteristics are the result of biology and environment rather than inheritance; (iii) the various characteristics grouped together as racial and said to be transmitted *en bloc* are in fact transmitted individually; (iv) human beings belong to a single species and are derived from a common stock; (v) although different human groups may be loosely referred to as 'races' it is not justifiable to attribute cultural characteristics to genetic inheritance; (vi) human evolution has been greatly affected by migration and cultural evolution and the capacity to advance is shared by all *homo sapiens*.

2 Collins (1990) argued that an Afrocentric feminist epistemology can be identified which is based upon the personal experience of black women and is characterised by emotion, ethics and reason. She suggested that white feminism seeks to question the position of men in social hierarchies, whilst black feminism questions the actual hierarchy of oppression itself.

3 Giddens' (1990: 51) assertion that 'we have mot moved beyond modernity but are living precisely through a phase of its radicalisation' reflects wider concerns that the concept of postmodernity is being applied prematurely. Crook, Pakulski and Waters (1992), for example, preferred the term 'postmodernisation', and suggested that the intellectual shifts described in this section of the thesis amount to an ongoing development rather than a decisive break with modernity. The authors discussed here broadly agree on the characteristics of intellectual doubts about truth, rationality and scientific methods, even though they disagree about the terminology used to denote it.

4 Cole (1996) discussed the extent to which seemingly positive stereotypes should be considered racist and argued that, since ultimately negative consequences result, they should be counted as such. He gives several examples of such stereotypes, including that which suggests that African Caribbean youth are good at sports. He suggested that '... like most stereotypes it is distorted and misleading and typically appears as part of a discourse which works to justify black children's exclusion from academic activities' (1996: 450). Another illustration Cole provided was the stereotype that Jews are an especially intelligent or superior 'race', a perception which, he pointed out, partly led to the holocaust.

2 Liverpool, 1919: '...To Make An Honest Bread'?

Introduction

The riots that occurred in Liverpool during June 1919 were just one of a series of disorders that happened in various parts of Britain during that year. Not all the other incidents were understood in racialised terms. Indeed, there was unrest in Liverpool during August 1919 which occurred during the only police strike that has occurred in Britain. Disorder broke out elsewhere during many events held to celebrate the Armistice. In Luton, for example, the town hall was razed to the ground by rioters angered at their exclusion from the official Peace Day celebrations. The riots considered in this Chapter share many similarities to others which occurred in London, Glasgow, Cardiff, Newport and Newcastle-upon-Tyne around the same time. All were characterised by hostility between white residents and black, largely male, communities regarding, amongst other things, employment on ships sailing from those ports.

The attacks consisted of assaults on black residents in the streets of Liverpool and arson attacks on their lodging houses. In one case, such a confrontation led directly to the death of a young black sailor, Charles Wootton. Wootton was chased by undercover police officers from his lodging house in Upper Pitt Street to the Queen's Dock where a crowd began to attack and beat him. Although the police tried to protect him they were beaten back by the crowd. The Chief Constable's report into the disturbances noted that 'he [Wootton] either jumped, was swept or thrown into the dock and drowned but it was too dark to say how he actually got there'.[1] The inquest into his death could only conclude that he died by drowning, no firm evidence of how he came to be in the water ever emerged. Wootton appears to have been the only fatality arriving from the disorders in Liverpool, although there were other deaths elsewhere, for example in Cardiff where three black men were killed (Fryer, 1984: 303). Nonetheless, the severity of the events and their extreme violence remain apparent.

The extent of the attacks grew so great that hundreds of black people were removed into police custody for their own protection and an 'anti-black reign of terror raged in Liverpool' (Fryer, 1984: 301). One young man, newly arrived in England at the time of the disorders, recalled how the climate in Liverpool changed:

> Suddenly you couldn't go out. White people in groups started roaming and anytime they saw a black man: "There's a nigger, get him!, get him!". They used to come from all over to hunt black people to beat them up. It became a bit of fun for them.[2]

In the report of the Chief Constable of Merseyside into the 'race riots' a detailed description of the build-up in tension and the development of small-scale fracas into more serious and widespread disorder can be found. Several days after the death of Wootton the intensity of the attacks was escalating and three black Americans received non-fatal stab wounds:

> On the ninth and tenth [of June] a well-organised gang, consisting principally of youths and young men, soldiers and sailors, ages of most of them ranging from sixteen to thirty years and who split up into different gangs, savagely attacking, beating, and stabbing every Negro they could find in the street, many of the Negroes had to be removed under police escort to Great George Street fire station for their own safety. When no more Negroes were seen on the street these gangs began to attack the Negroes' houses ... and in some cases they completely wrecked them.
>
> At times the crowd of rioters would number from 8,000 to 10,000 people and they kept the disturbance going on for two days and nights, during which time the strength of the police was so severely taxed and they were so over-powered that no arrests could be effected.[3]

Arrests must have followed at some stage, since further details of the nature of the disorders are found in press reports of subsequent court cases. A report in the *Daily Telegraph* on 13 June 1919 is a typical example:

> Police evidence was that the prisoners were on the roof of a house occupied by Negroes. They broke up slates and threw them on the Negroes, three of whom were badly injured. It was also alleged that the accused had attempted to set fire to another house.

This Chapter explores the reasons why these disturbances occurred and the nature of the reactions to them. The perceived role of 'race' evident throughout these processes is then examined. It is argued that the disorders were understood in racialised terms so that the hostility towards the black victims of the violence was conceived as a natural outcome of a 'multi-racial' community. This effectively meant that the blame for what happened was focused on the black community living in Liverpool. Much of the material analysed here is drawn from national press reports. This reflects the fact that the events elicited little comment from politicians or other sources. First, though, the background and context of the disorders is discussed.

Background and context

The Liverpool 'race riots' of 1919 occurred during a period of extreme social change at the end of World War One and the subsequent demobilisation of soldiers and sailors. Many of those demobilised experienced a stark disjuncture between the rhetorical claims of Lloyd George's 'Land Fit for Heroes' and the reality of unemployment which faced so many. Jenkinson (1993: 92) shows that, between November 1918 and March 1919, more than 2,100,000 'other ranks' were demobilised and reports, both in the media and elsewhere, of the Liverpool disorders suggest that it was precisely this section of the population who were involved in the unrest. The ensuing competition for scarce jobs was undoubtedly a key factor behind the riots and, in Liverpool as elsewhere, this focused upon employment opportunities in the merchant navy, a feature that is discussed at greater length below.

It was this competition for employment that transformed perceptions of the local black population as an important group of migrant workers into a scapegoat for the frustrations and anger of the white rioters. The black population in Liverpool had been settled since the end of the Nineteenth Century and had arrived largely as a result of the presence of the Elder Dempster shipping company in the city. Elder Dempster sailed many routes to West Africa and was a major employer of black seamen who formed a cheaper labour force than could be recruited in Liverpool. One illustration of the importance of the company to the black community in Liverpool is that one man interviewed, who arrived in Britain in 1917, claimed that, as a young boy in Sierra Leone, the only place in England known to him (apart from London) was Liverpool, and that this was because the shipping line — which was so important to the Freetown economy — was based in the city.

Estimates of the number of black residents of Liverpool at the time of the disturbances vary from between 2,000 to 5,000.[4] No doubt more exact estimates are unobtainable because of the transitory nature of a sea-faring community. Unsurprisingly, given their occupation, the community was concentrated around the docks area of Liverpool. During the Great War many of the black population were employed in the merchant marine. Some of these ships were used to bring soldiers from the United States to Europe and others transported foodstuffs and other materials. A group of disgruntled former seamen, who left Britain for the Caribbean after the War, described their role to the Acting Governor of Jamaica:

> for a period of 4 ½ years [we] served in the interests of the Empire ... as soldiers, sailors, merchant marine sea-faring men, sailing to the four corners of the globe conveying foodstuffs and all other war materials to the mother country. When white men bluntly refused to do so we true loyal subjects of the West Indies risked our lives for King and Empire.[5]

As was the case during the Second World War, the demands of the war economy during the period 1914–18 enabled many to enter the workplace who were otherwise excluded. Contemporaneous accounts from newspapers suggest that the black population found it relatively easy to obtain work during the War,[6] as did women, in munitions factories, for example. It is interesting to note that the white women of Liverpool did not feature heavily in the subsequent attacks on the black community and often intervened to try and prevent violence occurring. Whether this was due to a common wartime experience cannot be readily ascertained, although the role of gender in explanations of the riots is discussed more fully later in this work. This reflects a central feature of the racialisation problematic, which is to explore the articulation between ideas about 'race' and other socially-generated concepts, such as gender.

Explaining the disorders

Four aspects emerge in the reactions to the events in Liverpool in June 1919. Most of the evidence has been derived from press reports, police files, and Colonial Office records. The themes are: concern about sexual relations between black men and white women; the competition for jobs; notions of citizenship and difference in respect of the various parties to the violence; and the loyalty of the black migrants to British society.

Fears surrounding miscegenation

Expressions of fear concerning possible and actual miscegenation between white women and black men in Liverpool do not appear as primary explanations of the rioting. None of the national papers examined, except *The Times*, highlighted this issue in headlines or in the first of the articles reporting the disturbances. Rather, the press began to refer to the fears of miscegenation that the white rioters may have had as explanations and accounts of the events that had unfolded began to be sought. *The Times*, for example, explained, by way of background information, that:

> during the war the colony of coloured men in Liverpool, largely West Indians, increased until the men now number about 5,000. Many have married Liverpool women, and while it is admitted that some have made good husbands, the intermarriage of black men and white women, not to mention other relationships, has excited much feeling.[7]

The acknowledgement that 'some of them have made good husbands' only seems to reinforce the suggestion that the more general experience had been less favourable. This reflects more recent arguments that the occasional apparently 'positive' press story about minority groups or individuals serves to reinforce, by contrast, more frequent negative coverage (Searle, 1989).

Newspapers from the other end of the political spectrum also referred to fears of miscegenation. The *Daily Herald* of 13 June 1919 included an article entitled RACE RIOTS: THE ROOT CAUSE, which quoted a Rev Dr F. B. Meyer who expressed his belief in both the 'brotherhood of man' and the equality of the races before God. Dr Meyer apparently saw no contradiction between these views and his claim that:

> a mixture of races must be resisted on behalf of the next generation. Mongrel races were always despised and found it hard to hold their own.

Meyer's solution was that the each race should be held separate and allowed to develop in 'its own country', it is hardly surprising to learn that Dr Meyer's only apparent qualification to speak on this subject is that he 'was at close quarters with a somewhat similar colour problem in South Africa'. Beyond the specific context of that country, however, the question of sexual relations between black and white people — along with the position of any subsequent offspring — has been a central feature of racist discourse since the mid-nineteenth century, a factor discussed at greater length in the conclusion of this study (McClintock, 1995).

The danger posed to the supposed genetic stock of the white 'race' was a popular press reaction to these events. Other examples show how racialised discourse connected with gendered accounts to criticise black men and white women at one and the same time, thus leaving white men, who appear to have instigated the riots, relatively blameless. The *Daily Herald*, 14 June 1919, quoted a representative of the Seamen's Mission who agreed with the reporter that 'sex contributed very highly to racial complications. White women are to some extent responsible'. The *Liverpool Courier* of 11 June 1919 contained two items which demonstrate this conjunction of racism and sexism in its most explicit form. An article entitled WHERE EAST MEETS WEST recounts the reporter's journey into the neighbourhood where many of the black residents lived:

> You glimpse beneath the gas lamps, and somehow you think of pimps and bullies, *and women*, and birds of ill-omen generally' [emphasis added].

The *Courier's* editorial of the same day compounds this perspective, explaining that:

> one of the chief reasons of popular anger behind the present disturbances lies in the fact that the average negro is nearer the animal than is the average white man, and that there are women in Liverpool who have no self-respect.[8]

One story reported a demonstration organised by the Society of Peoples of African Origin which was held in Hyde Park to protest about the ongoing racist violence. This is a good example of secondary groups and individuals being forced to respond to a primary news agenda set by others (Hall *et al*, 1978). The *Daily Herald* reported the following:

> Mr Elfred Taylor, president of the society, referred to allegations of immorality between white women and black men and claimed it was libellous to the women of England.[9]

Mr Taylor has been quoted in a way which reinforces rather than challenges the underlying notion that 'inter-racial' relations are problematic. Effectively this refutation of the 'allegations' relies upon an equally gendered stereotype of the white woman by suggesting that it was unthinkable for her to engage in a sexual relationship with a black man. Such a phenomenon seems to have more recent parallels in stories concerning immigration, a factor discussed extensively in the Chapter Four on the 1958 and 1959 disorders. Often those who wish to challenge the primary agenda which asserts the need for strict immigration controls respond by arguing that the critical threshold has not been reached — instead of questioning the fundamental equation between immigration control and good 'race relations'.

Various correspondents to the press also referred to relations between black men and white women as inherently wrong, or at least unwise. The *Daily Mail* carried two letters on 12 June 1919 both of which referred to this issue. The first, signed only *An Africander Officer*, began by earnestly warning 'young girls and women against association with Negroes', a warning the writer issued because, although many people regard 'negroes' as their equals, 'unfortunately, facts prove that Negroes are merely big children with no sense of responsibility'. This claim reflected the imperialist vision of black people as 'backward races' who, from their state of child-like innocence, need to be nurtured and developed by the white man's hand (Rich, 1990).

A similar view can be seen in a letter to *The Times*, which discussed the possibility of repatriating the black population.[10] The writer began by expressing his long association with 'coloured people' in the colonies and liberally expressed his 'kindliest remembrance' of those he had known. However, there remained 'an instinctive certainty that sexual relations between white women and coloured men revolt our very nature'. An ingenious argument followed: given that 'these men now find white women of a certain temperament encouraging their attentions and allowing themselves to be taken as paramours ... What blame to the coloured men if they take advantage of it?' The letter continued by excusing the violence perpetrated by the white men as an understandable reaction to these liaisons. The only group involved who are not in some way thus excused appears to be the white women who are prepared to engage in relationships with black men.

Myths and fears surrounding the supposed sexuality of black men are a familiar feature of racist discourse and have been identified in many and various settings: from the arguments of those defending slavery in the southern states of the United States of America to accounts of 'swinging London' during the 1950s, discussed more fully in Chapter Four.[11] Such notions were a prominent feature of the reactions to and explanations of these riots and were used as a means to rationalise the racist behaviour of the white men who attacked their black neighbours. It seeks to explain and somehow justify the events that occurred.

Having mentioned these examples, it seems pertinent to refer to a letter responding to that from *The Times* already cited. It represents one of the few refutations of the apparently dominant explanation of these events. The Secretary of the Society of Peoples of African Origin, a Mr F. E. M. Hercules, effectively challenged the complacency of the arguments by drawing attention to the relations between white men and the indigenous women of the colonies. There were, he claimed, 600,000 'half-caste' children in South Africa alone who were the results of such unions. Mr Hercules continues by praising the white British women 'who can see behind skin and behind superficial skin difference and recognise the man inside'.[12] The idea that white women may have been more empathetic to the black men was reflected by an interviewee for this research who described the events as he walked the streets one lunch-time:

> They started chasing me, and a woman said "run, boy, run!". They saved me, in fact I was saved many many times by women: they are more sympathetic than men. A lot of women used to wear clogs in those days, and they took off their clogs [in order to beat the white men with them] and started shouting: "leave him alone! he hasn't done any harm!".[13]

Despite these exceptions, though, the prominent discourse which held that sexual relations between black men and white women were somehow responsible for the disorders were also evident in the attitude of the police, the government, and the civil service, as found in official reports and memoranda. The perception that miscegenation was unwise and provocative was clearly axiomatic reflecting the 'race thinking' of the colonial era. In the section which discusses the introduction of repatriation for the black seamen, further examples and discussion of the gender stereotypes that were at work within the overall governmental response are offered. Before that, though, the second theme in the responses to the disorders is considered.

Competition for employment

As previously mentioned, the end of the First World War saw the demobilisation of millions of men and led to intense competition for employment as they returned to their home towns and cities. Just as those women who worked in the Second World War were expected to relinquish their position to the returning soldiers, so too the black workers in the ports of Liverpool were, in the minds of many, expected to give up their employment to make way for the returning heroes of war.

As with the previous theme, the pressure of unemployment as a background factor in the riots was mentioned by all the newspapers examined, although, of course to different degrees and effect. The *Daily Telegraph* reported matter-of-factly: 'last week more than 100 black men were at work, but in consequence of the disturbances none are now employed, and are thrown on unemployment allowance'.[14] Such discrimination drew no comment from the *Telegraph* but competition for employment was considered by the paper to be an important causal factor behind the disorders.

An article from the *Daily Herald* offers one of the more complex, not to say contradictory, examples of explanations which refer to this competition for employment. The piece, entitled RACE RIOTS: THE ROOT CAUSE, begins with the straightforward assertion: 'the racial trouble — an outcome of the importation of coloured men during the war — is spreading with the return of our men to civil life'.[15] The article continues in this vein for several paragraphs, reporting that men who have fought for their country are being overlooked for jobs which are rightfully theirs. The paper's report that 'they are actuated only by patriotic motives. There is nothing against the majority of blacks', clearly indicates some sympathy with their position.

The *Daily Herald* was, at this time at least, an avowedly pro-union Labour newspaper, alone amongst those considered here in supporting the contemporary attempts to form a police union, for example, so perhaps this view is not surprising. As Carter (1986) has demonstrated, some trade unionists sought to prevent black people securing jobs even as late as the 1970s so it is not unexpected that such opinions should be countenanced in 1919.

This would be a simple deduction if it were not for the complete contradiction of this position with which the article continues. Having backed the claim that white workers should have priority over black workers the article continues by quoting an official of the National Sailors and Fireman's Union who says 'ninety per cent of the blacks are in our Union, they have all along been paid Union rates. As a matter of fact we have tried to get them taken on, but the officers are firm'. In one article, the *Daily Herald* is supporting discrimination against the black workforce and then quoting favourably a Union official who claims that the *employers* are maintaining the colour-bar despite the best efforts of the Union which the paper tends to support. This seems to be an attempt to have the argument both ways by conniving with the discrimination whilst overtly condemning it. The true position of the Union vis-a-vis the employment of black sailors is unclear. The view of the official quoted above suggesting that the Union was against the colour-bar was not the perception of the local police. In November 1920 the Liverpool police reported to the Colonial Office that:

> at the time and since the Negro riots of June 1919 white sailors declined to sail with coloured seamen and the National Seamen and Fireman's Union supported them.[16]

A similar argument was aired in the *Daily Herald* when a trades union official suggested that the solution to the disturbances was for the black workers to be given berths on long voyages and thus removed from the scene of the disorders. The official is quoted:

> if they [the ship owners] took them on a long voyage, as the P. and O. line take off the Lascars, they would not be here to cause the stirring up of *these old race hatreds* [emphasis added].[17]

In this instance as with others, the victims of racist attacks, and even of violent death, are defined as the 'problem' to be dealt with. Those who perpetrated such events are somehow excused on the basis of supposedly primordial characteristics of 'race hatred'. This naturalisation of racism serves to remove negative connotations which might hold those who instigated the disorders culpable. It would have been more accurate, in many respects, to refer to these events as rac*ist* riots rather than 'race riots' but, in 1919 at least, it seems that the press understood that the disturbances were a result of natural differences. As is argued later in this work, a similar conception was evident in response to the disorders surrounding the British Union of Fascists in the mid-1930s, as well as those of the late 1950s.

Newspapers of other political persuasions also identified employment as a key area of conflict between the white and black communities. The *Daily Mail*, for example, in discussing the riots at Cardiff, which were occurring at the same time and were often reported together with the events at Liverpool, offered the following by way of context:

> The coloured men in Cardiff are mostly seamen who have for years been voyaging to and from this country. They seem to have grown more arrogant of late. They have earned good wages and have been able to give free reign to their love of display and ostentation ... Some of the Negroes in Cardiff own their own houses, and demobilised Cardiff men who are lucky if they get a back room feel aggrieved at the black man's flourishing state.[18]

This example is instructive because of the lack of any distinction between the subjective description of the financial well-being of the black community and the apparent attempt to explain the motivations of the returning indigenous population. The reader is clearly invited to empathise with the returning soldiers, especially when contrasted to the 'ostentatious' black population. Interestingly, the report of the local police to the Colonial Office, which was written a day after the newspaper story mentioned above, uses similar language, blaming the events on the 'arrogant and overbearing conduct of the negroes...'.[19] This distinction between the worthy but downtrodden white population and the undeserving black community is considered again in the discussion of the disorders of 1958-59 in Chapter Four.

Reference to similar issues was also made in government documents regarding the disorders, suggesting that there was a certain degree of sympathy with the predicament of the white unemployed workers, although not — explicitly — with their actions. Some months after the disorders in Liverpool, the War Cabinet discussed amendments to the Aliens Restriction Bill, which had recently been defeated on its first reading and was to be re-presented to the Commons. In doing so it was minuted that ministers should remember the 'strong feeling in the country against the employment of aliens on board British ships'[20] and that many MPs had given pledges in the course of their electoral campaigns to regulate this matter. Interestingly, the Cabinet presented this as a matter of 'preserving the standards' of British seamanship, thus attempting to neutralise or deny the more crude racism evident elsewhere. At the same time, however, the government had different interests to manage. The position of the colonies was kept in mind and the discussion recognised that citizens of the Empire should not be excluded and that the standards that must be ensured on British ships need not be applied as stringently in 'distant waters'.[21]

Many of the passages described above implicitly assume that the black sailors were taking jobs that rightfully belonged to white people and, moreover, that they were living a life of relative prosperity. Obviously, this can be disputed as a valid justification for the attacks on black people that occurred. However, there is also substantial evidence that the reality of the experience for black people in British ports was less rosy and that they had difficulty obtaining work and — even when they did find employment — they were paid lower wages than white workers. Details of the letters written to the Colonial Office indicate the discrimination that many encountered. One man, William Samuels, wrote in 1918, before the disorders and during the period when black sailors were supposed to be 'doing well out of the war':

> we are badly treated by the British people ... Every morning we go down to shipping offices to find ourselves work so as to make an honest bread and are bluntly refused on account of our colour.[22]

Another man suggested to the Colonial Office in 1920 that '... you must have heard about Britishers (coloured) both West Indians and Africans ... being denied the right to earn their living'.[23] The response of the Colonial Office to both of these letters was similar and indicative of the fundamental understanding of the riots that is discussed in the next section. In both cases, the government responded by making arrangements to facilitate the repatriation of the correspondents.

Citizenship and 'difference'

Thus far two prevalent themes have been identified in the response to of the riots at Liverpool, and to some extent at Cardiff. To conclude the discussion of this episode an examination of a final theme is necessary, namely the contradictory representation of the black community as citizens of the British empire. The citizenship status of the black community was a central theme, both directly and implicitly, in the newspaper articles, civil service memoranda, and police reports. The position of the black population was called into question by two of the major responses to the disorder. First, the possibility of interning the black community in Liverpool and, second, the concomitant suggestion that they should be repatriated. Both these aspects of the argument served to reinforce the point already made in discussion of labour relations: namely, that the black victims of the disorders were identified as the problem to be dealt with.

The *Daily Telegraph* carried the following report under the headline LIVERPOOL INTERNMENTS:

> There is every reason to hope that the action of the authorities will prevent any further outbreak against the negro colony in Liverpool. To-day an official from the Labour Ministry conferred with the Lord Mayor and the Head Constable, and it was agreed to make arrangements for the internment of the negroes pending their repatriation.[24]

Although the article clearly presented the violence as being directed against the black community, and thus does not directly blame them, the prescription offered with *hope* is not one designed to confront the acknowledged protagonists of the disorders. Rather the solution which was endorsed amounted to the removal of the black people from the setting. The definition of events which prioritised the issues of competition for jobs was clearly shared by the authorities who were, on a national level at least, represented by the Labour Ministry. There was, however, no implementation of long-term internment largely, it seems, because such a policy was regarded as being too blatant a denial of civil liberties. Temporarily, though, a significant number of black people were held in police stations — either for their own protection or as a means of reducing the tensions in the city. The police report states that 700 black people 'took refuge with the police for their own safety'.[25]

On other occasions, however, the press did report the various demands of black individuals and spokespeople who presented their claims as citizens of the British empire who were entitled to respect and protection. As in its treatment of the competition for jobs, the *Daily Herald* provided some interesting material, not least for the contradictory arguments it offered, for example, in a piece headlined COLOURED MEN'S CLAIMS, which reported:

> Arabs, Somalis, Egyptians, West Indians, and other coloured men attended a meeting at Cardiff Docks yesterday to protest against their maltreatment and persecution. At present there are between one and two thousand of these men in Cardiff and they claimed protection as British subjects.[26]

In the relatively lengthy coverage the *Daily Herald* afforded to the disorders, this article contained one of only two remotely favourable references made to the status and rights of the black community. When considering the muted neutrality of this piece, acknowledging only the 'claims' of the black population, it is instructive to contrast this with another article published on the same page, which was cited earlier. This piece reproduced verbatim many quotes from a named union official who suggested that 'the problem itself is ineradicable, and strikes down to the roots of our different civilisations'. Thus, the views of one individual who stresses the inherent otherness of the black victims of racist violence was not only given a good deal more space, but also afforded legitimacy by the use of direct and extensive quotation. Unlike the opinions of the black community itself, such views were presented without comment and were not labelled as mere 'claims'.

Other references to the views of the black community also drew contrasts and a binary distinction between black and white. On 16 June 1919, the *Herald* published an article entitled BLACK AND WHITE IN CONFLICT which referred to a meeting held by the Society of Peoples of African Origin and remarked upon 'the unprecedented spectacle of coloured men appealing to a British crowd for 'fair play''. What makes this demonstration an 'unprecedented spectacle' is that the most British of virtues, the apparent devotion to 'fair play', or to the rule of law, should be invoked by individuals who were considered by colonial ideology to be cultural inferiors, incapable of civilised behaviour. This is another theme that can be identified in the media coverage of more recent disorders: a contrast was drawn between the legitimate values and aspirations of the indigenous white population, and the lawless behaviour and illegitimate culture of the black population. This point is considered further in the discussion of the disorders at Broadwater Farm in 1985 in Chapter Five.

The introduction of a voluntary repatriation scheme as a solution to the 'problem' of the black population in British ports was demanded by the Lord Mayor of Liverpool immediately after the disorders (Jenkinson, 1993). Initially, the Colonial Office refused such a scheme, but it was eventually instigated in June 1919 by an inter-departmental committee consisting of representatives of the Home Office, the Colonial Office, the Ministry of Labour and others. Although established by this central committee, the repatriation schemes were administered locally, by boards based in the ports — indicating the close link between the disorders and the shipping industry. To increase the attractiveness of the schemes, a fee was offered to those who left. One man who was in Liverpool at the time recalled:

> A leaflet was given to the black men in Liverpool to attend a meeting. I attended and this man was talking to us, telling us that they would give us free passage to go back to our country and that they would give us £6. One pound in Liverpool, in case we had anything in the pawn shop and then five pounds when you got to your country. They took us to Lime Street and then to London. We were put on the ship at the East India Dock. It was a cargo ship but there were lots of hammocks in the hold. There were 88 of us, some were from Cardiff, some were from Glasgow, from all over.[27]

The Liverpool police reported in 1920 that most of the unemployed black people in the city were refusing to take up the repatriation scheme. Similar reports from other towns confirm that it was not a great 'success' in terms of the number of people who participated. In order to encourage more people to apply, the government decided that the wives and families of the black sailors could also be repatriated. It was this issue which further exposed the conjuncture of racialised and gendered discourse that underpinned the response to these disorders. The Colonial Office had an interest in allowing wives to leave along with their husband on the grounds that the family could be kept together and the wife and children would not become dependent on public or charitable assistance. However, problems arose for officials when the wife in question was a white woman. Often the Civil Servants were reflecting the concerns of the colonial authorities who feared that the social hierarchy between the various ethnic groups would become untenable if 'inter-racial' families were established. The ambiguous status of any 'half-caste' children would also be problematic. Therefore, the Colonial Office tried to persuade and influence white women not to accompany their husbands. An internal Colonial Office memorandum suggested the following approach to the white wife of a 'coloured' returnee:

> I suggest we ask the Board of Trade to have the wife interviewed, to represent to her that the Governor does not consider it advisable that she should proceed to Jamaica, and that she would probably find the conditions of life amongst the coloured people extremely distasteful to her, and that in these circumstances she cannot be assisted to obtain a passage; and to enquire whether she has any objection to the provision of a passage for her husband alone. If she objects I think the Board of Trade should not give her husband a passage.[28]

Many of the themes already discussed in relation to sexual relations between black men and white women were magnified in regard to repatriation. In this context, though, the issue seems to be primarily connected with the implications for white wives of black men living in a colonised society. The maintenance of the 'colour line' (Du Bois, 1982) that kept the 'races' apart was the prime concern, both in the centre and the periphery of the colonial system. Although references to 'conditions of life amongst the coloured people' clearly smack of condescension or racism, there were no explicit references to 'inter-racial' marriage being morally or otherwise inadvisable *in principle*. Instead notions of cultural difference were used to caution against such developments. In other words the relatively privileged and well-educated civil servants did not resort to the crude racist attitudes expressed by their social inferiors on the Liverpool dockside. Although their terms of reference were culturally, rather than biologically, based, the conclusions reached by both social groups were broadly the same — black men were threatening to both white men and white women.

'Safe on sacred ground'

The primary response to the disorders was to remove, either by internment or repatriation, the black population. This implicitly identified the presence of that group of people as the fundamental root of the disorders. This racialisation of the disorder also occurred in the urban riots of the 1980s which in the press and elsewhere were commonly referred to as 'race riots', a feature outlined in Chapter Five which examines the Broadwater Farm disorder of 1985. In 1919, this portrayal relied upon the notions of difference and inferiority associated with the black population, which meant that their presence was considered the principal problem. An interesting contrast to this understanding is found in the pleas, petitions, and letters of the black people themselves about the disorders. It appears that many of the white population tended to regard their 'coloured' neighbours as foreign, different and inferior, whereas the black workers often emphasised their position as subjects of the Empire of equal standing with their English counterparts. The principle of *Civis Britannica Sum* was clearly understood by the migrant labourers from Africa and the Caribbean. As previously cited, in a letter to the Colonial Office, William Samuels wrote:

> What is the British motto? Are we not men and brothers, born of the same bone, or are our flesh iron and our sinews marble? Men who have fought for the glory of your country and for the emancipation of the world! Why treat us as mere brutes? Is it because we are mere dogs with neither bark nor bite?[29]

The reference to the contribution made during the war is a further piece of evidence which complicates the simplistic but apparently widespread belief that the black community had only benefited from the war. During the disorders some of the black men in Liverpool wore their medals as a demonstration of their loyalty and service to the war effort. *The Times*, warned its readers:

> it is to be remembered to their [the black sailors'] credit that during the war they faced the perils of the submarine campaign with all the gallantry of the British seamen. The negro is almost pathetically loyal to the British Empire and he is always proud to proclaim himself a Briton.[30]

Such patronising condescension rings of the Kiplingesque doctrine of the 'white man's burden' which informed much of the late imperialist period. It does, however, illustrate the expressed loyalty contained in many of the letters addressing the Colonial Office. The identification of England as both the motherland and the 'land of the free' by the men who had travelled there from the colonies suggests that the principle of equal citizenship for all members of the Empire, as propagated by the imperialists, was clearly taken on board by those who were the subjects of the colonial projects. The contrast between the expectations that migrants to Britain had about 'the motherland' and the subsequent reality of their experiences is a theme that recurs throughout this study. The following excerpt is from a petition delivered to the Governor of

Jamaica, signed by 44 people who had accepted voluntary repatriation following the disorders. It outlines the:

> ill-treatment that we received at the hands of white subjects of His Most Gracious Britannic Majesty in the United Kingdom — our motherland — while there we thought we were perfectly safe and on sacred ground free from any attack and ... that ... our colour as negroes would not debar us from living peaceably and contentedly under the British realm, we being loyal British subjects endowed constitutionally to find a home in any part of the British Crown.[31]

Conclusion

Several related notions have been identified in primary explanations of the 'race riots' that took place in Liverpool in 1919. All the newspaper articles, and police and government reports refer to the events as 'race riots' or 'colour riots' — a phrase which removes the negative connotations and attachment of blame that would arise from describing them as '*racist* riots'. This is not to suggest that this occurred deliberately, but only that it demonstrates a particular understanding of the events as a result of real difference. That there were virtually no dissenting viewpoints indicates the pervasiveness of this interpretation. Similar understandings were also evident in response to the events of 1958–59, which are discussed further in Chapter Four.

It has often been argued that the media coverage of the 1980s urban disorders tended to reflect the dominant political ideology of the time (see Murdock, 1984, for a discussion of this press coverage). As a broad generalisation this may be true, but, in comparison with the reporting of the events of the summer of 1919, the press coverage of disorder in the 1980s appears as a pinnacle of pluralist debate. No significant alternative agendas or arguments were apparent in the press coverage of the 'race riots' of 1919. The overt political character of the paper, or what van Dijk (1991) describes as the 'social personality' of the newspaper, appears to have had little bearing on the nature of the coverage. Although the *Daily Herald* consistently discussed the events and their background from the perspective of the trade unions, the resulting opinions were generally little different from those expressed elsewhere.

Another clear difference in the press coverage of the events in 1919 from that of the disorders of 1985, is in the actual quantity of column inches devoted to them. Whereas the disorders of 1958–59 and 1985 received considerable media coverage and generated much comment from politicians and leader writers, the 1919 disturbances excited relatively little attention. There may be several complementary reasons for this. The lack of press coverage can be explained by two broad factors. First, the technical and logistical nature of the media in post-First World War Britain meant that newspapers were physically thinner than in the later periods. Given this it may be expected that there was less press coverage of the disorder in 1919 in comparison with 1958–59 or 1985 because there were simply fewer pages and stories in any one edition. Another observable difference is that the newspapers contained little by way of commentary or features in 1919 compared with more recent periods and were more concerned with the presentation of newsworthy events in a straightforward reportage style. This does not mean that the press was an objective representation of reality — of course, selectivity and political agendas still operated as an inevitable feature of news production. Nonetheless, the style of the press was such that *analysis* of the events reported was largely non-existent in any daily newspaper.

One of the more convincing explanations of why crime stories in general feature heavily in newspapers refers to the centrality of such topics to the 'news agenda'. The concept of a 'news agenda' was advanced by the Glasgow Media Group (1976), who argued that items which provide violent and dramatic images tend to be considered as 'good copy' and feature prominently. One of the key issues which will determine the position of an item on the news agenda is the availability of striking photographs, which often result from urban unrest. In 1919, photographs of any sort were rare in newspapers, which meant that the 'news agenda' was less visually determined as it may have become in more recent times.

The second reason why the disorders of 1919 did not feature extensively in the press as in more recent cases concerns the social context in which they occurred. Just as press coverage is influenced by the logistics of a story, so too it is shaped by the perceived importance and relevance of an event to broader developments. There may be two explanations of why these disorders did not feature heavily in the 1919 press agenda. First, it may have been that other events were regarded as more important. Given that they occurred soon after the end of the First World War it may not be surprising that the Treaty of Versailles, which formally settled the conflict and was sealed in 1919, should receive more extensive press coverage. Another incident which received considerable coverage was Alcock and Brown's completion of the first successful trans-Atlantic flight. Events such as these served to relegate the disorders down the political and media agenda. Of course, this competition for space is a feature of any period and does not, in itself, explain why the unrest was not considered as more significant than, for example, an aeronautical breakthrough.

Another explanation could be that violence and disorder were so ubiquitous that they were unexceptional and did not merit a high place on the news agenda. As mentioned at the beginning of the Chapter, there were other disorders in 1919 and the multiplicity of such events meant that any single one was less visible than might otherwise have been the case. Given that other kinds of violence, for example, at sporting events, were also commonplace (see Dunning *et al*, 1984), it seems likely that the requirement of the news agenda to provide stories that were dramatic and unusual was largely unmet by the Liverpool 'race riots'.

The fundamental interpretation of the press appears to have been shared by the police and was reflected in the civil service documents examined. Elected politicians do not seem to have been particularly exercised by the disorders — no mention of them appears in *Hansard*, for example, and the press seldom quote their reactions. Perhaps this also indicates that the disorders were not regarded as especially significant on the national political agenda. All other discussions, though, share the dominant theme that the disorders were inevitable. They were 'an outcome of the importation of coloured men during the war', as the *Daily Herald* of the 13 June 1919 explained.

This racialised understanding of the disturbances was most clearly evident in the principal policy response — repatriation. The discussion amongst civil servants about the voluntary repatriation of the black population was primarily concerned with the practicalities of the scheme. Debates about who was entitled to be included, and especially about the position of wives and families, took place but the only grounds for tempering the drive for repatriation appears to have been the demands of the colonial authorities. No argument against the fundamental principle of repatriation was made — except by those who had been subjected to the violence. Those in the colonies who were concerned about the implications of repatriation of 'coloured' men and white women were adopting a gendered racialised framework. The underlying objective behind the Colonial Office discussion of the most appropriate ways to dissuade white women from migrating alongside black men, was to maintain what Du Bois (1982) famously called 'the colour line'. The principle that white and black people ought to maintain social distance was most obviously and fundamentally challenged by the sexual act. The role of gender in explanations of public disorder is considered further in later chapters, and is a primary example of the connection with other concepts that is central to the racialisation problematic developed in this study.

Although the position of white wives did prove problematic to the demands for repatriation, the multi-agency schemes established in the local ports involved varied attempts to encourage participation. As well as direct financial incentives, it is claimed that other methods were also used. A man interviewed, who accepted a passage to British Guiana and was cited earlier, argued that the British authorities relied upon false claims of the riches available to anyone who would leave Britain for the Caribbean. The logic of the scheme seemed to be to remove as many black people as possible, regardless of what awaited them. In this sense, the state acquiesced to the demands of the white people returning from war to face unemployment. Jenkinson (1993) suggests that this reflected a desire to appease working-class militancy in order to stave off Bolshevik agitation.

Newspaper reports, civil service memoranda, and academic accounts (Jenkinson, 1993) repeatedly referred to the programme to transport the black migrants to the Caribbean as a 'repatriation scheme' but it was, in fact, rather different. The removal of the black population, voluntary or otherwise, did not necessarily involve returning them to their country of origin, as the label 'repatriation' denotes, but instead removing them to one part of the colonial periphery, regardless of whence they came. Thus, the informant cited earlier arrived in Britain from Sierra Leone — so he was not 'repatriated' when shipped to the Caribbean, but rather migrated further within the colonial system. On one level, this point could be considered as no more than a matter of linguistic pedantry. It can, however, also be seen as symbolic of a more fundamental bipolar dichotomy between white and black, coloniser and colonised. When the presence of colonial migrants in Britain became problematic the solution chosen was to encourage them to migrate again to the Caribbean. This reflects a Eurocentric conception, which held the colonies as a singular entity — an internally undifferentiable Other, defined only by a collective separation from the 'mother country'.

Official reactions to the disorders, for example the comments made in court cases, did not condone the behaviour of the white working-class men who instigated much of the disorder but there was sometimes a certain implicit sympathy for their expressed grievances. Perhaps this, too, illustrates the wish by the state to be seen as reacting to people's concerns and demands. If so, this is a far cry from the almost universal mainstream condemnation of those engaging in disorder in more recent years. The concept of the 'racism of the interior' that Miles (1993) develops is applicable in this case. Miles argues that a dichotomy was established within emergent European states between the civilised, culturally superior elite and the uncivilised masses. He argues that Balibar's (1991) concept of 'class racism' is a useful way of explaining this creation of a distinct culturally-defined group who were separate and subordinate to the elite. Just as the subjects of European colonialism were racialised in terms of their culture, the racism of the exterior, similar — but not identical — process have been directed at those *within* European states. In this case study, the white rioters were criticised but not wholly condemned by those in power because they were somehow regarded as incapable of the civilised norms that would prevent their social superiors acting in such a base manner.

The riots were presented as the result of two 'different', and implicitly incompatible, populations living in close geographical proximity. Such inevitable frictions were exacerbated, the newspapers suggested, by three related factors. The first was the competition for employment — i.e. the black seamen had the jobs which rightfully belonged to returning war veterans — and the second factor were the sexual liaisons between white women and black men — although in this case culpability rested either with libidinous black men or with 'fallen' white women, or sometimes with both. These surface conflicts were explained by the third — and fundamental — issue of the 'difference' between the two communities in terms of their degree of civilisation and incompatible 'standards'.

Evidence of all three discourses can be found throughout the brief number of column inches afforded to these incidents. Overall, they served to define the 'race riots' that occurred in terms presenting the black communities in the sea ports as the problem to be both explained and dealt with, whilst the actions of the white rioters, who appear to have begun the riots and who contributed to the death of at least one black man, could be understood and 'explained' by referring to the social context in which they found themselves. By explaining the events in terms of 'old race hatreds', more fundamental concerns about the social problems that gave rise to the disorders could be ignored. The black population was a convenient scapegoat for the rioters on the Liverpool dockside, the journalists who reported the events, and for the civil servants charged with the policy response.

All four dimensions of the critical realist racialisation problematic which provides the framework for this exposition were evident in debates following the disorders in Liverpool during June 1919. It is apparent that ideas about 'race' were used to explain and simplify real material problems, such as unemployment, which existed in Liverpool and the other areas which witnessed similar unrest — as the first aspect of the critical realist model suggests. The importance of prevailing historical discourse in shaping racialised arguments was also evident in this case, and can be seen in the way in which the 'repatriation' scheme drew upon a distinction between the 'mother country' and an internally undifferentiated colonial other. This reflects the second feature of the racialisation problematic.

The third dimension of the critical realist problematic — which refers to the contradictory and inconsistent nature of racialisation — was apparent in the debates that followed the disorder discussed in this

Chapter. There were inconsistent accounts of the contribution black people had made to the war effort and to their loyalty towards the British Empire. The notion that black people had 'done well out of the war' was contradicted by other accounts which stressed the extent of their service, a claim made on occasion by the black people themselves. This reinforces the suggestion contained in the critical realist model that racialised ideas are diverse and may contain internal contradictions. The fourth feature of the racialisation problematic draws attention to the manner in which ideas about 'race' tend to articulate with other themes. This process was clearly evident in the sexual stereotypes of black men that were employed in debates about relations between them and white women, a feature that is also returned to in the chapters that follow.

Notes

1 PRO CO 318/352 *Liverpool Chief Constables Report on Race Riots*, November 15, 1919.
2 Interview notes.
3 PRO CO 318/352 *Liverpool Chief Constable Report on Race Riots*, 15 November 1919.
4 Fryer, 1984: 29.
5 PRO CO 318/349 *Petition to Acting Governor of Jamaica from Repatriated Seamen*, 29 August 1919.
6 See also Fryer, 1984: 295-6.
7 *The Times*, 10 June 1919.
8 Cited in Fryer, 1984.
9 The *Daily Herald*, 16 June 1919.
10 *The Times*, 14 June 1919.
11 Evidence for this can be seen in *Scandal!*, Christine Keeler's account of the Profumo affair, and also in *Absolute Beginners*, Colin McInnes' novel about fashionable London in the 1950s. See also McClintock (1995) for a more general discussion of the inter-woven discourse of gender, race and sexuality.
12 *The Times*, 19 June 1919.
13 Interview notes.
14 The *Daily Telegraph*, 11 June 1919.
15 The *Daily Herald*, 13 June 1919.
16 PRO CO 323/848 *Liverpool Police Report on Distressed Blacks in Liverpool*, 1 November 1920.
17 The *Daily Herald*, 14 June 1919.
18 The *Daily Mail*, 14 June 1919.
19 PRO CO 318/352 *Report from Inspector of CID, C-Division*, 15 June 1919.
20 PRO CAB 23 (15) *Minutes of the War Cabinet*, 24 October 1919.
21 *op cit*.
22 PRO CO 111/621 *William Samuels to Colonial Office*, 30 December 1918.
23 PRO CO 318/362 *M.E. Baptist to Colonial Office*, 19 May 1920.
24 The *Daily Telegraph*, 13 June 1919.
25 PRO CO 318/352 *Liverpool Chief Constables Report on Race Riots*, 15 November 1919.
26 The *Daily Herald*, 14 June 1919.
27 Interview notes.
28 PRO CO 318/349 *Repatriation of Wives*, 6 October 1919.
29 PRO CO 111/621 *William Samuels to Colonial Office*, 30 December 1918.
30 *The Times*, 13 June 1919.
31 PRO CO 318/349 *Petition to Colonel, Acting Governor of the Island of Jamaica from Repatriated Seamen*, 29th August 1919.

3 Political Disorder in 1930s Britain: 'Coloured Shirts and Tin Trumpets'

Introduction

This Chapter examines the campaign of the British Union of Fascists (BUF) to attract support in the East End of London, and elsewhere, during the mid-1930s, and the violence which often attended it. It considers the nature of the reaction to the clashes between the BUF and their various opponents, such as the Communist Party. Following the disorder that occurred in many British cities in the 1980s one reaction, which sought to deny social deprivation as a causal factor argued that there had been considerable poverty and unemployment during the 1930s, but that no disorder had occurred then. This Chapter will further demonstrate[1] that this assertion is manifestly untrue.

The reports considered in this Chapter are littered with references to disorders across the country as anti-fascists clashed with 'Mosleyites' at political meetings and in the streets. During this decade there seems to have been a widespread view of approaching social collapse. It was not only Sir Oswald Mosley who prophesied impending crises, for the Communist Party too had considerable support in certain areas. Such perceptions were not limited to the political margins — even the government were alarmed at the apparent frailty of public order in the 1930s (see Stevenson, 1975; Stevenson and Cook, 1977). This Chapter explores these debates and suggest that, underlying them, was a particular conception of English identity which drew upon themes of obedience to the law and toleration. All sides in this political conflict sought to define themselves as the heirs to this English legacy of respect for law and order. They all asserted that they embodied traditions of English political culture, in an attempt to legitimise their ideological position.

Background and context

In any discussion of history it is difficult to distinguish between the structural causes of events and the impact of particular individuals (Carr, 1961). In this case, the tribulations of the 1930s were rooted in social problems relating to the Great Depression and the political legacy of the First World War. However, it is difficult to consider these events in isolation from the manoeuvrings of the upper-class political maverick, Sir Oswald Mosley. One of the few people to cross the floor of the House of Commons from Conservative to Labour, Mosley ended his governmental prospects when, in 1930, he resigned his Cabinet position as Chancellor of the Duchy of Lancashire following a disagreement over his proposals to tackle unemployment.

In the same year, frustrated by what he perceived as the inertia of the conventional parties, Mosley formed the New Party, a precursor of the BUF. The New Party lasted for only one year and it 'failed spectacularly' (N. Mosley, 1983: 9) in the 1931 general election. In 1932, Mosley launched the BUF in an attempt to transcend the factionalism of the New Party and to unite a number of small sect-like fascist groups, that had existed in Britain at least since the 1920s, behind his dynamic leadership. Although many of those who inaugurated the BUF were committed anti-Semites the party did not, officially at least, take any position on 'the Jewish question' for some years. Considerable debate has taken place about Mosley's true opinion of Jews. Some have argued (for example, Benewick, 1972) that Mosley only adopted anti-Semitic views in order to garner support at a time when the BUF was waning. Skidelsky (1975), on the other hand, reflects Mosley's own account in arguing that the behaviour of the Jews themselves contributed to the anti-Semitic stance of the BUF, which is an issue discussed further later in this Chapter.

The period between 1932 and 1934, when Lord Rothermere, proprietor of the *Daily Mail*, withdrew his support in response to the BUF's emergent anti-Semitism, appears to have been the high-water mark for Mosley's movement. Membership of the BUF is difficult to ascertain with any certainty, largely due to the questionable reliability of the figures presented by particular interests giving a number that was either too high or too low. However, the number was relatively large and geographically spread. Durham (1989) suggests that the membership reached 40,000 by 1934, and Nicholas Mosley (1983) claims that there were in the region of 300 branches across the country by this date. Whatever the support in terms of numbers, Mosley certainly received favourable attention from notable sources. Nicholas Mosley (1983) quotes the favourable opinion of George Bernard Shaw, for example, and

Rothermere's support was announced on the front page of the *Daily Mail* of 8 January 1934 under the headline HURRAH FOR THE BLACKSHIRTS!. Many of those who had belonged to pre-BUF fascist parties and continued to play a role in Mosley's organisation were part of the establishment, and often they were former military officers. Indeed, one of the problems that the BUF sought to overcome in order to attract greater mass support was the perception that fascist politics was the domain of upper-middle and upper-class eccentrics.[2]

After 1934 the fortunes of the party waned. This was due to a number of factors including the negative images of the BUF following the violence at Olympia, the withdrawal of support by Rothermere in July 1934, increasing negative parallels being drawn with developments in Germany and Italy, and the considerable expense of maintaining the extensive organisation Mosley had devised. Anderson (1983: 137) outlines events that overshadowed the BUF's activities:

> In 1936, King George V died, Germany remilitarized the Rhineland, Italy conquered Ethiopia, the Spanish Civil War began, and Edward VIII gave up the throne to marry the woman he loved. In the year of three kings it would have been hard to keep a minority political movement before the public eye. That Mosley was once again able to gain headlines in 1936 was not an indication of the growth of his movement, but of the renewed intensity of anti-fascist activity.

It was against this background of decline that two related initiatives were launched in the mid-1930s. First, the BUF developed an overtly anti-Semitic stance, where previously the official policy had been ambiguous with some of the movement's leaders openly and proudly declaring themselves anti-Semites and others, including Mosley, trying to maintain that the BUF took no policy line on Jewish people *per se*. The second development was the launch of the campaign in East London. This effectively represented tacit recognition that the movement did not have the resources to agitate nationwide and the belief that a concentration of effort would bring greater reward. It was this campaign that brought the issue of violence back on to the agenda and culminated in the famous Battle of Cable Street in October 1936. Despite Mosley's efforts, the party's fortunes did not recover. Some suggest, rather naively given the history of anti-Semitism in Britain,[3] that the BUF's adoption of explicit anti-Semitism never received mass support because it was at odds with Britain's tolerant character and democratic past. Whatever the reason the party never regained its momentum. By 1938, the Metropolitan Police, who had been instructed by the Home Secretary to undertake surveillance on BUF and anti-fascist activities, were reporting that the movement was having little success in response to its summer campaign (Stevenson and Cook, 1977: 210).

The advance in fascism elsewhere in Europe throughout the 1930s saw the BUF develop another theme which also reflected the anti-Semitism they were propagating in the East End. Towards the end of the decade, Mosley and the BUF had entered into what Nicholas Mosley (1983: 148) has described as the third phase of their history: campaigning against war with Germany. Using the slogans 'Mind Britain's Business' and 'Britain Fights for Britain Only', the BUF argued that Britain should only enter a war if directly invaded or threatened. Their anti-Semitism was evident, as they argued that Jewish interests were dragging Britain into a war in which it had no 'real' concern. Mosley's campaign continued, with some apparent success in terms of pubic support. In May 1940, though, the Cabinet authorised the Amendment to the Emergency Powers Act so that the Home Secretary could imprison any person considered a danger to the national interest. The day after the amendment was passed, Mosley was arrested and sent to Brixton prison. Effectively this was the end of the BUF, and it was disbanded later that year. Mosley remained in prison until 1943 and, although he attempted a brief political return in the late 1950s, his brand of fascism never reappeared with anything like the same impact it had in the 1930s.

As shown in Table 4.1, violence often surrounded the activities of the BUF. It is clear that not all of it emanated from the Blackshirts, and both the BUF and anti-fascist groups were keen to distance themselves from the disturbances and to claim that their opponents were principally culpable. Both parties in the disorders attempted to exonerate themselves by claiming that they represented the authentic legacy of the British political tradition. If Mosley ever admitted that any of his followers engaged in violence — and he would usually stress that this was a matter of self-defence or to protect the other inviolable tradition of free speech — he would claim that they relied upon the 'good old English fist' rather than the more invidious methods of his opponents (Fielding, 1981: 21). Both the fascists and anti-fascists also claimed that the police offered their opponents undue protection and policed street politics partially.

It is difficult to prove an accurate picture of the extent and origin of the violence and the selective nature of the account in this Chapter indicates that no comprehensive attempt to do so is being made.

Table 1: A Selection of Violent Incidents Involving the BUF, 1932–36

Place	Date	Comments
Trafalgar Square, London	15 October 1932	First public meeting of the BUF. Largely peaceful but there were minor scuffles.
Farringdon Street, London	24 October 1932	Three hecklers thrown out of an indoor meeting by members of the Fascist Defence Force: 'this set the tone for many fascist meetings in the future' (N. Mosley, 1983, 11).
London	May 1933	Violent clashes between BUF and opponents at a rally in London, and clashes during an anti–Hitler demonstration (Benyon, 1987: 40).
Bristol	27 March 1934	4–500 fascists clashed with crowds outside a meeting hall. This incident was discussed in Parliament on 9 April 1934, '... the first example of a typical conflict situation in the 1930s, one which was to give the police some of their greatest headaches ...' (Skidelsky, 1975: 354).
Edinburgh	1 June 1934	Clashes as police intervened during a counter demonstration to protest against a BUF rally in the city.
Bristol	1 June 1934	*Parliamentary Debates* mentioned these disturbances after the police had to close a meeting of fascists following clashes with opponents.
Finsbury Park, London	3 June 1934	'Scuffles' between fascists and communists at a BUF meeting.
Olympia, London	7 June 1934	Major disturbances inside the venue where thousands had gathered for a key speech by Mosley. This is often seen as a major reversal in the fortunes of the BUF as it never managed to disassociate itself from violence after this point.

Table 1 (continued)

Place	Date	Comments
Plymouth	13 June 1934	Around a thousand people took part in an anti-fascist demonstration.
Leicester	15 June 1934	Police called to clear market place of thousands of anti-fascist demonstrators.
Bristol	22 June 1934	12 injured in a fight between 40 fascists and 150 communists.
Sheffield	28 June 1934	Major demonstration against Mosley's meeting in the City Hall. *The Times* described the police's 'elaborate preparations' to prevent rioting.
Worthing	9 October 1934	Mosley and followers charged with riotous assembly after disorder at a BUF meeting — all were subsequently acquitted (Skidelsky, 1975, 354).
Leicester	April and October 1935	Disorder at various BUF meetings in Leicester (Benyon, 1987: 41).
Merseyside	June 1935	A woman died during violence at a BUF meeting at Bootle (Benyon, 1987: 40).
Hull	12 July 1936	Six Blackshirts were knocked unconscious during Mosley's speech to an open-air meeting; as Mosley's car drove away its windscreen was shattered by a bullet.
East End of London	4 October 1936	'The Battle of Cable Street'. Contrary to folkloric accounts this was not a clash between the people of the East End and Mosley's fascists, but between anti-fascists and the police. Mosley diverted his proposed march through Cable Street following pressure from the Chief Constable of the Metropolitan Police, Sir Philip Game.

Source: Compiled from contemporaneous press accounts, parliamentary debates and the books referenced

Whatever the true position, the association of the BUF with violence became established in the public mind by the mid-1930s. Although somewhat superseded in the public imagination by the skinheads of the 1970s, the image of the violent fascist of the 1930s remains and is evidenced by the continuing connotations of violent thuggery sometimes associated with the black shirt, which was the uniform of the BUF stewards in the 1930s. From the distance of several decades it is not of prime importance to discover how much violence there was or who was responsible for it. Of course at the time these questions were of central concern but what is of greater interest in this study are the arguments that explained this violence, and the discourses that were employed around it.

The next section of this Chapter examines some of these incidents in greater detail and explores both the events themselves and the reactions to them. Particular focus is placed on the violence which occurred at the 1934 Olympia meeting and the 'Battle of Cable Street' of 1936, although other incidents are also mentioned.

Olympia, 7 June 1934: 'wholly unnecessary violence'

As has been shown in Table 4.1 the events at Olympia in June 1934 marked a turning point in the fortunes of the BUF. Prior to this violent confrontation between fascists and their opponents, the BUF had enjoyed a relatively respectable, if eccentric, image. Often they were regarded by the mainstream press as an interesting party, led by an exceptional orator, who, whilst not posing any serious threat to the status quo, provided an intriguing political distraction. Press coverage of the BUF after these events became increasingly focused on the issue of violence, with their political rallies and meetings usually being reported in terms of whether or not violence had occurred. After Olympia it was regarded as newsworthy to report a BUF meeting where there was no violence, suggesting that a peaceful event was regarded as unusual.

This shift in the image of the BUF did not simply reflect an increase in levels of violence associated with their activities. Whilst there may have been more disorder, in terms of the number of people involved, once the party became established, this may have been because the profile of the party had risen and interest in it, both in favour and against, had increased. If there were more rallies, meetings and processions occurring, it is not surprising that the likelihood of disturbances also increased. However, violence had always been associated with BUF meetings and was a common feature of much political campaigning between the wars (Dunning *et al*, in Gaskell and Benewick, 1987). What was significant about the Olympia meeting was not the disorder *per se*, but rather the way in which it was publicly mediated. The fact that these events occurred in front of the ranks of the 'great and the good' meant that their impact was much sharper than in other circumstances. Whilst this case may not amount to a moral panic in the usual sense (Cohen, 1972) it does reflect a broad theme in criminology which refers to the ways in which crime is socially constructed (see, for example, Matthews and Young, 1992). Skidelsky (1975: 365) makes a similar point when he argues that:

> for both fascists and anti-fascists Olympia was the epic battle of the 1930s ... [but] ... today it is clear that Olympia's notoriety owes less to the events of the meeting itself than to the context in which they took place.

Although it is often suggested that it was the 'Battle of Cable Street' which led to the passage of the 1936 Public Order Act it was actually Olympia that was the precursor to the debate that eventually led to the law. Stevenson and Cook (1977: 204) sum up the importance of these events when they argue that:

> the Olympia meeting focused attention upon the British fascist movement, brought the government to the brink of legislation, and frightened off more conservative support.

The Olympia meeting was not the first large scale rally held by the BUF. In April 1934 the Albert Hall was the venue for a rally which attracted some 10,000 people and passed off relatively peacefully. Nicholas Mosley (1983: 58) reports that Olympia was intended not only to consolidate the momentum that the BUF was building as a political movement but also to attract a more 'intellectual' and elite audience. As Skidelsky (1975: 369) states:

> Olympia was not a typical fascist audience. The enormous publicity had built it up into a social occasion; the startlingly rapid rise of fascism (more apparent than real) had made many people curious to see the new phenomenon. For the first and only time in the BUF's history Mosley was able to get into one of his halls a substantial percentage of Britain's establishment. It did not like what it saw.

From its inception the meeting received a high profile and was controversial. The Communist Party announced in mid-May that it would launch a counter-demonstration, whilst Rothermere's *Evening Mail* offered tickets to the venue as competition prizes and supplied black shirts for the stewards' uniforms. In the immediate build-up to the rally the *Daily Worker* printed maps showing how to get to the venue and urged anti-fascists to travel together on the tube in order to qualify for group discounts on their tickets. Skidelsky (1975: 368) records that four columns of communists marched to Olympia and that there were around 2,500 anti-fascists present, 500 of whom managed to secure entry to the venue. The BUF also marched to Olympia, and approximately 2,000 uniformed fascists were inside to hear Mosley's speech. By the time the meeting began there were approximately 12,000 people inside the hall and Mosley proclaimed the gathering to be the largest of its kind ever held in Britain.

Almost as soon as Mosley's speech had begun he was interrupted by members of the audience shouting anti-fascist slogans. Although Mosley ordered his BUF stewards to remove the hecklers they were organised in such a way that, as one was removed, another began to shout slogans from some other place within the hall. Pauses to deal with these interruptions prolonged Mosley's speech by almost an hour,[4] but it was the nature of the treatment meted out to the anti-fascist protesters that quickly became embroiled in controversy. Although the police recorded that there had been no serious violence (Skidelsky, 1975: 370) the more common reaction was horror and outrage at the actions of the stewards who, it was claimed, had assaulted protesters. Three MPs who had witnessed these events acted quickly to draft a letter to *The Times* recording their impression of events:

> We were involuntary witnesses of wholly unnecessary violence inflicted by uniformed Blackshirts on interrupters. Men and women were knocked down, and, after they had been knocked down, were still assaulted and kicked on the floor. It will be a matter of surprise to us if there were no fatal injuries.[5]

A number of those ejected recorded their experiences in a pamphlet published shortly after the rally (Vindicator, 1934). It is worth mentioning a few accounts to illustrate the nature of the events under discussion. One man recorded how:

> close by a man seemed to be protesting against the brutal treatment. He received a punch on the jaw that knocked him back into his chair, where a mob of Blackshirts proceeded to beat him up, one of them standing behind the man (held down in his chair) and hammering the side of his face with all his might.[6]

Another eyewitness recorded how the spotlight trained on Mosley would be swung around on to an interrupter in order to single them out, she stated:

> I saw several Blackshirts using knuckle-dusters near me in attacking hecklers, I saw male Blackshirts attack women who interrupted, and a man brutally thrown out who had just stood up in his seat and not even spoken.[7]

A victim of the stewards' violence recorded how he had witnessed others being assaulted. When he protested to two Blackshirts who were beating a woman, he claimed:

> [I] was immediately set on by twenty to thirty Blackshirts in the corridors towards the exit, after having been passed from gang to gang of Blackshirts who each in their turn beat me. I was knocked down and covered by at least thirty Blackshirts, who punched and kicked me whilst down, while others tried to twist my legs and arms in an attempt undoubtedly either to dislocate or break my limbs. During this time I was hit on the arm by one Blackshirt wearing a knuckle-duster. Finally I was thrown out of the door, practically unconscious, with one shoe lost, being wrenched off as they tried to twist my left leg.[8]

Despite the scale of the violence only 23 people were arrested. This was largely because the police were not present inside the venue where much of the disorder occurred — all the arrests were made outside after the rally was over. At that time the police had no clear right to enter a private meeting uninvited, and it was for this reason that Mosley often argued that he was entitled to use his own stewards to protect his meetings.

Although most condemned the violence, some commentators defended the activities of the stewards on the grounds that they were provoked by their opponents. Others argued that they were trying to ensure that Mosley could be heard and were upholding the democratic principle of free speech. Two correspondents to *The Times*, for example, claimed that:

> it is scandalous that a small minority [of the audience] should have it in their power to render nugatory the proceedings. A forcible ejection of such intruders is the only remedy left to the majority, and if these intruders violently resist they have no one but themselves to blame if they suffer.[9]

The same correspondents also noted that the women interrupters were dealt with by female stewards, a 'thoughtful courtesy' from the BUF. This view was often contradicted by other accounts. In Vindicator (1934), for example, there are several accounts of women being assaulted by male BUF stewards and, in one case, of the woman's clothing being torn off in the process.

Soon after the Olympia rally the Cabinet met to discuss the Home Secretary's proposal to grant the police powers to enter private meetings without permission. On 20 July 1934, the Cabinet discussed legislation which would ban the wearing of political uniforms, restrict local and national marches and provide for meetings to be banned.[10] Some of these measures had been on the agenda before the violence at Olympia and were not, in any case, acted upon for another several years. Anderson (1983: 121) suggests that this was primarily because the issue faded from the political agenda and that 'the National Government, never disposed to quick action, began to procrastinate'. The activities of the BUF and their opponents began to receive more attention during 1936, when the campaign in the East End of London was launched, culminating — at least in terms of the debate surrounding disorder — in the 'Battle of Cable Street' in October of that year.

'The Battle of Cable Street', 4 October 1936: 'they shall not pass'

In many respects the events in October 1936 have come to be seen as most significant in their symbolic value. It has been argued[11] that they led to the passage of the 1936 Public Order Act, which would have credited them with greater material impact, but this overstates the case, since the legislation had been contemplated for some years. Furthermore, the legal development was also provoked by the perceived threat from the left — in the form of the National Unemployed Worker's Movement and the Communist Party — as well as problems of disorder emanating from the far-right. Whilst the Battle of Cable Street may have provided further impetus towards legislation, it has enjoyed longer currency in anti-fascist history as the occasion on which the masses rose up and defeated British fascism.[12] Deakin (1978: 167) recognises that the violent scenes of 4 October 1936 have acquired a status out of proportion to their severity when he argues that 'these simple, if dramatic events, have become overlaid by a series of heroic legends with little foundation in fact'. In some respects, the place of these events in the anti-fascist pantheon can be considered quite separately from what actually occurred. Although the Battle of Cable Street was more complex than accounts in folklore often imply, this does not affect its position in myth or legend. Michael Keith (1993: 92) recognises that such events have parallel existences when he writes of more recent disorders:

> what an event *means* is not the same as what an event *was*. Again the difference between the 'private' and the 'public' lives of a riot' [emphasis in original].

The following account seeks to examine the 'private life' of the Battle of Cable Street —by exploring the perspectives of some participants. Following this, the reactions to the events and the themes that emerge from these debates are examined. These show the simplicity of the argument which holds that the events in October 1936 involved the working class of the East End rising up against fascist interlopers.

The Battle of Cable Street occurred at the end of a summer that had seen the BUF focus their attention on the East End of London. In October 1935, Prime Minister Baldwin had called the general election earlier than had been anticipated, leaving the BUF unable to field candidates for every seat and financially unprepared to wage a significant campaign. In order to avoid electoral humiliation, the Party decided not to contest the election, declared them a sham, and sought to operate with the aim of 'Fascism Next Time' (Cross, 1961: chapter 10; N. Mosley, 1983: chapter 12). A large part of this extra-Parliamentary effort was to be focused upon the East End of London. The decision to concentrate the Party's resources on a relatively small geographical area is explained differently by those with different perspectives on Mosley and the BUF. Those commentators who appear to some degree sympathetic to Mosley (for example, Skidelsky, 1975, and N. Mosley, 1983) suggest that the Party was encouraged to develop in the East End by the local population who had, real or imagined, grievances against the Jewish population. Other, more hostile accounts (for example, Jacobs, 1978), stated that the Party created anti-Semitism in the area and were 'outsiders' who never really 'belonged' there.

Whatever the truth of these conflicting claims, the East London campaign was significant as it saw the BUF's anti-Semitism become firmly entrenched and its effects become concrete for the first time on any scale. Skidelsky (1975: 398-99) suggests that much of the disorder occurring in the area at this time was relatively minor, consisting of graffiti and 'petty teenage fights'. Others record different perspectives which saw the activities of the BUF as more threatening. One woman who lived in the area at the time recalled:

> If you were a youngster brought up in the East End in the 1930s, you weren't a stranger to politics. They had political meetings on every

> corner, the Labour Party, the Communist Party. We'd also listen to the fascist meetings, and they were held on many corners too. For a Jewish kid, they were belting out their message of hate, and we'd hear of the attacks on Jews in the East End by them, and we learnt to hate back.[13]

Other accounts of the period record the extent of fascist and anti-fascist agitation in the area.[14] By October 1936, the extent of political activity in the area was such that *The Times* commented that 'the East Ender can do his work, have his supper, and then enjoy politics from 8 p.m. to bed-time every evening'.[15] Indeed the extent of the political agitation by both sides became such that the policing of other areas of the capital was adversely affected.[16] This commitment of police officers to monitor fascist activity in the East End was partly the result of political pressure from the Home Office. For example, the Home Secretary issues an *aide memoire* on 16 July 1936 reminding senior officers that:

> grossly abusive language about the Jews either individually or as a race is a serious offence and that there can be no question in this matter of good-humoured toleration of language which in other circumstances might not call for instant action.[17]

The extent to which the police enforced this principle is unclear, with some claiming that the police often tolerated the activities of BUF members whilst effectively preventing the Communist Party, for example, from mounting their opposition (Jacobs, 1978; Lebzelter, 1978; BBC TV, 1994). Whatever the truth of the claims about policing, one indication of the extent of anti-Semitic activities in the East End was the establishment of a Jewish Defence Campaign by the Board of Deputies, an organisation often criticised for lacking radicalism during the fight against fascism in London during this period (Lewis, 1987; Mullings, 1984).

It was against this background that Mosley announced that the BUF were to stage their biggest demonstration yet — through the East End on 4 October 1936, stopping at four points *en route* for meetings. The march met with opposition organised on a comparable scale and through similar newspaper campaigns as with Olympia. The influence of the international dimension to the fight against fascism could be seen in the adoption by anti-fascists of the phrase coined by those defending Madrid against Franco. One woman present recollected how:

> There appeared the whitewashed signs all over the pavements: "They Shall Not Pass", there were posters, there were leaflets, asking

> everybody in the East End to form what I can only describe as a human wall. You weren't asked to go and fight, you were asked to block the streets, block the roads so the fascists couldn't get through.[18]

Jacobs (1978) drew attention to the importance of the anticipation of Mosley's march and the role that rumour and expectation had on subsequent events. This is a factor also noted in respect of the disorders of Broadwater Farm in 1985, discussed in Chapter Five. Jacobs recalled how (1978: 235):

> In Stepney we heard a rumour that Mosley intended organising a mass march of uniformed fascists through the heart of the Jewish areas. In fact, the *Blackshirt* carried a notice saying full information about a proposed march and meetings would appear next week. The next week's issue announced a march ending in four meetings, at Aske Street, Shoreditch, Salmons Lane, Limehouse, at 5 pm in Stafford Road, Bow, and at 6 pm at Victoria Park Square, Bethnal Green. Before these announcements, the air was full of foreboding. Speculation was mounting. Rumours multiplied. The immediate response was that this could not be allowed to happen and that if it did, the outcome would be disastrous.

When the time came, however, the Blackshirts were not able to march through the East End. Mosley's wish to be provocative in his choice of location was fulfilled, perhaps beyond his expectation, and the number of people who turned out to block the street was sufficient to prevent the procession. One anti-fascist activist remembered that:

> They reckoned there was about a quarter of a million people at Aldgate, I think there was about 200,000, and we went to Royal Mint Street where they were parading and we smashed up banners and the police chased us. In the meantime Tubby Rosen and Phil Piratin, who became a Communist MP afterwards, set up a barricade because the police wanted them [the BUF] to march through Cable Street which would lead on to Victoria Park. They had to divert it because they couldn't get through Aldgate, it was just a mass of people. One thing you must remember, not a shop window was broken or anything looted. You see the Communist Party were very disciplined.[19]

Although the protesters prevented Mosley and his supporters from marching they did not confront the fascists face-to-face. Instead, the clash was with the police who tried without success to clear the streets to facilitate the march. The previously cited view claims that the affair was relatively orderly, a point reinforced by Mullings (1984, 266). Other accounts suggest that the clash with the police was violent at times. One eyewitness claims that a group of officers were forced to surrender to the protesters:

> Cable Street was very narrow at that time and we forced open lock-ups and pulled out lorries, carts and things and made barricades. Then the police charged the barricades. Above these stores were tenements and the women just leaned out and threw everything they could lay their hands on down onto the police. And when I say everything, I mean everything: hot water, boiling water, kitchen oil, fats and things, and they [the police] ran into these sheds to hide. Then a lot of women came down and started banging in and kicking at the shed doors. Finally they came out again, and surrendered with their hands in the air. Well, we were rather nonplussed, who ever saw a policeman surrender, and what do you do?! So we took their helmets and told them to shove off.[20]

In advance of the march, Home Secretary Sir John Simon had agreed that the Sir Philip Game, Chief Constable of the Metropolitan Police, could decide to ban the march should the circumstances demand. It was this course of action that was taken and Mosley agreed to reroute the procession away from Cable Street. In his subsequent report (Metropolitan Police, 1936) Game explained that:

> it became necessary to take steps to prevent a march through the East End owing to strong local opposition. There is little doubt that serious rioting and bloodshed would have occurred had the march been allowed to take place.

Nevertheless, fighting between the police and demonstrators did occur, leading to 88 arrests and 70 people being treated for injuries. More than 5,000 police officers had been employed to prevent the physical confrontation of Blackshirts with anti-fascists. After the march was redirected Mosley issued a statement claiming that the events marked a victory for the opponents of democracy and claiming that the government had '...openly surrendered to Red terror',[21] which was contrasted unfavourably with the law-abiding actions of the BUF.

A week later the Communist Party organised a rally in the East End to celebrate the successful 'show of strength' against fascism. The events have often been hailed as a triumph of the ordinary working-class people of the East End over fascism. Skidelsky (1975, 406-07) points out that this view is simplistic, ignoring that the BUF also had 'successes' in the area at this time. Indeed, exactly a week after Cable Street, Mosley addressed a meeting of thousands in Victoria Park and marched to it at the head of a procession through Limehouse, all with little significant opposition.

Explaining the disorders

An analysis of the main themes in the reactions to the events at Olympia and in East London shows that there were two main discourses in the debates about violence, disorder and the BUF. These discourses can also be identified in some of the cases discussed in other chapters in this book. First, the racialised portrayal of the settlement of the Jewish community in the East End is outlined and discussed. Second, the suggestion that political disorder was somehow alien to the national character is analysed. This understanding of the disorders relies upon a conception of a liberal, tolerant and law-abiding political tradition in Britain. This view of British history was often evident following disorders in the 1980s and is further discussed in Chapter Five on the Broadwater Farm disturbances. It is interesting that the BUF, their direct opponents, and mainstream political commentators, all drew upon aspects of this discourse to try to justify their position.

Jews in the East End of London: 'you've got to be a good Yiddisher boy'

A Jewish community has been established in Britain since Roman times and has suffered persecution for centuries. In 1190 Jews were massacred in York and a century later Edward I expelled the Jews from Britain (Cohen, 1994). The bulk of the recent migration came between 1881 and 1914, when Jewish refugees fled from pogroms in Russia, Poland, and the Baltic States[22]. There was anti-Semitism directed against these migrants, and the 1905 Aliens Act was designed to curtail their entry. By 1911 there were some 240,000 Jews living in Britain, many of whom were settled in the East End (Deakin, 1978: 161),

There are several explanations of the development of an explicit officially-sanctioned policy of anti-Semitism by the BUF as it concentrated its efforts on the East End of London. The development of anti-Semitism was regarded by all as a crucial factor in the escalation of disorder in the mid-1930s. As stated earlier, there were individuals within the BUF who had made little effort to conceal their virulent anti-Semitism, but Mosley refused to adopt such a position as a matter of policy until late 1934. Prior to this, he had issued orders that no BUF representative should indulge in anti-Semitism during their speeches.

Although the BUF included speakers such as William Joyce and Mick Clarke, who regularly abused Jews during their speeches, Mosley himself maintained that the official position of the BUF was that they only opposed individual Jews who were members of the Communist Party or were anti-fascist activists, and that the Jewish 'race' *per se* had nothing to fear from them (N. Mosley, 1983; Skidelsky, 1975). In the rally at the Albert Hall on 28 October 1934, Mosley marked a broadening of his opposition to Jews when he stated that:

> I have encountered things in this country which I did not dream existed in Britain. One of them is the power of *organised Jewry* which today is mobilised against Fascism. They have thrown down their challenge to Fascism, and I am not in the habit of ignoring challenges. Now they seek to howl over the length and breadth of the land that we are bent on racial and religious persecution. That charge is utterly untrue. Today we do not attack the Jews on racial or religious grounds: we take up the challenge they have thrown down because they fight against Fascism *and against Britain.* They have declared in their great folly to challenge the conquering force of the modern age. Tonight we take up that challenge: they will it: let them have it![23] [emphasis added].

From this point Mosley maintained that the BUF opposed the Jews on the basis that their internationalism was contrary to the elevation of the nation of a symbol of political and emotional unity. Holmes (1979: 181) suggested that this argument was 'neatly copied' from Joyce. This rather confused argument[24] was perhaps interpreted differently on the streets, where less grandiose complaints were made against the Jews. Mullings (1984) argues that there were two bases to this anti-Semitism. First, the complaint that Jewish landlords were exploiting their tenants by charging exorbitant rents, and, second, that Jewish business people were harming the commercial efforts of the indigenous petty bourgeoisie. The second of these amounts to the rather bizarre complaint that one group were working too hard, too efficiently, and simply being so good at business that their neighbours could not compete. Similar racialised arguments have been used, of course, against other migrant groups — some of the reactions to the arrival of 'West Indians' in the 1950s, as discussed in the next chapter, reflect similar economic fears.

One explanation of the BUF's adoption of such issues was that they were responding to the pre-existing concerns of the people of the East End, an area generally neglected by the mainstream parties. Certainly, Nicholas Mosley (1983, 108) explains the development of his father's party in these terms when he suggests that the BUF were using anti-

Semitic propaganda to make political capital in response to the demand from the people of the East End:

> During the course of 1935 there had sprung up in East London a movement which, almost uniquely in the history of the BUF, gained a large and spontaneous local following without direction from headquarters or at first the impetus of the leader as a speaker.

Others offer a similar perspective, but not one related to a specific characterisation of the area involved. Skidelsky (1975) outlined the position most resembling the justification provided by the BUF itself when he suggested that Mosley was not a committed anti-Semite but rather that the issue was adopted opportunistically to garner support.[25] Skidelsky went further than this, however, arguing that the Jews in the East End were themselves culpable for the hostility directed against them. This argument is underpinned by the notion that the racism exists in response to the actions of minority ethnic groups and is thus rooted in material reality. Skidelsky (1975: 381) argued that 'what started to change was the attitude of the Jews themselves, and they must take a large share of the blame for what subsequently happened'. He also echoed the theoretical stance of the BUF when he suggested that the Jews were over-concerned with international fascist developments[26] at the expense of domestic national interests. Given that many of the Jews in the East End at this time were either recent migrants who had escaped pogroms in Eastern Europe, or were related to those who had, and that events in Germany were increasingly hostile to Jews, it is hard to agree with Skidelsky's claim.

Other important actors also explained the disorders in a manner which, implicitly or explicitly, suggested that the Jewish population was itself responsible for the hostility directed against it. In 1938, for example, a deputation from the Board of Deputies met the Chief Constable of the Metropolitan Police, Sir Philip Game, to discuss the policing of BUF meetings and demonstrations. Having stated that he felt support for the BUF was waning, Game argued that officers resented having to give up their leave to police such events 'to which the Jews had contributed by their very presence' (Benewick, 1972: 256). Soon after the 'Battle of Cable Street', *The Times*[27] explained that the cause of the unrest was working-class attitudes, stating that there was an 'uncrystallized dislike of the Jews' which amounted 'to the traditional grumbles against Jewish price cutting, clannishness, and their problematical wealth or dirtiness'.

In contrast to the attitude expressed by Nicholas Mosley, others have argued that anti-Semitism was foisted upon the people of the East End, who, at the Battle of Cable Street and elsewhere, physically demonstrated their resistance to the doctrine of fascism. Often such commentators have argued that anti-Semitism was an 'alien' doctrine that was incompatible with the history of the area. Jacobs (1978), for example, outlined the response to the BUF from the people of the East End in terms suggesting that they were rising up against a doctrine that was unfamiliar to the traditions of the area. Mullings (1984, 165) recognised this point but argued that it should be treated with caution:

> Many of the people who stressed this harmony [between Jews and Gentiles] were, however, Liberals, Labour and Communist Party members. In general these parties attracted those who were devoted to the ideal of the "Brotherhood of Man" and who consciously sought harmony between different communities. Such people found it difficult to acknowledge the latent racism of the working class whom they sometimes tended to idealise, endowing them with their own ideals and principles.

In many respects, these arguments were grounded in ideas about national identity which suggest that extremism is somehow incompatible with British political tradition. Certainly, there is evidence that the people of the East End, in large number, resisted the overtures of the BUF and fought anti-Semitism. The 'Battle of Cable Street' was certainly an example of this trend and there is anecdotal evidence that the people of the area were more determined in their opposition to the fascists than were the organised political parties.[28] This anti-fascism notwithstanding, there is also evidence that there was a level of support for the BUF and that the Blackshirts drew recruits from the population of the area. As mentioned earlier, Mosley held a rally in Victoria Park soon after the 'Battle of Cable Street' which drew large crowds and proceeded with little notable opposition. Given this kind of evidence, it is clearly simplistic to argue that fascism was anathema to the people of the area. In fact, there was both support and opposition from the people of the East End who, like any other community, demonstrated a variety of political allegiances and sympathies. Holmes (1979: 187) made a similar point when he noted that:

> The East End was not in fact some kind of inert mass waiting to be picked up and moulded by Mosley; what developed was a symbiotic relationship between the two.

What is interesting about these competing arguments about the progress of and resistance to fascism in the East End is that they rarely question the assumption that this was a real 'race relations problem' between Jews and non-Jews: those of different *races*. The accounts are concerned with establishing a number of facts: whether the Jews were really exploitative landlords; whether they were unduly influenced by international developments; whether Mosley was trying to 'invade' the area with an unwelcome doctrine of anti-Semitism or whether he was responding to genuine demand from a harassed and threatened Gentile population. As time passes, it is increasingly difficult to answer these questions with any certainty. All that can be done is to sketch the nature of these debates, rather than resolve them. What is interesting, though, is the fact that all of those arguments take the reality of the disputes as given and simply argue about the nature of the outcome. Those who appear sympathetic to Mosley (such as Skidelsky, 1973) and those who were hostile and campaigned against fascism (such as Jacobs, 1978) share a theoretical stance that here was a 'race relations problem'.

Academic accounts also tend to imply that there was a real material basis for Mosley's introduction of anti-Semitism in the East End. Mullings (1984: 139), for example, argued that the campaign was introduced in that area because 'only here and in a few other pockets could Mosley find people with grievances on any scale'. Lewis (1987: 105) claimed that 'having decided to adopt anti-Semitism it would appear that the BUF's leadership sought for its application that area of Britain where such a policy would have most relevance — London's East End'. Both of these arguments rest on the assumption that anti-Semitism develops because of the presence of Jews: it is this which gives people 'grievances' and makes anti-Semitism 'relevant'. As has been shown in Chapter Two, a similar perspective was evident following the disorders in Liverpool in 1919 when the violence perpetrated was seen as an understandable, if regrettable, result of natural 'racial differences'.

The object of analysis in 1936 need not have been whether the majority of the people were pro- or anti-fascist and should be thus condemned or exonerated, but how and why the Jewish community were *racialised*. In the response to the disorders surrounding fascism in the 1930s, a number of features can be noted in respect of the Jewish community of the East End. First, they were presented as a distinctive group who did not 'belong' to the area. Second, this difference was constructed in terms of a bipolar contrast between Jews and non-Jews, with no other effective identities, or areas of overlap — for example, there was little to suggest that differences between Jews and other local people could be subsumed beneath class relations or a more general identity as 'East Enders'. Another feature of the racialisation was that the Jews were considered as an alien presence who threatened to 'contaminate' the indigenous population, either directly, through disease or vice, or indirectly, through promoting 'foreign' political movements such as fascism or communism. Finally, the presence of the two 'races' was taken as a deterministic factor that led inexorably to social problems and to disorder. Just as the arguments discussed in the previous chapter were predicated around the existence of separate racial groups who naturally fell into conflict in Liverpool in 1919, so in the case of the BUF and the Jews the problematic status of the concept of 'race' is not questioned. Small (1994: 29) makes a general criticism of studies of 'race relations' which appears particularly relevant:

> One problem with many social scientific analyses of 'race' is that while they often acknowledge that 'race' is a social construct that is flexible and fluid they then go on to talk about 'race' as if it was a naturally occurring phenomenon, treating it as real and adding credibility to its status as an explanatory factor in social relationships.

The literature on the events in the East End of London is often ignorant of the debates within social science pertaining to racism and racialisation. Of course, many of the studies were conducted before many of these theoretical developments gained currency, and it should not be assumed that this point is a specific criticism of particular authors. Nonetheless, it can be argued that these explanations of the anti-Semitism of the BUF in the 1930s and its role in promoting disorder rest on the false premise that different 'races' exist and that their coexistence is inevitably problematic. The theoretical literature on 'race' and racism tends to marginalise studies of anti-Semitism,[29] focusing on the experiences of black and Asian minority ethnic groups. There are, of course, some exceptions to this (Lebzelter, 1978; Holmes, 1979), but these tend to be historical studies which overlook theoretical developments in the study of racialisation, whilst most of the theoretical examinations remain silent on the subject of anti-Semitism. Clearly this has meant that theoretical debates about racism continue to focus on the experiences of those with different somatic characteristics — the visible minority ethnic groups, and the positions of others are still relatively overlooked.

The next section develops some of these points and considers the manner in which ideas about British political culture and traditions were employed to define these disorders as aberrant and alien. The 'extremist' ideologies of the fascist and the communists were also contrasted with a supposed British tolerance and liberalism.

Fascism, violence, and the British tradition: 'un-British weeds in British soil'

A common reaction to incidents of public disorder in Britain is for politicians, the media, and other commentators, to proclaim that such events are alien to the British tradition of Parliamentary democracy and obedience to the law, what Pearson (1983: 243) concludes by describing as 'the stubbornly immobile myths of law and order'. The disorders in the East End in the 1930s provide as good an illustration as any of the ignorance of this perspective. Not only did many of the reactions to the events deny that Britain had any legacy of disorder, but they did so in terms of a supposed national character which abhorred extremism and stressed the virtue of toleration. Such explanations emanated from those at all points on the political spectrum.

In introducing the second reading of the Public Order Bill in 1936, the Home Secretary argued that extremist political movements, on the right and the left, had grown considerably since the end of the First World War. The proposals before the House were necessary, he claimed, because:

> If these foreign doctrines get a footing in this country ... then Parliament must secure that the methods which are employed in support are consistent with our tolerant traditions.[30]

In many respects this extract sums up the reaction of the political elites to the 'extremism' of the BUF and their, predominantly Communist Party, opponents. The government adopted an approach whereby the principle of free speech should be extended as far as possible to the BUF, providing that they did not threaten the democratic freedom of others. In the same debate, the Home Secretary contrasted the activities of the opposing groups on the streets with '... the grand characteristic of British political life ... its tolerance'. In private correspondence, Simon further emphasised that he regarded the activities of the BUF as un-British:

> I am very deeply impressed with the danger of letting this silly business of 'playing at Mussolini' to go on in this country ... Our young people are accustomed to fresh air and healthy exercise without the folly of coloured shirts and tin trumpets.[31]

Other Parliamentarians also portrayed the violence on the street as alien. After the disorders at Olympia, for example, W. J. Arthuser-Gray, Conservative MP for North Lanarkshire, talked of the 'brutality which is so foreign to the British race'.[32] During the second reading of the

Public Order Bill, in November 1936, the decline of the fascist movement was predicted by the Unionist MP for Leeds North West, Major Vyvyan Adams, on the grounds that 'it is the most un-British weed that has ever pushed itself above British soil'.[33]

Left-wing opponents of the BUF were also keen to claim that fascist political ideology and the related street violence were inconsistent with the national character. Labour's Herbert Morrison, who was later Home Secretary himself, wrote to Sir John Simon in October 1936 pressing that the government take more determined action against the BUF:

> Recently a fascist organisation, meticulously following the technique it has learned from foreign countries, has taken action in East London which appears to be provocative and calculated to produce social disorder, racial hatred, and strife which, fortunately, are contrary to British traditions and the best instincts of the British public.[34]

The *Manchester Guardian*[35] reflected this approach by arguing, a few days after Morrison's letter was reported, that 'the fascists can be rendered harmless if we keep our heads and are not afraid to curb their un-English manifestations'. Perhaps the most enduring contemporaneous example of the left position claiming that fascism and political violence was alien to British traditions is found in Orwell's 1941 essay *England Your England*. It was here that Orwell (1982: 40) asserted his vision of the English character:

> Like all other modern people, the English are in a process of being numbered, labelled, conscripted, 'co-ordinated'. But the pull of their impulses is in the other direction, and the kind of regimentation that can be imposed on them will be modified in consequence. *No party rallies, no Youth Movements, no coloured shirts, no Jew-baiting, or 'spontaneous' demonstrations.* No Gestapo either, in all probability[36] [emphasis added].

Academic studies of fascism and disorder during this period have also occasionally explained the restricted success of such parties in Britain in terms of the 'traditional values' of the people. Geiger (1963: iii) offers the best example of this tendency, arguing that:

> It [fascism] failed of success [*sic.*] in Britain due partly to the fact that democracy, civil liberties, and freedom were too highly respected and deeply rooted among people to whom fascist ideas of racial hatreds, and the suppression of liberties were repugnant.

Few of these arguments distinguish between the ideology of fascism and the manifestations of public disorder which accompanied its activities in the 1930s. Both are condemned as un-English in the same breath. Of course, on one level it is easy to see why the argument has been framed in this sense. Britain did not have a significant fascist movement throughout the period in question. However, only three European countries had a fascist or national socialist political party in government, meaning that Britain was one country amongst the majority in Europe where fascism was resisted. This hardly makes a convincing case that it was the national *character* which decided the matter — unless the national character was shared by the residents of many other European countries. In many respects, the arguments outlined above are the mirror-image of those which seek an explanation for Hitler's popularity in terms of the 'authoritarian personality'[37] of the German people, and they suffer from the same problems of generalisation and oversimplification. The suggestion that fascism was incompatible with the British people is little more than a tautology. It is plain that Mosley failed to win widespread support. However, it is disingenuous, and a potentially dangerous delusion, to explain this in terms of 'national character'. Britain has a long tradition of political violence and of anti-Semitism and racism. Lewis (1987: 260-61) made the point effectively, arguing:

> Why did fascism fail in Britain? There is no simple answer to such a question, of course, but it is as well to dispense at the outset with the popular myth that fascism was eliminated by the moderation and tolerance of the British character, or culture. In reality neither nations or races have inherent common traits of character. Nor even is there such an entity as a single national culture.

Interestingly, the BUF itself also sought to establish itself as indigenous to Britain. This assertion of their Britishness can be seen in several aspects of the BUF's history. For example, Mosley went to great lengths to deny that the Party received any funding from Mussolini's Italian government.[38] The attempt by the BUF to link their anti-Semitism with the interests of the British nation has already been highlighted, but there were other ways in which they tried to legitimise their actions in terms of 'the national tradition'. One of Mosley's supporters, a former Conservative MP, argued in 1933 that there was a British tradition of fascism. He linked Mosley's economic proposals with Elizabethan statecraft, arguing that they both emphasised the needs of the nation as a whole above any one section of it (Allen, 1933). The BUF also explained its opposition to the Public Order Bill in terms of

Britain's democratic legacy. In a leader in the *Fascist Quarterly*, in October 1936, the BUF argued that:

> the struggle of British freedom is arising. The question is whether Englishmen shall be allowed to plead their country's cause on their own streets, or whether they are to be silenced by an oriental army of occupation.[39]

Perhaps those who adopted such positions did so because appeals to 'the national character' provided an easy means of legitimation for those in the political mainstream to act against those on the extremes. That the only Communist MP of the day was one of the few opponents of the Public Order Bill illustrates this point. What is clear is that those on the extreme, most notably Mosley himself, tried to present themselves as true Britons, not bearers of a suspect 'continental' style of politics.

Conclusion

It has been demonstrated that violence was an endemic feature of the political campaigns by the British Union of Fascists and their opponents during the 1930s. Whatever may have been claimed after more recent disorders, social instability in that decade did engender considerable unrest. The fact that the press explicitly reported BUF meetings in terms of the occurrence or otherwise of disorder reinforces the claim that violence was a commonplace feature of day-to-day politics. In the case of the rally at Olympia in 1934, it is apparent that both the BUF and their opponents were prepared for, and virtually organised, the conflict which erupted. The printed and oral propaganda circulated by both sides could often be considered as tantamount to incitement to violence. The extent of disorders on a more day-to-day level was such that the policing of other parts of London was disadvantaged as resources were directed into the East End. This policing attention towards the conflict between the BUF and their, often Communist Party, opponents reflected political directions from the Home Office. One example of this occurred in 1938 when the Home Secretary directed the Commissioner of the Metropolitan Police to undertake surveillance of BUF meetings. Despite this specific political intervention from the centre, it is simplistic to argue that the violence which occurred at Cable Street in October 1936 led directly to the 1936 Public Order Act which granted greater powers to the police to prohibit marches and demonstrations. In fact, this legislation was engendered by more widespread fears of social unrest which were a response to the activity of the left as much as the right.

One factor which makes this case study different from the others considered here is that the participants in the disorders were relatively organised. This means it is possible to consider representations and arguments made by those involved in the disorders — voices that are often marginalised in the aftermath of unrest. The people who took part in the racist violence in Liverpool in 1919, or Nottingham and Notting Hill in 1958 and 1959, or the urban unrest in Tottenham in 1985, were generally unrepresented in the media or political debates thereafter. Most of the public debate following those events was conducted by politicians, newspaper columnists, and senior police officers. In the 1930s, though, the BUF and Communist Party routinely offered their perspectives on the disorders which took place. On other occasions, it may be that individual participants are able to offer insights into their motivations or reactions but not in the organised or routine way which applied in the case of the 1930s. Whereas the media more generally have to rely upon the police or politicians for responses to urban unrest, journalists in the 1930s could also easily seek the views of those who directly represented the participants. Of course, there remained many who engaged in violence whose views were not articulated because they were not members of any organised party. There were no doubt others who did belong to an organised political party, but who had divergent views from the official party position. It cannot be assumed, therefore, that the media and other reports offer a complete account of the disorders. Nonetheless, the involvement of organised and relatively mainstream political parties meant that a more representative range of opinion on the disorders are available than has been the case in other instances considered in this study.

Two general features of the explanations of the violence offered by all of the parties to the disorders have been highlighted. First, it is apparent that a widespread assumption has been that the apparent tensions between Jews and non-Jews in the East End of London were based in material reality. This assumption has tended to be made in academic explanations as well as in the contemporary reports and debates. Even when the anti-Semitism and violence of the BUF has been condemned the basis of their campaign, that the presence of Jewish people in the area was at the root of the problem, has often been implicitly endorsed. As in other incidents described in this work, the reality of the 'race relations' problem was accepted as given and the question of alleviating the resultant conflict became the key area of debate.

Another feature of the discourse surrounding these events can be seen in the positions adopted by all of the main players involved. All the major parties to the conflict claimed to represent genuine national political traditions and all sides invoked the culture of the 'people' as a source of legitimacy for their political position. This was done in specific and general ways by the BUF, the anti-fascist Communist Party, and politicians and ministers at the political centre. The BUF, for example, sought to portray itself as the guardian of traditional rights of free speech that were under threat from those who ascribed to either foreign or internationalist political movements. The BUF also expended great efforts to deny that it received any money from abroad — a controversy that was to dog Mosley until his death — and, in one instance, it presented itself as an advocate of an Elizabethan practice of statecraft. All of these arguments were employed in an effort to portray the party as a genuinely British political movement.

On the other hand, opponents of the British Union of Fascists also presented themselves as the true embodiment of the national political tradition. Part of this approach was directly designed to discredit Mosley and the BUF as essentially foreign incursions into the British scene. Although this strategy may have represented little more than a convenient way of trying to undermine the ambitions of the BUF, it is nonetheless interesting that the language of national tradition and political identity was invoked to this end. It has been shown that many of these arguments against British fascism have assumed that an innate character of the British people meant that far-right politics failed in the 1930s. However, this is a dangerous assumption which cannot account for the varying levels of support that far-right parties have had in Britain.

Those at the political centre appear to have found it easiest to express their contempt for both the BUF and the Communist Party in terms that stress their departure from the law-abiding and tolerant nature of British politics. To reiterate the point made earlier, such a view is based upon an extremely partial reading of British history, which ignores such events as the Suffragette and Chartist movements, the Gordon riots of the late eighteenth century, and the Peasants Revolt of the fourteenth century — to name but a few examples. Political violence, then, was not a new and sinister development which copied an inferior politics from the continent. Such conceptualisations, however, did allow mainstream political actors to condemn extremists of both left and right who represented a relatively minor, but potentially much more serious, threat to their own position.

In conclusion, it should be remembered that there was considerable connection between the two themes outlined above in the reactions to the disorders of the mid-1930s. Anti-Semitism, as well as political violence, was presented as an unwelcome foreign manifestation of inferior political traditions. As in the other case studies, that assertion owed less to historical truth than to political expediency. Unfortunately, it is clear that anti-Semitism, like other forms of racism, has a longer pedigree in British society than is often admitted. The explanations of the anti-Semitism expressed by the BUF during this period nearly all take for granted the reality of the 'race relations' problematic and readily assume that it could be explained in terms of genuine grievances between Jew and non-Jew. The notion that the process of racialisation should be central to any discussion has generally been neglected by writers on this subject.

Participants from all quarters, including those directly involved in the violence, suggested that the development of this public order problem was inconsistent with British history. This perception provided an explanatory framework for the disorder, and allowed mainstream politicians to distance themselves from it. It seems that all of those involved, directly or indirectly, in the disorder saw political advantage in claiming that national political traditions supported their actions. Government ministers claimed to be upholding the 'tradition' of peaceable Parliamentary politics; the British Union of Fascists said they were exercising the tradition of free speech; and the left argued against fascism in the name of the tolerance of the ordinary people of the East End. All of these claims were highly questionable, but they did allow mainstream political parties to legitimise themselves in the face of opposition from the street. The contemporaneous reaction of the Conservative MP Geoffrey Lloyd to the disorders at Olympia in 1934 could be taken as symbolic of the more widespread response to the events:

> I could not help shuddering at the thought of this vile bitterness copied from foreign lands, being brought into the centre of England.[40]

Many aspects of debates which surrounded the violence accompanying British Union of Fascists' activity in the mid-1930s reflect the critical realist racialisation problematic developed in Chapter One. Contemporary analysis of the disorder by the media, police officers, and politicians were often based on an assumption that genuine 'racial' differences existed between Jews and non-Jews, and that these explained the real problems and violence which arose. It has been shown that a similar perception is also apparent in more recent historical accounts of the period. This reflects the first aspect of the critical realist model which indicates that racialised discourse is used to understand and interpret specific problems.

The second and third features of the theoretical model refer to the importance of prevailing racialised ideas, which are not specific to a particular situation, and to the diversity of myths which are applied to different groups in divergent circumstances. Both aspects of the model were apparent in responses to the unrest outlined in this Chapter. When *The Times* referred to 'traditional grumbles against Jewish price cutting, clannishness, and their problematical wealth or dirtiness', as detailed in a previous section, it highlighted long-standing myths which have been specific features of anti-Semitism but do not necessarily appear in other racialised discourses (Cohen, 1988).

Just as it was claimed that anti-Semitism was incompatible with British culture, so public disorder was held to be aberrant from national traditions. Although prejudice against the Jews was often condemned, it was still implied that they constituted a distinct 'racial' group, but often it was maintained that the inherent tolerance of the British people served as a bulwark against the 'inferior' politics evident elsewhere in Europe, a key feature of which was violence. Thus the racialised debate corresponded closely with notions of national culture and related suggestions that Britain was superior to many of her neighbours. This process of articulation reflects the fourth feature of the critical realist racialisation problematic.

Notes

1 See Benyon (1987: 38-41), for a fuller account of disorder in the 1930s.
2 Geiger (1963: 51) records that leaders of pre-BUF fascist groups included Rt Hon. Vincent Fitzalan [Imperial Defence League], Major General Sir Alfred Knox [National Citizens Union], and Lord Duncairn [Ulster Volunteer Movement].
3 For a fuller account of the history of anti-Semitism in Britain see Lebzelter, (1978).
4 It seems likely that there was no real need for Mosley to wait for the protesters to be removed. Given that he had a powerful public address system it seems feasible that he could have continued and 'drowned out' hecklers. It has been suggested that he preferred to pause so that he could claim the violent response was necessary to permit free speech. If he had simply continued speaking the grounds for justifying the removal of hecklers would have disappeared.
5 *The Times*, 8 June 1936.
6 *Vindicator* (1934: 18).
7 *ibid*, 25.
8 *ibid*, 33-34.
9 *The Times*, 9 June 1934.
10 Stevenson and Cook (1977: 236).
11 See, for example, Anderson (1983).
12 Jacobs (1978) presents his account of events in these terms.
13 From BBC TV (1994).
14 For example, Cross (1961: chapter 11); Jacobs (1978).
15 *The Times*, 20 October 1936.
16 See Lebzelter (1978: 129).
17 Cited in Mullings (1984: 183).
18 From BBC TV (1994).
19 Interview notes.
20 From BBC TV (1994).
21 Reported in *The Times*, 5 October 1936.
22 Searchlight, (1995).
23 Cited in N. Mosley (1983: 85).
24 The argument was made with no evidence to support it and it seems highly likely that the Jewish community had allegiance to Britain. They are not the only group of migrants who have displayed great attachment to their new home, perhaps to a greater degree than the indigenous population. One interviewee who's parents had arrived from Eastern Europe at the turn of the twentieth century described the attitude of the Jewish community at this time as follows: 'England is the most tolerant country in the world. It is you know. My father and all the people living in the east End used to speak broken English, but they loved England because, as my father said, when he came here, the policeman didn't have revolvers, they couldn't believe it. It is a free country, but we used to say 'free without a doubt, if you have no dinner you're free to go without'. What is more the BUF's position assumes that

political and emotional identity is unifocal and ignores the fact that one individual can have allegiance to multiple local, national, or supra-national identities.

25 Skidelsky (1975) takes the unusual step of allowing the subject of his biography a direct platform to comment on a matter of some controversy when he includes a justificatory endnote written by Sir Oswald Mosley to his chapter on anti-Semitism (see pages 391-92).

26 Skidelsky (1975: 381) argues that 'a Jewish malaise of this time was to be obsessed with fascism'.

27 *The Times*, 20 October 1936.

28 Jacobs (1977) records that even the Communist Party were reluctant to organise against Mosley's march through Cable Street in October 1936 and only did so when it was obvious that the protest would go ahead without them.

29 See Cohen (1988) for a fuller discussion of the marginalisation of the study of anti-Semitism.

30 *Parliamentary Debates*, 1936-7, vol. 317, col. 1349, 25 November 1936.

31 Cited in Lebzelter, 1978: 115.

32 Cited in Anderson, 1983: 103.

33 *Parliamentary Debates*, vol. 317, col. 1422, 25 November 1936.

34 Quoted in *The Times*, 17 October 1936.

35 *Manchester Guardian*, 19 October 1936.

36 Orwell (1968) acknowledged the presence of anti-Semitism in British history and society, but suggested that a counter-veiling tradition of tolerance would prove stronger.

37 See Adorno *et al*, (1950), and Nicholls, (1981).

38 See N. Mosley (1983: 304) for a fuller discussion.

39 Cited in Anderson (1983: 169).

40 Cited in Vindicator (1934: 11).

4 Nottingham and Notting Hill 1958–59: ‘Ostentatious Blacks and Rowdy Whites’

Introduction

The ‘riots of 1958–59’ were not a set of coherent or unicausal events. Of course, this is true of any incident of public disorder involving disparate groups with myriad motivations for their participation. Such an observation applies, to some extent, to the unrest in 1919, the mid–1930s, or 1985, described in other chapters here. One of the more problematic arguments advanced by Keith (1993) concerns the difficulty in generalising about ‘disorder’ and the need to recognise the local, specific, character of such events. Whilst it is salutary to be reminded of the particular local relations that generate disturbances, Keith raises a methodological difficulty in that social science needs to discuss such disparate events at some level of generalisation and in relation to macro-level developments. The dilemma is how to balance the need to acknowledge specificity whilst recognising that, as contagion theorists of disorder emphasise most strongly, isolated incidents occur in concert with others which often share similar features. As mentioned in the previous Chapter, Keith (1993: 92) distinguishes between the ‘public and private life of a riot’ and the events described in this Chapter neatly illustrate how disparate private events have entered public histories as a unified incident of disorder.

The incidents under discussion, however, cannot accurately be described as ‘riots’, even if one puts to one side, for the moment, the argument that ‘riot’ is a pejorative and contested term. In the case of Nottingham, there were two weekends during August 1958 when relatively large numbers of people engaged in street disturbances in a small area. These were disorders of the kind that became more familiar during the 1980s and 1990s. Otherwise, however, the incidents explored here can be more aptly described as a series of comparatively small-scale confrontations involving relatively few people, formed into gangs, who carried out attacks directed at specific others. There were not, on the whole, scenes of looting, arson and destruction which one might normally refer to as 'riots', uprisings, or disorders. Not only were the events of a smaller scale than disorder in the sense usually taken, but they also occurred over relatively long periods of time. In fact, in the case of Notting Hill it is not possible to mark a definitive beginning and end point of the events. Certainly, there were press reports of street disturbances in August 1958 yet the racist murder of Kelso Cochrane was not committed, in North Kensington, until May 1959. Compared, for example, to the disorders in Manningham, Bradford, or in Luton, in June 1995, which lasted for a few days, the incidents in Notting Hill in the last years of the 1950s were clearly of a different temporal character.

Even the localities that have been named must be treated with some caution. The disorders in 'Notting Hill' actually occurred over a fairly broad area, not all of which is labelled as such on the map. Several contemporary reports, for example Glass (1960), refer to Notting *Dale* as well as Notting *Hill*. Jacobson (1958: 6) was one of a few commentators who recognised this confusion at the time:

> The name "Notting Hill" has been given to the riots, but the area in which disturbances of one kind or another took place — ranging from attacks on individual coloureds to the stoning of houses, attempts at arson, and street brawling on an extensive scale — is very wide indeed. It stretches from beyond the Edgware Road on the west to Sheperd's Bush on the east; and from the Bayswater Road on the south to somewhere north of Westbourne Park. It includes the highly respectable — the almost Kensingtonian — squares and crescents of Holland Park; and the slums just to the north of Paddington.

This point is further evidenced by the frequent reference at the time to the disorders of *North Kensington*. This confusion is indicative of a broader tendency, elaborated further in this Chapter, to over-generalise about the disparate events that occurred in Nottingham and Notting Hill in 1958 and 1959.

It is thus important to explain why this Chapter, to some extent, might be criticised for repeating this distortion. Unreliable as it may have been, it is clear that contemporary and subsequent analyses of these disorders did assume a certain coherence to them and it is the themes and implications of such reactions which are the main focus of what follows. Clearly, it is important to delineate the events themselves and to give some flavour of what happened. This is not to say that what is being offered is a retelling of the disturbances as they unfolded. Instead some attempt is being made to understand the related themes of 'race', national identity, and public disorder as deployed in response to these disturbances. It should be remembered that the debates often misrepresented and distorted what actually happened, but it is neither surprising nor unprecedented that this was the case.

This Chapter focuses upon the reactions to the events themselves. Unlike the events of 1919 or the 1930s, these were the subject of contemporary sociological analysis, and the themes of these explanations are also considered. It is suggested that the disorders of 1958–59 relied upon a racialised account of community tensions and that this represented an early example of what is now often referred to as the 'race relations' approach. This racialised discourse is discussed as it was evident in the ways that various problems were identified: the housing shortage, immigration, and the activities of lawless white youths. The response of liberal and charitable groups, and the role of gender in the debates arising from the disorders, are also examined. Prior to this analysis an overview of the disorders is given.

Background and context

In terms of the history of public disorder in Britain, the first events in what have become known as the '1958 race riots' were not without precedent. Taken on their own merit, and from a perspective nearly forty years later, it is not immediately apparent why they became symbolic and disturbing to contemporary commentators. On 23 August 1958, a Saturday night, a fight occurred between a black man and a white man outside the Chase Tavern on the St Ann's Well Road in Nottingham. The fight escalated until some 1,500 people were involved and the police had been called both to the Chase Tavern area and to another site some streets away. The extent of the disorder was such that all available officers from across the city were called to the scene and senior officers were dispatched to the area (Popkess, 1960: 675). The nature of the violence is evident from the Chief Constables subsequent observation that 'the mob were now attacking any coloured person in sight, whether they had been implicated in any way in the disturbances or not' (Popkess, 1960: 676). Glass (1960: 131) suggests that it took the police until midnight to restore order, by which time the disturbances had been in progress for about ninety minutes and seven civilians and one police officer had been hospitalised.

In contrast, the disorders that occurred in the Handsworth area of Birmingham in autumn 1985 lasted for somewhere in the region of twelve hours, two civilians were killed when their Post Office was set on fire, 122 other people were injured and damage to the order of £7.5 million was reported (Benyon and Solomos, 1987: 5). When the events in Nottingham are considered in the light of this more recent example, it is clear that the attention they have received in academic literature owes more to their symbolic importance than their inherent properties. The disorders received such scrutiny, not because of their intensity as scenes of violence, but because of their portentous nature as signifiers of social malaise. This reflects the point made previously about the unrest at Olympia in 1934 — that the social context in which events occur is central to the way in which they are understood.

The impact of these events in a postwar austere society which was unused to public disorder on any large scale was considerable. At one level, the impact can be seen in the widespread national and local press coverage that the unrest received. An article in the *Nottingham Courier* on 26 August 1958 predicted that the St. Ann's district would witness further violence. Under the headline RACE RIOT CITY IS LIVING IN FEAR OF NEW CLASH, the article suggested that gangs of 'teddy boys' and 'coloureds' were preparing to descend on the area for further battles. Such press coverage, no doubt, also contributed to the attraction of other visitors and highlights the role that expectations can have on subsequent developments. The following weekend witnessed the unusual phenomenon of parties of tourists arriving in the area to witness the 'race riots', attracted partly by the 'sensational press reporting' (Popkess, 1960: 676) and partly by the coach tours advertised in the local press of nearby towns such as Melton Mowbray and Leicester. Indeed, The *Times* reported on 16 September 1958 that the city authorities had asked the police to approach bus companies in nearby areas to ask them to stop these 'sight-seeing trips'.

The tourists were not disappointed as disorders resumed on the weekend of 29 and 30 August when 'teddy boys', local residents, and assorted reporters formed a crowd of some 4,000 or so people. According to contemporary sources, there were very few 'coloured' people on the streets as they had been warned to stay indoors. As in the Liverpool disorders of 1919, 'coloured' people had been taken into protective custody the previous weekend, a move that the Chief Constable recognised they resented (Popkess, 1960: 676). However, some black people did venture out. Glass (1960: 132) reports the fate of three black people who tried to drive their car through the area:

> Cries of 'let's lynch them', and 'let's get at them', went up as the crowd, many of them teddy boys who had poured from public houses, tried to smash their way into the car. Beating on the windows they tried to overturn it ... Finally the police forced a path through them and told the coloured men in the car to 'go like hell'. They did.

Perhaps it was because the local black population largely kept off the streets that this second weekend of disorder was largely conducted against the police. A rather literal flashpoint in the disorders was created by a newspaper photographer's magnesium flare. The *Leicester Mercury* reported how:

> the flare was burning with great intensity, and gave the impression that buildings were on fire and the crowds were converging on this point. The officer remonstrated with him. By then the crowd had become angry and fighting had started.[1]

Little mention was made in contemporaneous accounts of how the disorder died down, how long it lasted, and at what, financial or other, cost. *The Times* reported on 1 September 1958 that the Chief Constable stated that the police had been forced to 'use strong methods in self-defence against the white population'. Some fifty people were arrested following the second weekend, twenty four of whom were charged with public order offences.

Following these incidents in Nottingham attention switched to events in Notting Hill. As has been indicated, although it is rather inaccurate to use this name to describe a wide and heterogeneous area, for the sake of this discussion it will be retained. The events in Notting Hill occurred over a longer time period than those in Nottingham. They escalated from a series of isolated racist attacks into more widespread violence involving large numbers of people and attracting the attention of Mosley's Union Movement.[2] Accounts of those who lived in the area suggested that there was some recognition that disorders might occur in the light of the events in Nottingham. The article in the *Nottingham Courier*, cited above, concluded by reporting that 'police chiefs' in London recognised the possibility of disorder and that extra street patrols had been deployed in Notting Hill and other parts of London. The possible significance of local people, including police officers, anticipating unrest is a factor that recurs throughout this examination of urban disorder.

The first incident reported in the press and other contemporary accounts involved a group of nine white youths who embarked upon a series of racist attacks through the Notting Hill area on the night of Saturday 30 August 1958. According to Jacobson (1958) most of the young men seem to have been in their late teens. Jacobson (1958: 4-5) suggests they:

> had been drinking in a pub and decided to go on a "nigger-hunting expedition", armed with wooden staves, knives, an air pistol, a table leg, and iron railings. Between midnight and five am they cruised the

> streets and attacked single coloured men, leaving them unconscious in the street. The group of nine never attacked more than two coloured men at one time.

At their trial the nine youths were sentenced to four years imprisonment for actual bodily harm. Justice Salmon told them that they committed 'extremely grave and brutal crimes' and that:

> It was you men who started the whole of this violence in Notting Hill. You are a minute and insignificant section of the population who have brought shame on the district in which you live and have filled the whole nation with horror, indignation, and disgust.[3]

For several years afterwards these sentences were the subject of Parliamentary questions and a debate that argued that they too severe and urging that the youths be shown clemency.[4] However, the Home Secretary, R. A. Butler, persistently refused to intervene.

Despite this 'determined action' (Butler, 1971: 206), the disorders did not abate at this stage but continued with greater ferocity. Fryer (1984: 379) described how:

> By the end of August brawls, disturbances, and racist attacks were a daily, and nightly, feature of life in North Kensington. A Jamaican was shot in the leg. Petrol bombs were thrown into black people's homes, including the homes of pregnant women. Such attacks were often preceded by a threatening letter or a shouted warning: "We're going to raid you tonight if you don't clear out". Crowds hundreds strong shouted abuse at black people. A young African student, a stranger to the area, emerged from an Underground station to find himself chased by a hostile crowd shouting "Lynch him!". He took refuge in a greengrocer's shop whose proprietor gave him sanctuary by locking and bolting the door and defying the mob.

Hiro (1973) provided some indication of the reactions of local black residents to the violence that threatened them. He suggested that, following the actions of the police to take them into protective custody, referred to earlier, the black residents of Nottingham were noticeable by their absence from the streets in the St Ann's area. The response of the black residents in London was also noted:

> Once the blacks in Notting Hill had overcome their initial alarm, shock and despondency, they tried to help themselves as best as they could. They avoided, as far as possible, leaving their homes; and when they

> had to, they avoided walking alone after dark. They provided elaborately arranged escorts for those black London Underground employees who had to work late-night or early-morning shifts, and formed vigilante groups which patrolled the area in cars.[5]

One black man who became involved in the disorders recalled a more direct response from those who were subjected to attack:

> During the day we made preparations for the attack and I can quite clearly remember standing on the second floor with the lights out in Blenheim Crescent when I looked out and could see from Kensington Park Road and Portobello Road a massive lot of people and I distinctly heard when they said "burn the niggers", "lynch the niggers", and from those spoken words I said "start bombing them" and then the Molotov Cocktails came out from number nine Blenheim Crescent. Then we saw that they were bombing us too, I said "open the gate and throw them back where they are coming from". When the police saw the amount of people that was in number nine, they drove the Black Maria, rammed the gates, and said "not another one of you black bastards is coming out", I was arrested immediately. But from then on the police took over. It was a very serious bit of fighting that night, because we were very, very angry and we were determined to use any weapon, anything at our disposal for our freedom. We were not prepared to go down like dying dogs.[6]

Extreme right-wing groups appeared in the district in September 1958 — but not for the first time — although it seems that their involvement alone cannot explain the disorders. The number of people involved was simply too great for right-wing groups to be entirely responsible. Glass (1960: 141), for example, describes the extent the disorders had reached by 3 September:

> petrol bombs were flung into the homes of coloured people in Notting Hill and Paddington. There was by then the usual 'anti-nigger' shouting and bottle throwing. Even the most ordinary encounter between a white and coloured could still set off new turmoil. When a coloured mother's perambulator brushed against, and became entangled with, a white mother's push chair at a road junction in North Kensington, a crowd of about 150 people collected instantly, and the police had to be called to restore order.

As was the case with the events in Nottingham, there is little evidence to explain how or when the disorders died away. As previously mentioned, the racist murder of Kelso Cochrane did not occur until May 1959 but it seems certain that the intense disorders of September 1958 did not continue until this point. Rather it may be that, as Fryer (1984: 380) suggests, all that happened was that 'by mid-September the situation in North Kensington had returned to normal — or, rather, to what passed as a "normal" incidence of racist violence'. As Fryer also pointed out, there had been racist attacks in the area for several years before 1958 and they continued afterwards, albeit at a less widespread level. This indicates that the incidents in 1958–59 came to represent social changes not directly related to the events themselves. The activist Michael X made a similar point in his recollections of life in Notting Hill during this period (Malik, 1968: 76):

> The situation, as far as I could see, was being created by newspaper sensationalism and police hysteria. Together they were having quite an effect. There was no doubt by now that a 'situation' did exist.

Explaining the disorders

This section will examine some of the responses to the 1958–59 disorders. The explanations offered by the media, police, politicians, government, and sociologists and social workers, are the main focus of the discussion. Four broad themes are identified: those which refer to the housing shortage as a causal factor, those that assume that the number of 'West Indian' immigrants arriving escalated tensions, those which focus upon the role of lawless 'rowdy' white youths, and those which identify sexual relations between black and white people as a causal factor. The response of liberal, charitable groups is also considered. It is suggested in the conclusion what lay beneath all of these explanations, whether they were broadly conservative or liberal, pro- or anti-immigration control, was an assumption of racial antagonism and a conception of 'race relations' as inherently problematic.

Housing, unemployment, and national assistance

One of the central themes of the reactions to the disorders in 1958–59 was the socio-economic problems of the localities in which they occurred. In particular, many commentators drew attention to the shortage of good quality housing and the problems of unemployment in both Nottingham and Notting Hill. A common view was that the migrants arriving from the Commonwealth were exacerbating, if not creating, the problems of housing and job shortages. Reference was also made to the poor-quality, over-crowded, accommodation that the newcomers had to endure and allegations were made that they were drawing national assistance because they were unemployed.

The provision of affordable decent housing was one of the keenest political issues of the 1950s and was accepted as such by Labour and Conservative governments. In their manifesto for the 1951 general election, the Conservatives had promised to build 300,000 houses a year, more than the Labour government's previous high of 248,000 new houses in 1948 (Adams, 1992). Although this figure was not achieved, the Conservative government oversaw the building of 180,000 new houses a year between 1951 and 1957 (Hamnet, 1992). Such unprecedented public-sector house building was partly necessitated by the destruction of housing during the Second World War and also by the political consensus of the era which saw a broad agreement that the state had a responsibility for the well-being of the population. The desire to eradicate the slums associated with the 1930s' depression was evident by the scale of the programme.

Despite the extent of the new house building there appeared to be some agreement that, at least in Notting Hill and St. Ann's, Nottingham, there remained a serious shortage of adequate dwellings. In their survey of St. Ann's, conducted some years after the disorders, Coates and Silburn (1967) found that the housing density of the district was much higher than for other nearby council estates and for the City of Nottingham as a whole. The low quality of the housing in the area is a marked feature of their survey and the St. Ann's district, as it existed in the late 1950s, was eventually razed as part of a slum clearance programme.[7] In various debates about the disorder, and about immigration more generally, MPs suggested that the housing problem was exacerbated by newly-arrived migrants. For example, in a Parliamentary debate on the sentences imposed on the youths arrested in the Notting Hill disorders, Frank Tomney MP (Labour, Hammersmith North) described the build-up to the disturbances:

> Into this huge city, where people scramble for houses and where the Rent Act is in operation, streamed thousands of colonial nationals. They had a perfect right to come here under the Constitution of the country and their associations with the Commonwealth, but nevertheless, they aggravated a problem which was already acute.[8]

Other politicians from both the Conservative and Labour parties also made reference to the lack of decent housing in their response to the disorder. James Harrison, Labour member for Nottingham North reportedly suggested that housing problems, coupled with 'ominous unemployment trends', were responsible for the unrest and argued that action by central government was needed to rectify the situation. The Cabinet was also directed to this issue in its discussion of the violence. The Lord President of the Council, Lord Hailsham, explained in a memorandum that:

> Property has been bought up by coloured landlords, who have then made the position of white tenants intolerable, and entire streets have gone over to a coloured population.[9]

Beyond Westminster, other commentators also referred to housing problems as an important background factor in the escalation of tensions. Writing in the *New Statesman*, Mallalieu (1959), suggested that housing shortages coupled with broader social problems had caused the disorder:

> In fact such race troubles as there have been have themselves sprung from the nature of the area itself and especially from the acute shortage both of space and of houses, which above everything else is the area's great curse. People of one race and similar habits would have difficulty living in such an environment; but the difficulties are greatly increased when one group, the West Indians, have different habits from their neighbours.

Such concerns had been expressed prior to the disorders,[10] but there were others who recognised that such shortages were not simply a result of immigration into these areas. In a Parliamentary debate about immigration control, held on 3 April 1958, Christopher Boyd MP (Labour, Bristol NW), pointed out an inconsistency in the prevailing debates about housing and immigration. He stated that:

> the housing aspect of this problem is actually helped by the greater volume of emigration than made more difficult by the smaller volume of immigration.[11]

A commonplace contradiction often existed in the public imagination about the socio-economic position of the black migrants, just as stereotypes about the Jews in London during the 1930s were confused. On one hand, newcomers from the Caribbean were held to be responsible for the shortage of quality housing available for whites, but at the same time they were seen as living in overcrowded, undesirable housing and it was said that this aspect led to other problems with neighbours. This reflects the third feature of the racialisation problematic, the framework delineated in Chapter One, which is that such discourse is often contradictory and inconsistent. It was noted by several observers in the late 1950s[12] that the migrants from the Commonwealth often had trouble finding suitable accommodation of a reasonable quality. Of course, this position was not only caused by a lack of housing, but was also a result of the attitudes of prejudiced whites who refused accommodation to black people. One commentator suggested that it was for this reason that many black people in Notting Hill came into contact with one of the more notorious individuals of the period, the 'slum landlord' Peter Rachman. His dilapidated properties were no doubt the sort that many had in mind when they condemned the living conditions of black people in Notting Hill. Malik (1968), however, casts a different perspective on the role of Rachman and his relation to black people in the area at that time:

> I'm not eager to run to his defence. But I object to him being used as a scapegoat to conscience in this country. The real villain was not Peter Rachman. It was, and still is, all those who put up notices saying: 'no coloured' ... 'no Irish' ... 'no children' ... 'no dogs' ... the 'no' people: nasty, mean, ignorant, joyless people. They're the ones who made it possible for Rachman to provide his particular kind of service.

Concern was also expressed about the impact of the black immigrants on the labour market. Although migration from the Commonwealth was initially encouraged in order to satisfy the demands of the labour market, by 1958 unemployment was beginning to reappear as the government took steps to control inflation. Just as they were, at least partly, blamed for the housing shortage, black people were often regarded as guilty of taking jobs from the white workers who had a stronger claim upon them. In this vein, an early champion of immigration control, Cyril Osborne MP (Conservative, Louth), demanded such a measure 'with a view to controlling all immigration in order to safeguard the jobs of workers already in this country'.[13]

As was the case in 1919, employers and trades unions were often reluctant to employ black workers. Employers tended to speak in terms of the need to maintain harmonious relations amongst their workforce — whilst trades unions also referred to concern about the job security and wage levels of the white workforce (see Phizacklea and Miles, 1980; Fryer, 1984; Carter, 1986). The contradictory argument which held that black people were enjoying housing provisions that 'rightfully' belonged to whites, whilst also holding that black people were causing a problem due to their overcrowded and insanitary housing conditions, could also be seen in respect of unemployment. Just as the newly-arrived migrants were blamed for occupying jobs belonging to others, the black workers were more likely to be unemployed and often were the first to be made redundant. Pilkington (1988: 39-40) records that 'West Indians' in Nottingham experienced higher levels of unemployment than the white community, and cites the explanation offered by one employer:

> Whenever I have to put off staff, I sack the coloured ones first. The trouble is that whenever you dismiss West Indians they make such a fuss. They say you have done it because of colour prejudice, and that makes you feel a rotter. But there would be a riot if I did anything else.

Not only were black migrants regarded as having a deleterious effect on unemployment but their receipt of national assistance when unemployed was also occasionally raised. Although Cyril Osborne often expressed concern about the lack of reliable information regarding the number of migrants and their subsequent circumstances after arrival into the country, he did find statistics to support his pro-control argument in the Queen's Speech debate of October 1958. Osborne suggested that there were 10,000 Commonwealth migrants in receipt of unemployment pay and public assistance and that this effectively meant that indigenous white workers were financing their upkeep. He concluded:

> it seems reasonable and fair to the British people who are paying money into these funds that a limit should be placed upon the number of people coming here and drawing upon those funds to which they have made no contribution.[14]

It should be remembered that, in the concerns expressed about both housing and employment issues, the black migrants living in Britain during the late 1950s were rarely blamed by mainstream politicians or the media for creating such problems where none had previously existed. The campaigns emanating from far-right groups, who attempted to make political capital from the disorders, may have blamed them on occasions but 'respectable' analysis more usually suggested only that they were adding to pre-existing social problems. However, as in other times and at other places, for example in 1919, the black migrants were effectively victimised twice by a racialised understanding of the genuine problems of housing shortages and rising unemployment. Not only were higher levels of emigration compared to immigration largely overlooked, the comments of Christopher Boyd notwithstanding, but the fact that white people formed the substantial majority of immigrants,[15] and yet attracted little or no concern for their impact upon social conditions, indicates that the arguments were not about immigration *per se* but about 'coloured' immigration in particular.

Immigration

It is clear that the very presence of Commonwealth immigrants in Britain was seen by many as a causal factor in the disorders. Demands to control immigration from the Commonwealth were made immediately after the disturbances and continued over a longer period, not always with direct reference to the events in Nottingham and Notting Hill, leading up to the Commonwealth Immigrants Act of 1962. In the immediate aftermath to the unrest, both the MPs representing Nottingham (one Labour and one Conservative) demanded that Commonwealth immigration should be curbed.[16] The following day, the Conservative MP for Kirkdale, Norman Pannell — an early postwar supporter of control — argued:

> the Nottingham fighting is a manifestation of the evil results of the present [immigration] policy and I feel that unless some restriction is imposed we shall create the colour bar we all want to avoid. Unless we bar undesirable immigrants and put out of the country those who commit certain crimes we shall create prejudice against the immigrants, particularly the coloured immigrants. We must avoid this.[17]

This argument appears to assume that racism is an inevitable feature of the human condition which can only be prevented by stopping or at least limiting regular contact between the different 'races'. As in 1919, it was argued that the 'colour line' (Du Bois, 1982) needed to be enforced if direct confrontation was to be avoided. Such a conception reduces racism to the level of individual psychology and ignores the social process of racialisation, a point considered further in the conclusion to this Chapter. There is a contradiction in this discourse in that it remains relatively silent in respect of the migration of white colonialists to the Caribbean. As was seen with the issue of miscegenation surrounding the 1919 disorders in Liverpool, the principle of separation between the 'races' was extended to the colonies, where the prospect of mixed 'race' marriages was seen as threatening the social hierarchy of the colonial societies. Conversely, the presence of the white people in the colonies was regarded as beneficial to the indigenous populations (McClintock, 1995; Young, 1995). When the position was reversed, however, and black people were present amongst the indigenous white population in 'the motherland', the supposed dangers of moral, sexual, and socio-economic 'pollution' were feared.

Pannell's fellow-traveller on the immigration control issue, Cyril Osborne, put the claim more starkly. In his contribution to the Queen's Speech debate, in October 1958, he argued:

> it is time someone spoke for this country and the white man who lives here, and I propose so to do ... Sooner or later some control would have to be put on. If it is not put on soon we shall, whether we like it or not — this is what I fear and I am very frightened about it — have Little Rocks [*sic.*] and Notting Hill incidents over and over again.[18]

A common theme underpinning such demands was that Britain faced an increasing and apparently open-ended process of immigration from the Commonwealth that posed material and psychological problems for the indigenous white population in the areas where they settled. However, the official statistics for immigration from the New Commonwealth indicated that the numbers arriving during the period

Table 2: Commonwealth Immigration to Great Britain, 1956–61, by Country of Origin

	1956	1957	1958	1959	1960	1961
West Indies	12,700	5,500	7,800	1,700	14,800	26,000
East Africa	350	250	200	15	–60	650
West Africa	500	525	250	nil	–425	900
Cyprus	825	425	65	–200	825	1,800
Gibraltar	80	nil	–75	–150	–75	–175
Malta	275	200	80	–175	–250	225
Aden	525	nil	15	275	60	75
Hong Kong	75	300	70	300	350	600
Malaya	275	175	325	225	–200	nil
Singapore	75	90	–110	10	–30	275
India	2,650	2,200	3,300	1,300	2,000	6,700
Pakistan	800	1,200	4,200	–175	–125	6,000
Ceylon	250	250	100	–10	–225	125
Total	**19,380**	**11,115**	**16,220**	**3,115**	**16,645**	**43,175**

1. A minus sign denotes a net *outward* movement.
2. Figures are not available in respect of other Commonwealth countries.

Source: *Parliamentary Debates*, vol. 642, 1655–62.

1956–1961 fluctuated rather than increased year-on-year. Although there are reasons to believe that these official statistics do not provide a wholly reliable record of such immigration,[19] there does not appear to be a more reliable source available. Table 2 shows the number of immigrants arriving during these years and their countries of origin.

Whilst the number of migrants arriving did increase before the introduction of controls in 1962, the number of migrants arriving from the 'West Indies' fell sharply in 1957, 1958, and 1959 compared to the figure for 1956. It is thus misleading to argue that the disorders were a direct result of increasing numbers of migrants arriving from the Caribbean who caused material and other problems in the districts where they settled. The arguments proposed by Pannell, Osborne, and their supporters, were not supported by the facts. Immigration from the Commonwealth was not rising during this period and so the disorders could not have been simply caused by a 'natural' reaction to a changing world, as they tended to suggest.

Even those who opposed controls appeared to accept implicitly the assumption that immigration itself posed a social problem. A common problem for those arguing against immigration control was the danger of becoming embroiled in the 'numbers game', whereby the argument focused on disputes about the volume of actual or potential migration rather than on the more fundamental issue of why immigration was regarded as problematic in the first instance. In arguing against control, the *New Statesman* illustrated this tendency in 1959:

> The volume of West Indian immigrants has fallen off rapidly since 1957 and will continue to decline. The problem of assimilating the immigrants, all of whom are British citizens, is thus definable and measurable.[20]

The reason why the *New Statesman* opposed the demands of those who regarded immigration *per se* as the problem was that the numbers involved were not escalating. This was an early instance of the thinking underlying Roy Hattersley's influential dictum that 'integration without limitation is impossible; limitation without integration is indefensible'.[21] The logic of this argument can be counterpoised with that illustrated by a *Daily Telegraph* editorial of the time. Although numbers are mentioned in the extract, the logic of this paragraph is very different from that which is evident elsewhere:

> There is no "colour problem" in this country. To discuss it endlessly is to discuss nothing endlessly: it does not exist. What there is is a British problem, and it is a grave one, a very grave one indeed. When a

> great and apparently prosperous country cannot peacefully absorb some 250,000 people (a mere 0.5 per cent of its total population), there must be something gravely wrong with that country. By these sudden disturbances what strange and monstrous manifestations have been churned up from the depths of our society! What hatred, bitterness, and spite is suddenly revealed, what anger and frustration, what boredom and what rootless, aimless hooliganism, what envy, perhaps (yes, envy: are not West Indians envied if they look happy and well-dressed?). There was no "Jewish problem" in Germany. There was a German problem, however, as we and the world know to our cost.[22]

As Solomos (1988: 34) suggested, the events of 1958 have often been regarded as a watershed in the politics of immigration in Britain. Many writers (for example, Katznelson, 1976; Ramdin, 1987) have regarded them as a catalyst which transformed the laissez-faire open-door attitude towards immigration from the Commonwealth into one which recognised the need for control. This understanding was reflected in the subsequent memoirs of Macmillan (1973: 74) who admitted that immigration control had been discussed by the Cabinet as early as 1955, but suggested that 'no action was taken until the matter was brought forcibly to public attention by the so-called "race riots" which took place in 1958'. The Home Secretary in 1958 was R. A. Butler who also claimed that the disorders were a vital precursor to the legislation of 1962 (Butler, 1971: 206):

> As Home Secretary I had been gravely troubled by the Notting Hill riots in 1958, and I cannot praise too highly the determined action of the Judiciary in the person of Mr Justice Salmon who pronounced the most stringent sentences on the racist trouble-makers. But whilst disturbances on this scale did not recur, I was by 1961 persuaded that *the rise in racial tension could be avoided only if it were anticipated* [emphasis added].

There are two reasons why the suggestion that it was the disorders of 1958 which forced the issues of immigration control onto the political agenda is somewhat simplistic. First, this argument underestimates the demands for control that were being made before the disturbances. In other words, it is not the case that there were no calls, or even only isolated calls, for immigration control until the disorders 'brought forcibly' the issue to public attention. The issue of immigration control was discussed by the Cabinet at several stages in the early 1950s. The Labour Government under Attlee discussed the matter in 1951 and commissioned a committee of civil servants and ministers to review the 'means which might be adopted to check the immigration into this country of coloured people from the British colonial territories'.[23] In 1955, Macmillan later recalled (1973: 73-4):

> after some desultory discussions in the Cabinet, it was agreed that a Bill should be tentatively drafted. I remember that Churchill, rather maliciously, observed that perhaps the cry of 'Keep Britain White' might be a good slogan for the Election which we would soon have to fight without the benefit of his leadership.

At the local level, too, demands for immigration control were being made prior to 1958. Rich (1994: 177) recorded that:

> Leading a delegation of Council members to the Home Office in January 1955, a former Lord Mayor, Alderman William Bowen, urged the government to focus on economic development programmes in the Westindies [*sic.*] in order to try and prevent further immigration.

It is thus misleading to believe that calls for immigration control could only be heard from 'maverick' MPs (most notably Cyril Osborne and Norman Pannell) on the backbenches. These demands for, and discussions of, immigration control did not lead to legislation until after the disorders of 1958. This was not because the issue was seen as unproblematic for domestic harmony, however. Rather, it seems that a broader interest in maintaining good relations with other Commonwealth governments (Rich, 1994) and the need to ensure the free movement of labour (Phizacklea and Miles, 1980) were the primary reasons for lack of action on immigration control.

The second reason why it is simplistic to regard the disorders of 1958 as the principal cause of legislation to control immigration is that the Act of 1962 represented a change of method rather than of political aims. Before immigration was formally controlled in 1962 there was a period of immigration unregulated by law. However, other, more informal and perhaps illegal (Carter *et al*, 1987), measures were taken to discourage immigration. Macmillan (1973: 75) recorded how his discussions with Norman Manley, Prime Minister of Jamaica, in September 1958 centred upon the possibility that immigration could be influenced by non-legislative means as it had been previously.[24] In this respect, the aim of controlling, and reducing, levels of immigration began long before the 1958–59 disorder. What was changed by the 1962 Act was that this goal was explicitly stated or, as Osborne had put it, control should be '… a condition, instead of a plea'.[25] In other words, immigration control became a matter of legislation rather than negotiation.

Youths, crime, and social nuisance

Another theme that can be identified in the reactions to the disorders of 1958–59 related to the characteristics of the localities in which they occurred and the black and white communities who inhabited them. Images of black criminality have become a common feature of arguments relating to the presence and position of minority ethnic groups in British society (see Hall, *et al*, 1978; Gilroy, 1987) and the debates arising in the late 1950s suggest that this had, on occasion, been an issue before the 'crisis' period of the 1970s. However, there were also concern and condemnation expressed of the criminality and 'hooliganism' of young white males living in the areas concerned. In an editorial, *The Times* argued that:

> The troubles are certainly the latest manifestation of that youthful ruffianism … which has variously expressed itself in raids on post offices, the wrecking of cinemas and cafes, and gang clashes and stabbings. West Indians and other coloured residents, neither better nor worse than their white neighbours, but certainly different, are the latest "novelty" target for gangs out for trouble.[26]

In his article, Mallalieu (1959) explained the disorders in the following terms:

> Clearly there is tinder here waiting for a spark; and, since a few of the later West Indian arrivals have been the worst riff-raff from Barbados, it is not surprising that there should be clashes between them and such white riff-raff as had already battened on the place.

Such arguments tended to explain the events in terms of the incivility of those involved. Often it was suggested that the black migrants' lifestyle and living conditions led to tensions between themselves and the indigenous community, some of whom responded in a violent way. Reference was made, for example, to the involvement of the migrants in 'pimping', drug dealing, and illegal drinking clubs, as discussed further in the next section. As with other themes in the debates about the disorders, such concerns were evident prior to the events of Nottingham and Notting Hill,[27] although the Joint-Under Secretary of State for the Home Office stated in April 1958 that Commonwealth immigrants were not over-involved in criminal behaviour compared to other sections of the population.[28]

The politicians and commentators who focused on the lawlessness of those involved in the disorders produced a reassuring explanation of the events which located the problem in the disreputable areas of the cities, inhabited by culpable 'ruffians'. The black and white participants were blamed in equal measure as both were condemned as uncivilised and problematic. Often, though, the participants were regarded as victims of their social situation or culture. Those youths imprisoned following their 'nigger hunting' in Notting Hill, for example, were occasionally portrayed as impressionable individuals who were swept along by the circumstances in which they lived. Although the judge who sentenced them suggested that 'it was you men who started the whole of this violence in Notting Hill',[29] MPs pleading for leniency in their case tended to portray them as uneducated and uncivilised youths who should not be so severely punished for their understandable, though unacceptable, behaviour. The MP representing the constituency where the most of the youths lived, Frank Tomney (Hammersmith North) argued in the Commons that the background in which they had been brought-up should not be forgotten:

> In these circumstances, among people who have been reared in working-class districts, one gets a slow simmering to boiling point ... finally erupting in the mob violence that the judge punished very severely. I am the last to decry the ability, the impartiality and fairness of our judges but ... it is impossible ... for a man to divorce himself from his environment, his emotions, his upbringing, and his passions.[30]

Similar arguments were made about the black people who, although the subjects of the violence, were regarded as culpable by dint of their lifestyle and behaviour. The playing of loud music late at night, for example, was reported in the press as causing social tensions.[31] The Commonwealth migrants were often portrayed as though compromised by their changed social setting — one liberal argument held that they were acting in a manner 'natural' in their own environment but out of place in British cities. Wickenden (1958: 20) argued that friction arising from cultural differences between black migrants and the indigenous white population contributed towards the disorder:

> Although the West Indian thinks of himself in a certain sense as British, his customs and basic assumptions are radically different from those of England. He has been used in the Caribbean to living a great deal in the open air; doors are seldom closed in the West Indies; anyone may walk

> into a neighbour's house; privacy is little known and not much wanted. In England, because of the climate, doors are kept shut and an Englishman's house is his castle. There are still strong Puritan elements in the English character and to a West Indian the English will seem staid, reserved and prudish.

Contradictory arguments about who was responsible for the disorders are evident, however. Whilst several reports blamed the black population, to some extent, this was not a universal response. Welfare and charitable groups were established to help the migrants 'integrate' into society and the Chief Constable of Nottingham praised the actions of the immigrants, saying 'the coloured people behave in a most exemplary way by keeping out of the way. Indeed they were an example to some of our rougher elements'.[32] Even the common suggestion that the white youths imprisoned after the events in Notting Hill were victims of their deprived environment was not without contradiction. All of the youths had jobs and their employers kept their positions vacant during their imprisonment. Jacobson (1958) suggested that the youths were well-paid and came from 'good homes'.

Although responsibility was not placed definitively on one group or another for the violence, all of these cultural explanations suggested a certain inevitability to the disorders. They were predicated upon the notion that antipathy and suspicion were inevitable between people of different 'races', and that criminality and 'anti-social' behaviour exacerbated such problems. As was evident in the reactions to the disorders of 1919, such 'natural' differences were regarded as especially problematic in the context of urban areas with populations 'brought up in an atmosphere and in a district where justice is swift'.[33]

Pimping, sex, and 'silly girls'

A key feature of the arguments about the problems that the 'riff raff' migrants were causing in British cities referred to sexual relations. As was the case in 1919, it was taken for granted that 'sexual jealousy — the sight of coloured men walking along with white women'[34] was a central cause of the grievances of the white men. A further parallel with the earlier case study was the manner in which white women were occasionally blamed for aggravating the insecurities of white men. Just as the *Liverpool Courier* explained that, in 1919, there were 'women in Liverpool with no self-respect', the press reports of the disorders in 1958–59 also sometimes drew attention to the behaviour of local women. One interviewee attributed the disturbances in Nottingham to the fact that:

> There's a lot of jealousy caused by white girls — usually rather undesirable characters, silly teenagers with no moral standards — setting out to attract coloured men.[35]

Once again, the actions of the white men involved in violent attacks could be rationalised and explained — if not actually condoned. Relationships between sexually threatening black men and immoral white women were regarded as an obvious provocation. A Gallup Poll conducted in December 1958 revealed the issues that concerned white people about black migration. Whereas 37 per cent expressed concern about the unemployment situation, and 54 per cent about housing conditions, the most commonly identified 'problem', at 71 per cent, was 'inter-racial' marriage (Glass, 1960: 247). Pilkington (1988: 92) suggested that 'disapproval of miscegenation was rife at all levels of British society' and he indicated the role that some scientists and academics played in this concern:

> As late as 1963, for instance, Dr Ernest Claxton, Assistant Secretary to the British Medical Association, asserted that chastity should be enforced among black people in Britain in order to minimise the risk of producing children of mixed blood which he thought was becoming an increasing problem. Another medic, Dr Bertram, fellow of St John's College Cambridge and a member of the Eugenics Society, wrote in 1958, just before the riots, that when a community dominated by one race is invaded by a small number of men of a different race those men tend to mate with women of inferior social and biological standing, thus limiting the prospects of their offspring.

Unlike the position in 1919, however, there also allegations of a more sinister threat to women from the black migrants. Some of the key proponents of immigration control argued that Commonwealth migrants were disproportionately involved in 'pimping'. Parliamentary questions were asked about the number of convictions for living on immoral earnings passed on those from West Africa, the West Indies, Malta, and Cyprus.[36] Cyril Osborne suggested that crime was the second most significant problem that the migrants caused, after unemployment, and that the two main forms of crime were drug trafficking and pimping.[37] Although she stressed that the problem was limited, the Under-Secretary of State at the Home Office was moved to claim that '...certain types of immigrant possess a propensity to live off the immoral earnings of women'.[38] The power of stereotypes about sexual relations between black men and white women was such that one black man resident in Notting Hill during the postwar era reportedly remarked that 'if I was seen walking down the street with the Queen of England, people would assume she was a prostitute' (Pilkington, 1996: 13).

So it seems that some of the vague and rather non-specific fears about the effects black migrants might have on the social fabric of the community crystallised around well-established stereotypes of the black man as a sexual threat.[39] Whilst this concern was rarely expressed in terms of the biological impact this may have on future generations of the 'race', as it had been in 1919, it was still regarded as problematic and an obvious source of tension. The threat was also explicitly criminalised in this context. Whereas the same 'problem' of sexual relations had been identified in 1919, in the late 1950s it had become more serious in as much as it was characterised by the coercive crime of pimping.

Liberal, charitable, and community groups

Much of the recent literature discussing the disorders of 1958–59 ignores an important and interesting kind of response which involved the establishment of voluntary groups intending to promote 'racial tolerance' and integration (Fryer, 1984; Miles, 1984; Pilkington, 1988; Solomos, 1993). On the surface, it appears that these initiatives were based upon different assumptions to those implied in many of the arguments above, because they were more sympathetic to the position of the black victims of the disturbances. Such initiatives were reinforced by the statements condemning racial discrimination that were issued by various bodies, including the Labour Party, the British Council of Churches, the Conservative Commonwealth Council. The 'Keep Britain Tolerant' (Glass, 1960) groups varied in their membership and longevity, with many of them apparently fading as soon as the initial violence waned. The local authority for the Notting Hill area appointed a black social worker and the Mayor established a 'Racial Integration Co-ordinating Committee' consisting of representatives of various local organisations and members of the public with 'the general, rather vague purpose of promoting harmony in the borough' (Glass, 1960: 195). As a direct result of the disorders, the British-Caribbean Association was established in order to develop 'friendship and understanding' between the peoples of the Caribbean and Britain.

Although apparently divergent from the more common arguments outlined in earlier sections, the operations of these groups were based upon a similar model of 'race relations' which assumed that racial discrimination was a 'real' phenomenon — arising from cultural differences and misunderstanding. Educational initiatives, in the broadest sense, could enlighten those sections of the white population whose ignorance led to antipathy towards 'strangers'. Forty years later many of the initiatives seem naive and patronising to all concerned and they certainly failed to consider the structural and ideological nature of racism. Other objections were raised at the time. Malik (1968: 79) recalled with some incredulity how:

> As a result of the trouble, Notting Hill gained official recognition as a problem area and sociologists, professional and amateur, began to flood the area, together with their cohorts of students, titled ladies and do-gooding young middle-aged women. They literally came in droves — all of them terribly well-intentioned, quite clueless and full of questions. They all wanted to do something for the poor, unfortunate residents of Notting Hill and they were desperate to meet us.

The objections raised by others assumed that the initiatives would be unlikely to succeed. Glass (1960: 197) cited an interview with Councillor Olive Wilson, reported in the *Kensington News* on 30 October 1958. Under the headline WILL TOO MANY DO-GOODERS PAVE THE PATH TO NOTTING *HELL*?, Wilson argued that the various bodies that had been formed were 'bedevilling' the situation:

> It's time somebody realised that the ordinary decent coloured working folk don't want to go to meetings and sit on committees; they want to lead ordinary lives and *forget* they are coloured [emphasis in Glass].

In many respects, the notion that ethnicity can be forgotten, as expressed by Wilson, reflects the broader assumption made by the assimilationist groups. As was noted in relation to the debates about immigration, these liberal discourses assume that racism is a given phenomena, based upon real biological and cultural differences between the 'races'. By equating it to individual ignorance, broader structural or ideological dimensions of racism, are marginalised, a criticism already noted in Chapter One.

Conclusion

The reactions to the disorders of 1958–59 clearly involved a racialised construction of the causes of the events. As the first feature of the racialisation problematic outlined in Chapter One suggests, this does not mean that there were no problems arising from a housing shortage or unemployment. Such problems undoubtedly did exist but the racialised construction meant that they were understood through a framework which assumed that they were exacerbated, if not actually caused, by migrants from the Caribbean. The lobby for immigration control, which was stimulated by, but did not arise from, these disorders, was based on the assumption that racial prejudice was a 'natural' response by white people when faced with new and different groups arriving in their localities. This view is based on the premise that a 'multiracial' society is inherently problematic. As with many responses to the disorders in 1919, 1936 and 1985, underlying the reactions in 1958 was, an understanding of a British national character and history which emphasised traditions of tolerance, obedience to the law, and respect for law and order. The migrants from the Commonwealth were considered problematic because they were not considered to share these characteristics, and so were outside of the tolerant British community (Holmes, 1991). The idea that British political culture was inherently tolerant has been identified in the previous two case studies discussed here and this factor demonstrates the fourth aspect of the racialisation problematic, which is that ideas about 'race' articulate with other themes. The precedents for this articulation also illustrate the second aspect of the racialisation problematic which is that debates in any one period refer to historically prevalent discourse.

The reactions also drew upon negative counter positions of 'race relations' in other countries, most notably in this case, the USA. Parallels between Britain and other countries were often drawn in response to the disorders in Nottingham and Notting Hill. Just as the 'mugging' panic of the early 1970s (Hall *et al*, 1978) occurred in the shadow of developments in the 'ghettos' of US cities, so the events of 1958–59 were considered as an aberration from the British tradition. The historical precedents for inter-ethnic and religious violence (Pearson, 1983; Fryer, 1984; Panayi, 1993) were forgotten by those who suggested that such things did not happen in Britain. Whilst the *Economist* accepted that it was mythical to suggest that the English were unexceptionally welcoming to 'strangers', it argued that:

> they have had two great saving graces. One is that they tend to be easy-going in their prejudices; they are often xenophobic in word but only seldom in deed. The other is that, generally, they are law-abiding; they do not press their prejudices with the knife or the boot. The appalling feature of the recent disorders first in Nottingham and then in the so-called Notting Hill district of London is that they have shown what can happen in this land of the free where these *natural, national* restraints are off[40] [emphasis added].

This account reflects many of the dimensions of views of 'the British character' which were considered in Chapter Three, suggesting that this had been a major bulwark against fascism and anti-Semitism. These, highly contestable, national 'saving graces' were frequently contrasted with the position in other countries. Osborne's reference to events in Little Rock, Arkansas, cited earlier, were echoed in the press. In Nottingham's *Sunday Evening News*,[41] for example, a generally sympathetic article portraying the victimisation of the black population was carried beneath a photograph of violent scenes from the USA, with the caption IT MUST NOT HAPPEN HERE! *The Times* carried several reports of the reactions to the disorders from Rhodesia and South Africa which included salutary warnings that Britain, too, had a 'colour problem'.[42] Such comparisons contribute to the particular context in which the disorders in Nottingham and Notting Hill occurred and, as the first aspect of the racialisation problematic suggests, are vital to a full understanding of how ideas about 'race' were used to explain the unrest.

The link between the disorders and the subsequent demands to restrict immigration was considered earlier. The racialisation of immigration that continued through the late 1950s, and into the 1960s and beyond, was based upon an understanding that 'good race relations' could only occur with restricted migration. This was regarded as the liberal alternative to the apartheid and segregation practised elsewhere, and assumed that racism and prejudice were inevitable occurrences which could only be managed if the numbers of non-indigenous 'races' were carefully controlled. Contradictorily, this problem was not an issue when white British imperialists migrated around the globe.

The socio-economic issues were interpreted through a racialised account which effectively blamed the migrants for exacerbating the housing and unemployment problems. These arguments often appeared confused, as they suggested that the migrants were causing unemployment and housing shortages and yet represented a significant drain on national assistance and occupied accommodation of such poor quality that it caused a nuisance to neighbours. As the third feature of the critical realist problematic contends, racialisation is an inconsistent and contradictory process. Pilkington remarked (1988) upon the illogical nature of many of the attitudes expressed by the media and white residents of Notting Hill. He reported several such perceptions about the black immigrants (Pilkington, 1988: 91):

> They were criticised for taking lower wages than whites, then accused of being flash and ostentatiously wealthy. But how could West Indians be both poorly paid and rich? One man said: "They live like dirt in private and like kings the rest of the time". Another said: "Oh well, they work for lower wages so they can't get nicked for living off prostitutes".

As was the case with the immigration debates, these arguments also assumed that those of different lifestyles and cultures could not live alongside one another without difficulty. This argument was well-expressed in a statement issued by the Labour Party (1958: 4) which abhorred 'every manifestation of racial prejudice, and particularly condemns those instances which have recently occurred in this country':

> However, difficulties inevitably arise when a large number of immigrants settle in one place. Housing shortage, periodic unemployment, and differing social customs may combine with *natural* strangeness to exaggerate community tensions [emphasis added].

This quote draws many of the themes together. The 'problem' was caused not simply by immigrants, but rather by large numbers of them concentrated in a specific area coupled with social problems and a 'natural strangeness' between different peoples. As Miles (1984b: 271) observed this latter point serves to define the problem as natural in origin, caused by the differences between 'races'. This argument is reminiscent of that expressed by the leader of the French *Front Nationale*, Jean Marie Le Pen, in defence of his anti-immigrant stance. Le Pen argues that his dislike of *l'estranger* is natural and no different from the fact that: 'I prefer my daughters to my nieces and my nieces to my neighbours like everyone else ... all men are the same'.[43] The understanding of racism adopted by these arguments suggests that it exists at the level of personal psychological prejudice — a question of the inherent wariness that humans are assumed to express towards that which is different. This socio-biological conception of racism has been identified in more recent British history by Barker (1990).

Many of the themes evident in the reactions to the disorders of 1958–59 have subsequently recurred. Subsequent debates around the various pieces of legislation which have further restricted immigration into the UK have not moved far beyond the logic underlying arguments in the 1950s. The assumption that 'racial tensions' are inevitable has also had a long currency. It was certainly apparent in 1919 and has become a key theme in the 'new racism' identified by Barker (1981; 1990). The understanding of racism which locates it only at the level of personal ignorance or suspicion underpins much of the logic of multiculturalism, which promotes the education of individuals as a key way of reducing prejudice and racial discrimination.

It has been shown that many of the racialised arguments about the alleged problems that the migrants posed also had gendered undertones. As considered in previous chapters, this connection between 'race' and sex encapsulated rather vague threats to morality that many appeared to believe were posed by immigration. Well-established stereotypes of black people, and particularly black men, allowed this issue to become a self-evident explanatory framework for the tensions which led to violence. Sexual promiscuity was seen as crucial evidence that black people were culturally and morally inferior to whites, and this was seen as a key indicator of the problems that a 'multiracial' society would inevitably face. At the same time that black men were held to be inferior to white males, they were also considered a sexual threat, in much the same way as was described in the context of the 1919 disorders. This clearly illustrates a key dimension of the racialisation problematic explained in Chapter One, which is that racism articulates with other discourses, and combines contradictory and incompatible elements.

The debates on the restriction of migration from the Commonwealth also drew upon the notion that Britain had a noble reputation as the welcoming 'mother country'. Of course this reputation did exist and was very powerful, as the expectations and testimony of many of those who arrived from Africa and the Caribbean as long ago as 1919, as well as in the postwar era, indicates. The origin of this discourse is difficult to locate precisely, but the ideology of Empire was certainly legitimised by it. It is apparent from personal memoirs and newspaper reports that, as in 1919, the notion that British citizenship was of equal status across the Commonwealth was firmly entrenched in the minds of many of those migrating to Britain in the years after World War Two (Fryer, 1984: 374; Carter, 1986: chapter two).

The events of 1958–59 represent something of an epitome of other debates about 'race', ethnicity, and British national identity. They were not responsible for a fundamental shift in immigration policy and may not, compared to more recent events, appear to have been particularly violent. They did, however, represent a key point in the further development of racialisation in the postwar period, as Britain moved away from the Empire and towards a new role in Europe.

This analysis of the disorders in Nottingham and Notting Hill in the late 1950s has further illustrated the critical realist model outlined in Chapter One. Each of the four dimensions of the racialisation problematic can be identified in the above discussion. The first element draws attention to the need to consider the temporal and spatial context in which ideas about 'race' are formed, in this case it can be seen that the relative privation experienced in the areas concerned contributed to the unrest. Furthermore, instances of 'race riots' (as they were usually labelled) in the United States and more general concerns with lawless youth also contributed to the specific milieu in which the debates outlined in this Chapter were conducted. However, the racialisation problematic also refers to the importance of historically prevalent ideas about 'race', and these too can be identified, for example, in references to Britain as a traditionally peaceable country, threatened by those deemed to be at odds with this culture, and in arguments which suggested that black men posed a sexual threat to white women, a long established notion (McClintock, 1995).

Inconsistent and confused aspects of the racialisation of the disorders have been illustrated and explored, particularly in relation to the impact that black immigrants had upon socio-economic problems. This aspect of the debates clearly reflects the third feature of the critical realist model which stresses the importance of recognising the mutual incompatibility and diversity of racialised myths and stereotypes. The articulation between racialised discourse and other issues has been clearly illustrated in this Chapter, and is the fourth aspect of the racialisation model. In this discussion it has been shown that racialised debates about immigration combined with concerns about gender roles and the supposed lawlessness of relatively new youth subcultures. Given the range of issues evident in debates following the unrest in 1958–59, the critical realist model of racialisation allows for this diversity of factors to be fully considered.

Notes

1 *Leicester Mercury*, 1 September 1958.
2 Mosley subsequently contested North Kensington in the General Election of October 1959, where he lost his deposit.
3 Cited in Jacobson (1958: 5).
4 For example, on 17 November 1960 Fenner Brockway (Labour, Eton and Slough) appealed for a remission to the Home Secretary on the grounds that the lengthy sentences were passed on the basis of the temporary and severe situation prevailing at that time in Notting Hill. This was refused on the grounds that the trial judge had stressed the seriousness of the crimes (*Parliamentary Debates*, vol. 630, cols. 544-5, 17 November 1960). Similar arguments were advanced in a parliamentary debate on the sentences in February 1960. MPs suggested that the youths had been given unfair exemplary sentences but again the Home Office maintained that there could be no political interference in the judicial process (*Parliamentary Debates*, vol. 618, cols. 331-40, 23 February 1960).
5 Hiro (1973: 41).
6 BBC TV (1994).
7 According to the survey conducted by Coates and Silburn (1967) 92.6 per cent of the houses in St. Ann's had an outside lavatory, 85 per cent had no bathroom, and 53 per cent had no hot water system.
8 *Parliamentary Debates*, vol. 618, col. 332, 23 February 1960.
9 *Sunday Telegraph*, 1 January 1989.
10 In 1957, for example, see *Parliamentary Debates*, vol. 577, col. 217-8.
11 *Parliamentary Debates*, vol. 585, col. 1422, 3 April 1958.
12 For example, Hill (1959) details the expensive and low-quality housing available to black migrants and that the number of their complaints to rent tribunals had increased.
13 *Parliamentary Debates*, vol. 586, col. 33-4, 17 April 1958.
14 *Parliamentary Debates*, vol. 594, col. 198, 29 October 1958.
15 Even Cyril Osborne conceded this point: 'It is true that it was estimated in another place that only 25 per cent of the immigrants were coloured. I am asking that there should be control irrespective of colour or race. But it is useless denying that opinion in the country is most exercised by the coloured immigrant', (*Parliamentary Debates*, vol. 596, col. 1555, 5 December 1958).
16 *The Times*, 27 August 1958.
17 *The Times*, 28 August 1958.
18 *Parliamentary Debates*, vol. 594, col. 197, 28 October 1958. In the US town of Little Rock, Arkansas there had been violent conflict between white and black people in 1957 as states paratroopers were deployed to enforce desegregation in schools. Many media reports also drew comparisons between the two sets of events.
19 At least two, probably minor, problems exist with these figures. Clearly they are rounded to the nearest 5 cases, and they do not include migrants arriving by air (although most immigrants, from the Caribbean at least, appear to have travelled by sea).

20 *New Statesman*, 23 May 1959.
21 Cited in Solomos (1988: 39).
22 Cited in *Encounter*, December 1958.
23 *The Times*, 2 January 1982.
24 For example, following a report in 1955 the Jamaican Government had established the Migration Advisory Service designed to discourage the emigration to Britain of those unlikely to acquire employment and press and newspaper reports in Jamaica warned of the worsening employment situation in Britain (see Davison, 1962).
25 *Parliamentary Debates*, vol. 596, col. 1558, 5 December 1958.
26 *The Times*, 3 September 1958.
27 See, for example, the question of black migrants involvement in crime raised in February 1958 (*Parliamentary Debates*, vol. 583, col. 17, 24 February 1958).
28 *Parliamentary Debates*, vol. 585, col. 1424-5, 3 April 1958.
29 Cited in *Encounter*, December 1958.
30 *Parliamentary Debates*, vol. 618, col. 333, 23 February 1960.
31 See, for example, *The Times*, 27 August 1958.
32 *The Times*, 1 September 1958.
33 *Parliamentary Debates*, vol. 618, col. 331-2, 23 February 1960.
34 *The Times*, 27 August 1958.
35 *Sunday Evening News*, 31 August 1958.
36 *Parliamentary Debates*, vol. 583, col. 17, 24 February 1958.
37 *Parliamentary Debates*, vol. 594, col. 199, 29 October 1958.
38 *Parliamentary Debates*, vol. 585, col. 1425, 3 April 1958.
39 Fryer (1984: 153) indicated that stereotypes of the black man as pimp were evident as long ago as the mid-eighteenth century.
40 Cited in *Encounter*, December 1958.
41 *Nottingham Sunday Evening News*, 31 August 1958.
42 *The Times*, 30 August 1958.
43 Cited in Lloyd (1994: 234).

5 Broadwater Farm, October 1985: 'This is not England'

Introduction

The disorders which occurred at the Broadwater Farm estate, in Tottenham, north London, in October 1985 represented a landmark in Britain's history of urban unrest. Not only did they result in the murder of PC Keith Blakelock — whose killers remain at large — but they were also the first time that plastic bullets were deployed (although not used) during public disorder on the British mainland. The scenes took place during an era in which many British cities had experienced violent unrest. In his report into the Brixton disorders of 1981, Lord Scarman (1981: 1.2) told of the 'horror and incredulity' with which the public responded to events rarely experienced in postwar Britain. By autumn 1985, however, scenes of violent confrontation between the public and the police were relatively familiar images of urban Britain (see Benyon and Solomos, 1987), and racialised arguments could be employed to explain the events. It seems clear that the racist criminalisation of the black community served to simplify the complex story of the Broadwater Farm disorders. The notion that these were simply 'law and order' events relied on this racialisation and meant that more difficult and fundamental questions about the role and function of policing, structural socio-economic issues, and institutional racism, could be down-played by many commentators.

This Chapter identifies a number of themes evident in much of the reactions of the media, politicians, and police to the Broadwater Farm disorders. These include the dominance of the law and order paradigm, the racialisation of the causes of the disorder, and the 'demonisation' of Broadwater Farm. It is suggested that previous academic explanations of the process of racialisation have not paid sufficient attention to the different stereotypes applied to black men compared to black women. It is argued that whilst culturally-based racist explanations demarked black people *per se* as separate and inherently different to the mainstream population, these arguments were applied differently to men than to women. In conclusion, it is argued that the racialisation of these events can only be understood in terms of the broader context of Thatcherism. The coded discussion of 'race' in relation to urban unrest is typical of the 'new racism' and the incidents of civil disturbances allowed dominant themes in New Right discourse to converge. However, it is equally clear that the discourse surrounding these events drew upon and expounded other racialised themes which have been apparent in various contexts for many decades. Indeed, some themes already discussed in relation to other case studies re-emerge in an analysis of the coverage of the Broadwater Farm disorders. Before embarking on this discussion, however, it is necessary to outline in brief the events themselves.

Background and context

The unrest which occurred in Tottenham on 6 October 1985 can be understood both as a specific event in itself and as part of a broader series of disorders in Britain during the 1980s. Relations between the local police and the people of Broadwater Farm were central to what happened. The broadly cordial relations which apparently existed between senior officers in the local division and community organisations on the estate were undermined by the activities of non-local policing units, such as the Special Patrol Group, and by the fast turnover of personnel policing the estate (Gifford, 1986: chapter 3). Further important factors specific to the local context of Broadwater Farm included the role and reputation of the Broadwater Farm Youth Association and the characterisation of the estate in the local media.

In other regards, though, it is hard to understand the disorders apart from the history of relations between minority ethnic groups and the police elsewhere in London and beyond.[1] The immediate event that led to the disorders was the death of a local woman, Cynthia Jarrett, during a police search of her home. This death was interpreted by many local people both as an indication of the deteriorating relations between the police and the people of Tottenham and in the context of other controversial incidents, in which members of the public were killed or seriously injured by the police.[2] The Broadwater Farm Youth Association, and other local organisations, explained the 'uprising' in these terms, arguing that 'during the summer of 1985 the people of the Farm ... came under increasing police pressure' (BFYA *et al*, 1987: 8). The Chair of the Haringey Police Committee, Councillor Stephen Banerji, suggested that a range of factors had a deleterious impact on relations between local people and the police:

> I'm talking about a stop and search operation, raids on people's houses, picking up people in the street, stopping black youths and asking them to empty their bags and empty their pockets on Tottenham High Road, that kind of thing was going on.[3]

In the light of disturbances at Handsworth and Brixton, police in Tottenham had made preparations in case of unrest. As is explained later, local divisional leaders had devised contingency plans to deploy officers in such an event. The impact of expectations of disorder on events as they subsequently unfolded was evident in the discussion in Chapter Four of disturbances in Nottingham in 1958. If some police officers and sections of the public anticipate that disorder is likely to occur this may be one reason why relatively routine contacts between police officers and small groups or individuals escalate into more unusual incidents of disorder. The context of anticipated unrest means that relatively innocuous events may assume catalytic dimensions (Waddington *et al*, 1989). Gifford (1986: 62) reported that the police had warned Dolly Kiffin, chairwoman of the Broadwater Farm Youth Association, in advance that there might be disorder on the estate. To some extent this warning arose from relatively small-scale confrontations between local people and police officers in the period leading up to the unrest. In September 1985, for example, two home beat police officers were forced off the estate under a hail of missiles after being threatened by youths.[4] Events elsewhere in the country were also regarded as warnings of future disorder in Tottenham. A Metropolitan Police report presented to the Haringey Police Community Consultative Group suggested that disorders in Brixton and Handsworth had increased the expectations that police had of disorder at Broadwater Farm (*Police Review*, 1986a).

Whatever the influence of events elsewhere, the catalyst for the disturbances in Tottenham was a particular event which illustrated tensions between the police and local black people. Officers had arrested Floyd Jarrett, Cynthia's son, on suspicion of motor vehicle offences and, acting on an unspecified 'tip-off', decided to search her house for stolen property. Gifford (1986: 70-73) records the claims and counter-claims about the legality of the police search and reflects the doubt as to whether the officers obtained a warrant before the event. The exact circumstances of Cynthia Jarrett's death were also contested — the police officers searching the premises admitted that she collapsed whilst they were present and insisted that they offered all the assistance they could. The Jarrett family, on the other hand, maintained that the officers pushed her over, thus precipitating her death, and only offered to help at a late stage. Whichever account was accurate, Cynthia Jarrett was certified dead when she arrived at North Middlesex hospital. The jury at the Coroner's Inquiry returned a verdict of accidental death (Gifford, 1986: 80).

The following morning, Sunday 6 October 1985, a demonstration was held outside the local police station in Tottenham High Road, which was roughly equidistant between the Broadwater Farm estate and the Jarrett home in Thorpe Road. Although the demonstration was noisy and angry most media reports agree that it was predominantly orderly (Gifford, 1986: 92) and the Broadwater Farm Youth Association argued that 'the people of Tottenham wanted to exercise their rights to demonstrate peacefully' (BFYA *et al*, 1987: 8). Meetings between councillors, council officers, community leaders, and the public were held during the afternoon of 6 October to express grief and anger and to register concern and criticism about the local police. At one such meeting, the counsel of established community leaders, such as Councillor Bernie Grant, that grievances should be expressed through conventional political channels, was rejected by the audience who preferred to return to the police station for a second demonstration.

It was around this time, late in the afternoon of 6 October, that pre-established police plans to respond to disorder on Broadwater Farm were activated, although they could not be fully implemented as events escalated quickly. Police vans containing officers with riot equipment were sent to the estate where, the Metropolitan Police (1986) claimed,[5] they were confronted by youths throwing bottles and establishing blazing barricades at the four vehicle access points to the estate. These barricades effectively prevented the police from entering the estate — which meant that all they could achieve was to seal-off the area and contain the disorder within.

During the next few hours the police could do little more than maintain this containment approach. The physical design of the estate, with raised walkways linking the tower blocks together, was such that any attempt by officers to enter the area would have left them vulnerable to attack from above. This aspect further illustrates Waddington *et al's*, (1989) acknowledgement that the physical environment plays a constitutive part in any incident of disorder. A senior local police officer also referred to the material structure of the estate in his analysis of the disorders:

> It's dangerous in as much as it is designed for crime. In 1970, it was architecturally given an award, in 1985 it's a disaster, in my view. It is a rabbit warren, there are walkways, there are many roadways, there are inter-linking hidden corridors and it's a trap.[6]

It was an outbreak of fire in one of the tower blocks, Tangmere, that drew fire-fighters onto the estate, protected by a group of police officers. However, both groups were attacked and PC Keith Blakelock was murdered as he attempted to flee with his colleagues. Another apparently new feature of these disorders, in contrast to others in the history of mainland Britain, was the use of guns against the police.[7] Media accounts often conveyed a sense that the events represented the most serious incident of disorder during the period. The *Guardian*, for example, referred to the unrest as the 'ugliest incident so far in Britain's wave of racial disorder',[8] whilst the *Daily Express* labelled the events as 'Britain's most horrific race riot'.[9]

References to 'race' in descriptions and explanations of the disorder, as made in both the above examples, is discussed in more detail later in this Chapter, but newspaper reports do convey a sense of the intensity of the violence. The *Daily Mail*, for example, reported that:

> Around 500 policemen in riot gear were fighting pitched battles in the streets of Tottenham against mobs attacking them with petrol bombs, bottles, bricks, lumps of concrete — and guns. The mobs set cars and buildings on fire and set up street barricades.[10]

The *Daily Mirror* reported the experiences of several local residents who had been trapped by the disorders, and told how some local people had fled the estate under police protection. One man described how:

> Every time the police charge the mob they are being pelted with fire bombs and paving slabs, some being thrown by people on the balconies of the flats.[11]

By 10.20 p.m. the police commander on the ground had received permission from Metropolitan Police Commissioner Newman to use baton rounds against the crowd. It was decided, however, that the intensity of the violence was waning by this time and the batons, and CS gas, remained unused. Although the disturbances appeared to have declined by midnight, officers did not enter the estate to 'sweep' it through and make arrests until 4.00 a.m. on 7 October. Despite the use of guns against the police, the murder of an officer, and the deployment of potentially lethal weapons by the police, the overall level of violence against the public and damage to the physical infrastructure of the estate was relatively minimal. The Metropolitan Police (1986: 35) recorded a total of 346 crimes reported following the disorders — 67 per cent of which were assaults on the police and 15 per cent criminal damage. By June of 1986 351 people had been arrested in connection with the disturbances, of which 147 were charged, 3 cautioned, and 201 were the subject of 'no further action' (Metropolitan Police, 1986: 36).

Explaining the disorders

Four main themes can be identified in the explanations that were offered for the disorders in 1985 in Tottenham. First, there were those arguments which adopted a law and order perspective. Secondly, some explanations racialised the disorders while other commentators portrayed the entire estate as fundamentally problematic. Finally, there were those explanations which were based around the role of gender and its relation to racialisation. In some respects these themes are mutually dependent and closely connected.

As previously indicated, the disorders occurred during a period where incidents of public disorder had been high on the political agenda for some time, and the explanations advanced formed part of the wider debates about law and order, inner-city deprivation, and the position and role of black people in British society. The points discussed in this Chapter do not represent an exhaustive catalogue, rather they are the predominant themes and those articulated by a number of key sources amongst the media, politicians, and the police.

The primacy of law and order

To a large extent, the press, police, and politicians understood the disorders primarily in terms of the law and order issues that were raised. Their common conclusion was that the most important response was to assert the need to restore and reinforce public order — by force where necessary. The manner in which this demand was articulated provided a good example of a primary definition of a news event becoming entrenched and setting the agenda to which others must respond (Hall *et al*, 1978: chapter 3).

Once the disorders were constructed in this way, the law and order debate largely dominated subsequent discussions. On the day after the disorders the Metropolitan Police Commissioner, Sir Kenneth Newman, held a press conference at which he put 'the people of London on notice' that he would authorise the use of plastic bullets and CS gas in order to tackle future instances of disorder. The press reported this claim widely,[12] and also reproduced photographs of weapons seized during and after the disorders. The crucial role of this senior police officer as a primary definer of the news agenda is evident from subsequent reports that the Home Secretary was endorsing the decision already taken by Commissioner Newman.[13]

A further aspect of the law and order agenda evident after the disorders was apparent in some of the media coverage of the events. Comparisons between what had occurred at Broadwater Farm and events in Northern Ireland were explicitly made by some newspapers. Newman's previous experience in charge of the Royal Ulster Constabulary was often referred to by the press to give his warnings about the future use of CS gas and baton rounds greater credibility, as these techniques had been used extensively in Northern Ireland. The *Daily Telegraph*, for example, reported that Newman was '... ready to bring Northern Ireland riot-police tactics to mainland Britain'.[14] Other press reports also made explicit comparisons with Northern Ireland. The *Daily Mail*, for example, ran an article headlined 'Ambush ... IRA-style'[15] which suggested that the rioters had adopted tactics developed by terrorists. The *Daily Telegraph* racialised images from the sectarian 'Troubles' when it described Broadwater Farm as being like 'the Divis flats with reggae'.[16]

Not only did these comparisons provide a recognisable framework in which the reader could understand the 'alien' events that had occurred, they also quickly led to a similar set of prescriptions. Media images of the Northern Ireland conflict have tended to portray both sides as religious fanatics bent on mutual destruction. Often this portrayal has relied upon stereotypes of the Irish as a violent, quick-tempered people driven by emotion rather than reason (Curtis, 1984). The repeated suggestion that the conflict in Northern Ireland is a religious dispute has provided a theological dimension to what is more accurately a political and nationalist conflict. Just as the mainstream media have rarely considered that the presence of the British army in Northern Ireland may have had some direct constitutive impact on the problem, so the media coverage of Broadwater Farm gave a relatively low profile to suggestions that the police may have been one of the causal factors behind the disorder. Furthermore, the comparison also led to a similar solution being endorsed in Broadwater Farm as in Northern Ireland — more emphatic policing from a more powerful police force.[17]

As with very many other instances of disorder in British history, various forms of conspiracy theory were put forward by the press to explain the unrest. The *Daily Telegraph*, for instance, suggested that:

> Special Branch intelligence reports indicate that a well-orchestrated conspiracy among Trotskyists, anarchists and other extremists is operating to stir up trouble in potentially volatile areas, and in some cases has led to riots in inner city areas. Special Branch officers report

> that up to a dozen political activists have been spotted moving between Handsworth, Toxteth, Brixton, Tottenham and other areas. Their visits have been followed by rioting.[18]

The *Daily Express*[19] put forward an even more elaborate version of a conspiracy theory which suggested that the riots were caused by conspirators trained not only in the Soviet Union, but also in that other country often vilified by the press in Britain, Libya. This story was quickly exposed as a hoax perpetuated by one 'Rocky' Ryan — a notorious 'con artist' who often fooled the press. Foot (1985: 15) pointed out that the falsity of the story is, in itself, revealing as Ryan's speciality 'is knowing what journalists and editors want to believe — and then "revealing" it to them'. As with other arguments analysed in this study the use of the conspiracy theory — with implications of treachery and plots, and, in some cases, the involvement of foreign countries — frames the events in terms of security, law and order. This understanding of the events was also evident in the *Express* editorial of the same day, entitled ENOUGH IS ENOUGH, which reflected the conservative understanding of disorder and denied socio-economic explanations of unrest. The newspaper's position drew links between the disturbances and other developments:

> The scenes of exultant rioters hurling petrol bombs and other missiles at helmeted police as cars and buildings blazed was like something from Dante's Inferno ... This was criminal violence for which there was no excuse, no sociological explanations, no twentieth-century heart-bleeding clichés. It was urban warfare ... in London N15 ... The softly-softly approach — foisted on [the country] by Scarman and left-wing police authorities — is not working as Brixton and now Tottenham bear witness.[20]

The primacy of law and order was also used by the government to resist calls for 'another Scarman' — another inquiry examining not only the policing, but also the social roots of the disorders. Although the 'original'[21] Scarman inquiry into the Brixton disorders of 1981 advocated better equipment, tactics, and resources for the police, in this context it was Scarman's emphasis on the need to improve socio-economic conditions in the inner cities that the government regarded as not only unnecessary but undesirable. The Home Secretary dismissed social explanations of the disorders on the grounds that they do not account for:

> many factors all too obviously present in the particular incidents we are discussing. It leaves out the excitement of forming and belonging to a mob, the evident excitement of violence leading to the fearsome crimes that we have seen reported and the greed that leads to looting — not the looting of food shops, but looting that leads to the theft of television sets, video recorders and other things that can be disposed of quickly. To explain all of these things in terms of deprivation and suffering leaves out some basic and ugly facts about human nature'.[22]

Given this identification of the problem, the Home Secretary was able to rebut opposition demands for a public inquiry on the grounds that the police investigations underway were sufficient.[23] Attempts to find broader explanations of the riots were condemned as efforts to excuse the criminal acts which had occurred. As Hall (1988: 75) remarked:

> as soon as the 'law and order' perspective prevails, all wider questions pale into insignificance. Anyone who raises them is immediately tarred with being a 'soft do-gooder' or — worse — a secret fellow-traveller with violence. Everything is concentrated on the black-and-white [*sic*] question of 'who broke the law?' [parenthesis in original].

The disorders were the inexcusable result of 'human wickedness', as the chairman of the Conservative Party Norman Tebbit argued,[24] and as such could only be prevented by a firmer police presence. Thomas Hobbes could hardly have put it better.

The racialisation of the disputes

The press coverage of the disorders quickly identified and problematised the ethnicity of those perceived to be involved in the disorders. Many reports talked about black or 'West Indian' youths attacking the police as though the fact of their skin colour was, in itself, a causal explanation. Even those papers which did not directly state that the rioters were black made only slightly more subtle reference by claiming that the estate's population was 'mostly black'.[25] It is tempting to engage in a discussion of the actual ethnic make-up of the crowds in an attempt to discover whether the newspaper reports were accurate. Methodological difficulties aside, such an exercise is not undertaken here, since to argue against this racialised portrayal of the disorders on the grounds that significant numbers of white people were involved misses the main point. Even if *all* of those involved in the disorders were black this would not serve as an explanatory factor in itself. It would be a matter of observation or of description, but not of *meaning*.

Often surveys of rioting crowds have tried to establish the 'identikit rioter' (Keith, 1993: 101) — an approach which mistakes correlation for causality. Other instances of public disorder where the majority of participants have shared somatic characteristics, for example, the 1984 'Battle of Orgreave' or the 1990 'Poll Tax Riots', have not been interpreted through the lens of 'race'. Of course, the ethnicity of those involved cannot be ignored, as if racism were not important. The emphasis in the explanations following the Broadwater Farm disorder, however, often was not on *racism* but on 'race'. In other words, they relied upon the racialised notion that the cultural proclivities of black people were the crucial factor in developing conflict with the police and wider society. The press coverage of the events was simplistic in that the complex web of variables, which included racism, was reduced to one predominant explanatory factor: 'race'.

Others moved beyond just identifying the rioters as black and explained why they considered 'race' was a significant aetiological variable. The *Daily Mail*, for example, suggested that the reason why black people engaged in such activities was cultural. In an editorial entitled 'The Choice for Britain's Blacks', the paper made it clear where it thought responsibility lay. It argued that 'Britain's blacks' must:

> forgo the anarchic luxury of these orgies of arson, looting and murderous assaults against the men and women whose task it is to uphold the laws of this land or they will provoke a paramilitary reaction unknown to mainland Britain ... They must do more to discipline their young. They must find themselves community leaders who preach co-operation, not confrontation. They must encourage black recruits to join the police and 'swamp' black areas with black constables on the beat; ultimately the only kind of community policing that is going to work. It's up to them.[26]

Similar arguments were expounded by voices from the Conservative backbenches. In many respects, these opinions replicate those discussed in regard to previous disorders where it was suggested that urban disorder was alien to the British tradition. Sir Peter Emery, MP, argued, for example, that the disorders were wholly unjustifiable and that 'the vast majority of people expect the precepts of Anglo-Saxon behaviour to be maintained. These standards must be maintained, despite what other ethnic minorities want'.[27] Emery's colleagues Anthony Beaumont-Dark and Jonathon Sayeed made similar remarks. The former contrasted the violence perpetrated by 'West Indians' with the law-abiding behaviour of

Asian and Jewish migrants and explained that the reason for this difference was cultural:

> In faiths and religions where people are self-disciplined, where people respect their families and have a sense of self-discipline, there are not riots and problems. Families, black or white, who abandon their old and their young tend to get into disputes.[28]

Sayeed implicitly endorsed this analysis when he argued that:

> Environment, unemployment and colour alone do not explain why the riots have been confined to areas that are predominantly black, for do not those from the Indian subcontinent suffer the same disadvantages? Perhaps there is something culturally different ... that explains this phenomenon and explains why Asians argue when West Indians would fight. While those from the Indian subcontinent set great store by education and, despite difficulties, build trading empires, I cannot name one equivalent West Indian concern.[29]

The Ulster Unionist MP, Enoch Powell, argued in the same Parliamentary debate that the changing ethnic profile of inner-city populations augured badly. He claimed that:

> What we have seen so far in terms of the transformation of the population, like what we have seen so far in terms of urban violence, is nothing to what we know is to come.[30]

These kind of arguments were also made by police officers who suggested that the black community as a whole were responsible for the disorders. The presence of black people in an area appears to lead to the identification of that locality as a difficult one to police in the eyes of some officers. After the disorders there were complaints made by officers who argued that they had been prevented from enforcing the law on the estate because senior officers were more concerned with preserving harmonious relations than enforcing the law in a style that other areas would have experienced (Police Review 1986b, 1986c). The debate about these two approaches to policing — that it should be an emphatic non-discretionary application of the law, or that it should be responsive and more concerned with preserving public tranquillity — assumes that sections of the community of Broadwater Farm was hostile to the police and somehow implicated in criminal activity. Gifford (1986: 52) relates how, in the Metropolitan Police Annual Report for 1983, Commissioner Newman referred to Broadwater Farm as one of:

> those areas identified as 'symbolic locations' where Black communities, often the young, come to view a particular location with something of a proprietorial attachment resenting intrusion, especially by the police to enforce the law.

Not only is this suggestion extremely simplistic,[31] it also ignores the logical outcome of the argument which is that police officers are also susceptible to such 'authoritative policing geographies' (Keith, 1993: 20). This conception of the estate as inherently problematic, coupled with the 'demonisation' it received in the local media, which is further discussed in the next section, is one explanation of the rumours of disorder that apparently circulated amongst the police before the disorders occurred.

It is ironic that this historical study of public disorder in Britain should show that, in each instance, that Britain's history of disorder was ignored or even denied in many reactions. In the case of Broadwater Farm, the process of racialising the disorders was an intrinsic aspect of this denial. By avowing that the cause of the violence was ultimately to be found amongst the black community the disorder could be regarded as 'foreign' to mainstream English culture. The debates reflect the legacy of Powellism in that they share his assumption that the problems of Britain's inner cities could be traced back to the cultural changes which followed from postwar immigration (Smithies and Fiddick, 1969). Suggestions that communal violence was antithetical to a longer British tradition were complemented by this process of identifying the black community as the problem. A by-line in the *Daily Express* encapsulated many of these claims about the lack of disorder in British history. The newspaper quoted the words of a police officer who had been present at the disorder and told reporters that 'this is not England, it's just madness'.[32]

'Demonising' Broadwater Farm

The process of racialisation of the disorders was accompanied and aggravated by the 'demonisation' of the population of Broadwater Farm by the press. The *Daily Mirror*, for example, ran the following story beneath a headline which read LIVING HELL: "YOU'VE NO IDEA HOW AWFUL DAILY LIFE IS":

> They sit there, these gaunt tower blocks, like citadels of disillusionment. They are scruffy. They are battered. They smell. Broadwater Farm estate sounds grand — the name conjures visions of

> some elegant, idyllic Tory land-owner's sprawl in the Cotswolds. It even borders on a lengthy road called Lordship Lane. The reality is a shoddy, graffiti-adornedset of looming unattractive flats that won an architectural prize in the bustling, progressive 1960s. Most of the people who live in the flats are black or brown.[33]

Such stories reflected the image of Broadwater Farm that local newspapers had been perpetuating for more than a decade before the disturbances. The impressions that such stories made in the minds of local people, including local police officers, can only be imagined, but the fact that residents of the estate occasionally wrote letters to the local press to protest about the coverage they received suggests that they were aware of the negative impact these could have.[34] It is not suggested that reports of social and environmental problems on the estate were untrue, no doubt there were real difficulties facing the residents and the local authority — but it is clear that, as in other contexts, the media concentrated on the worst dimensions. A few examples of headlines in the local papers illustrate the tendency to focus on negative aspects of Broadwater Farm. In 1976, the *Wood Green and Tottenham Weekly Herald* headlined a story FAMILIES WHO LIVE IN THE SHADOW OF VIOLENCE and wrote that 'fear haunts the gloomy passages, lifts and entrances of Broadwater Farm estate'.[35] In 1977, the same paper talked of 'concrete jungle blues'[36] in relation to the estate. Seven years later, the paper propagated a similar impression of the estate — in a slightly more implicit way — asking BROADWATER FARM — IS IT AS BAD AS THEY SAY? Although this article referred to some improvements in the policing of the estate, it still spoke of the area as 'north London's equivalent of Brixton — a battle ground where police, blacks and whites fight out their differences'.[37]

Such bleak views of the estate seem to have been shared by at least some officers within the Metropolitan Police. In the police inquiry (Metropolitan Police, 1986: 6) into the disorders it was explained that:

> It would be difficult to define 'normality' in respect of Broadwater Farm. It has an unenviable reputation and normal policing methods are resisted by a vociferous ill-disposed minority. Gratuitous abuse and violence towards the police became an almost daily occurrence during periods of tension.

Since the local press shared this bleak picture of the estate it is not surprising that the nationals adopted a similar approach, especially as the nationals often use the local press as a source. The Gifford Inquiry (1986: 13) reported that the views of the local press were often considerably more negative about the estate than the facts warranted. It certainly appears that there were enough positive features to counter-balance this impression, although they were not often reported. Certainly the estate received several 'VIP' visits which suggest that there were more favourable dimensions to be identified. In the months prior to the disorders Sir George Young, Environment Minister, praised the estate and, in February 1985, it was visited by the Princess of Wales. Platt (1985: 50) records that a three-year development programme had led to improvements in security and the physical infrastructure of the estate and that so many visitors were given tours of Broadwater Farm that the Department of Environment agreed to reimburse the local authority to cover the cost of showing them around. This was not the picture of Broadwater Farm that the tabloid press chose to paint.

As an urban public-housing estate with, a high proportion of unemployed residents as well as a host of other socio-economic problems, it is unsurprising that Broadwater Farm estate experienced relatively high levels of crime and disorder. Structural features of the estate also contributed to the physical problems that beset it from the outset. As mentioned earlier, the architecture of Broadwater Farm was a significant factor in the disorder itself. The estate was built on marsh land that had to be drained prior to construction, and in order to avoid damp in the housing the blocks were built off the ground on stilts, which created protected car-parking area underneath the tower blocks where the rioters congregated. Despite the socio-economic disadvantage that the estate and its residents faced, the impression offered by the local and national press was too bleak. Broadwater Farm was not the 'hell on earth' that the newspapers would have had their readers believe. Many of the local residents painted a different picture of the estate, highlighting declining levels of crime, increasing community activism, and growing possibilities for self-help economically — all factors that were generally absent from the press coverage of the disorders (Gifford, 1986).

Not only was Broadwater Farm portrayed as suffering from very high levels of socio-economic problems but community relations on the estate were also regarded by the press as intensely dysfunctional and conflictual. The Daily Mail, for example, included a series of profiles of different ethnic groups living on the estate in part of its coverage after the disorders.[38] Thus, readers were presented with the 'White View', the 'Asian View', and the 'Black View'. Not only did this article suggest to readers that the estate was divided on ethnic grounds but also that there was intense fear and suspicion between the different groups.

Other perspectives also played on the notion that the community was disorganised and in conflict. In many respects, the coverage given to so-called 'community leaders' reflected this perspective. Two such individuals were identified by the press — Bernie Grant and Dolly Kiffin. Grant, who later became the MP for Tottenham, was at that time the Leader of Haringey Council. He was a target for media attention after he stated in a press conference soon after the disturbances that, in the eyes of many of the young people on the estate, the police 'got a bloody good hiding during the disorders. The press picked up on this comment and criticised this point of view as irresponsible in the light of the Blakelock murder. The coverage of Grant reflected wider tabloid concern with so-called 'loony left' local authorities (Murray, 1989). The *Sun*, for example, ran a story DON'T CALL ME BARMIE BERNIE which listed a series of allegedly bizarre decisions made either by Grant or Haringey Council.[39] The story also relied upon racist stereotypes of Grant. One Labour councillor, who 'asked not to be named', was quoted as saying that: 'Bernie Grant is like the leader of a black tribe — always looking for battles and shaking his spear. He sees all whites as his enemies'. In an editorial on the same day, the paper commented that 'the *Sun's* earnest wish is that Bernie Grant should rot in hell'.

The community of Broadwater Farm was criticised by sections of the press following the acquittal of the 'Tottenham Three' who had been wrongfully convicted for the murder of PC Blakelock. The press portrayal of Winston Silcott during the trial has been thoroughly described elsewhere (Heller, 1991; Mullin, 1992; Rose, 1992), but the arguments that surrounded the eventual acquittal of Silcott, Mark Braithwaite, and Engin Raghip have received less attention. The *Sun* newspaper was referred to the Director of Public Prosecutions by the judge at the original trial for publishing a photograph of Silcott on its front page, and identifying him as the man the police believed killed Blakelock. As the (ultimately successful) appeal approached in 1991, the *Sun* ran stories about Silcott's criminal record and the continuing grief of PC Blakelock's widow.[40] When the convictions were eventually overturned the paper argued that the community itself was culpable for police malpractice. It was suggested that the police had to break the rules because they were faced with a 'wall of silence' from the people on the estate.[41]

Gender roles and racialisation

Much has been written about the racialisation of the disorders in the 1980s (Gilroy, 1987; Solomos, 1988; van Dijk, 1991: Keith, 1993) and this trend was clearly evident in the case of the Broadwater Farm disturbances of 1985. What has been less well-observed is the gendered nature of this racialisation. This reflects a more widespread ignorance of the impact of gender on racism in the criminal justice system. What has often been omitted from debates about minority ethnic groups and the criminal justice system is a recognition that the general over-representation of minority groups, whatever its cause, does not apply equally to both men and women.[42] There is no doubt that black people are over-represented, but a more detailed analysis of the position demonstrates that the problem is one which affects black men to a much greater extent than black women.

One of the key areas of interest in this respect has been the number of black people stopped and searched, and arrested, by the police. Of course the over-representation of black youths in the data has been a key background factor in the perpetuation of the 'tale of failure' (Scarman, 1981) between the African Caribbean community and the police. Smith and Gray's (1983) study was one of the earliest large-scale statistical studies of the rate of contact that different ethnic groups had with the police. They found that the group most likely to be stopped by the police in London was 'West Indian' males, 63 per cent of whom had been stopped in the previous twelve months. In comparison, 44 per cent of white males were found to have been stopped in the same period. Not only were 'West Indians' more likely to have been stopped, but they were more likely to be stopped several times — on average black males were stopped 4 times a year, compared to 2.5 occasions on average for white males. Other studies[43] tend to replicate the general tendency of these findings and also show that women, of whatever ethnic group, are under-represented in stop and search figures. Although there is much less agreement about what explains this difference, factors such as police racism, unemployment, housing tenure, vehicle possession, educational qualifications, and differential rates of involvement in crime, amongst others, are usually referred to.[44]

This gender differential in the racialisation of crime in general is also reflected in the more particular case of public disorder, although this feature has not received much academic attention. Most theories of public disorder have remained silent on the issue of gender. Whether seeking to explain disorder in terms of the psychology of the individual actors or in terms of the structural causes relatively little has been said to explain why the evidence indicates that in urban disorder, men very greatly outnumber women. One more concrete, if problematic, indicator of the gender difference in incidents of disorder can be gleaned from data relating to those arrested for such offences. Within the Metropolitan Police area in 1995, 3,326 arrests were made in connection with public order offences. In 3,174 (95.4 per cent) of these cases the gender of the person arrested was recorded, and of these females accounted for just 7.8 per cent of the total (Metropolitan Police, 1996).

Discussions of the racialisation of disorder have also tended to ignore the ways in which this process affects women and men differently. What is clear in the case of the Broadwater Farm disturbances is that different discourse operated in respect of the lawlessness of the young black males in contrast to the supposed 'nurturing' role of the black women. The threat of the black men to mainstream society was clearly identified in the case of Broadwater Farm. Newspaper stories spoke of 'hundreds of West Indian youths'[45] who were 'fearless because they hunt in packs, who seem to hate white people and who on Broadwater Farm Estate are the dominant force'.[46] Elsewhere, the press portrayed the black men of Broadwater Farm as a direct threat to local white people, who, allegedly, lived in a state of perpetual fear. There are several examples of this kind of story to draw upon, but the most lurid in its racism is that written by the *Daily Mail* columnist Lynda Lee Potter who argued that 'within ten years London will have totally black pockets where the police are impotent, where the law of the jungle rules and where no white person dare venture'.[47]

Although these accounts apparently remained gender neutral in language, the talk of black youth terrorising others was implicitly about young black *men*. This reflects more widespread conceptions about the supposed over-involvement of young black men in violent street robberies, drug-dealing and associated criminal activity (Hall *et al*, 1978; Gilroy, 1987). The position of women in respect of the disorders was indirect, the media tended to portray them as either matriarchs controlling the community or placed them in a nurturing role as mothers.

The most obvious example of the former applied to the case of Dolly Kiffin, co-founder of the Broadwater Farm Youth Association — which was often characterised in the press and by the police as an organisation akin to a local mafia. In fact, the activities of the Broadwater Farm Youth Association, which was formed in the early 1980s, were more mundane. As well as providing a meeting place for the young people on the estate, the Broadwater Farm Youth Association provided meals for the elderly residents and was involved in various attempts to stimulate local economic development.[48] Although Kiffin was a key mover within the Broadwater Farm Youth Association, she was not, and never claimed to be, the only person involved in its work. However, as far as much of the press and the police were concerned she was the linchpin of the Broadwater Farm Youth Association. The activities of the police in the build-up to the disorders and the press coverage afterwards tended to rely upon a particular stereotype of the black woman as matriarch of her community.

Two illustrations serve to exemplify this racialised and gendered stereotype. In the period prior to the disturbances, Kiffin was amongst a group of local people who were away from the estate on a trip to the Caribbean. On her return, the police asked her to 'invite' them onto the estate to deal with drug-dealers who had begun to congregate there. The local officers apparently felt that Kiffin's sanction was needed to legitimise their presence on Broadwater Farm. Kiffin, fearing the potential wrath of dangerous drug-dealers, refused to co-operate and argued that the police did not and should not need her permission to enter the estate.[49]

The second example came sometime after the disorders when various newspapers ran a number of stories that were highly critical of the Broadwater Farm Youth Association and Dolly Kiffin. Many of these stories centred around allegations that Kiffin and the Broadwater Farm Youth Association had expropriated local authority money to buy personal property in Jamaica. The stories frequently presented Kiffin as though she was the sole source of authority for the residents of the estate. The *Sun*, for example, published a story on 16 December 1985 which claimed that 'they call Dolly Kiffin the Godmother. Her word is law — the *only* law — on London's riot-racked Broadwater Farm Estate' (emphasis in original). Not only did this story draw upon one stereotype of black women — that of the domineering matriarch — it also suggested that the population of the estate were both homogenous and lawless.

The stories about both Bernie Grant and Dolly Kiffin reflected a broader tendency in the debate after the Broadwater Farm disorders about the nature of the black community and its leaders. The suggestion that young black males were lawless and out-of-control ran parallel to other arguments[50] which suggested that the lack of community cohesion meant that the usual informal means of social control were absent amongst the black community. These suggestions often tied in with other debates which blamed single mothers, for example, for being unable to control their children. In this case, such arguments were generalised to the extent that the question became one of the lack of legitimate leaders within the black community. The fact that there were many people from church groups, the local authority, and from within organisations on the estate itself, who were in effect 'community leaders' was largely ignored by the media, who preferred to concentrate on 'undesirable' figures like Grant and Kiffin.

This kind of portrayal of the people on the estate as leaderless was not exclusive to the tabloid press. An article by Sewell (1985: 12) in the *New Statesman* in October 1985 argued that the lack of leaders to 'bring reason to the rage of black youths' was due to an inherent contradiction of being the leader of a dispossessed ethnic minority group whilst being in a position of power within local or national political hierarchies. Not only did this comment ignore the fact that there was considerable evidence of an active and organised community on Broadwater Farm, it also played on the notion that the disorders were the result of mindless 'rage', and not a rational response to genuine grievances. Bernie Grant's refusal to condemn vigorously the youths involved in the disturbances may have been unpalatable to the general public, it did, however regrettably, represent the perspective of some of those living on the estate. One anonymous youth reflected this when he told a television journalist his perspective on the violence directed at the police was 'an eye for an eye, that is as far as we are prepared to go'.[51] Perhaps the question ought not to have been whether Grant would withdraw inflammatory comments, but why such opinions were apparently endorsed by some local residents.

The view expressed in the media and by the local police that Dolly Kiffin was the sole voice of authority on the estate drew upon a well-established stereotype of the black woman as matriarch, providing leadership and stability within the community. Whilst this stereotype may have positive connotations, in as much as it presents women as strong leaders, it serves to reinforce the idea that the black community at large is disaggregated and conflictual. Collins (1990: 73-4) pointed out that the supposed matriarchy of black women also often stigmatises these women by holding them responsible for the 'failure' of their children — because they are activists they do not have the time to devote to the role of socialising their children.

Collins also identifies another stereotype applied to black women, which was also evident in reactions to the Broadwater Farm disorders. The death of Cynthia Jarrett, the immediate precursor to the disorders, often was reported in the press as the death of a black *mother*, as though Jarrett had no status if described simply as a black *woman*. This emphasis on motherhood was also made by those within the community of Broadwater Farm. Wright (1985: 17), for example, reported how protesters on the estate claimed 'every time the police break down a door we fear the death of another mother'. One witness to the Gifford inquiry explained that the initial demonstration outside Tottenham High Road police station was held because 'there's is no way we can accept the death of a black mother within our community' (Gifford, 1986: 90). Collins (1990) argued that motherhood has been an important source of status for black women within the community and that this reliance has had both negative and positive implications. On the positive side, motherhood has been a source of power and identity for women denied access to other identities — such as those obtainable in the workplace, for example. On the other hand, the emphasis on motherhood has meant that black women have had to endure the burden of child-care that 'makes them partners in their own oppression' (Collins, 1990: 118) by denying them other social roles.

There are other important gender issues which contributed to the background context of the disorders. The press portrayal of the Broadwater Farm Youth Association as a source of terror to the local population mirrored the identification by some police officers of the Association as a problem. Gifford (1986: 43-44) recorded how the local police commander argued on a television programme that if the Broadwater Farm Youth Association were correct to claim credit for reduced crime, this only indicated that they had previously been implicated in it. One reason why the Broadwater Farm Youth Association was often considered a 'front' organisation for illegal activities seems to have been that many of its members were not really 'youths' at all, but were in their mid-twenties or even thirties (Gifford, 1986: 24). The reason for this again illustrates the effects of gendered racism. Black males living on the estate experienced higher levels of unemployment than other groups. Thus, many of those young black men who were well into their twenties had not been in work since leaving school. Just as women's status was associated with motherhood, men's has been drawn traditionally from employment. The status of black males as 'youths' was not only associated with their age — failure to obtain employment meant that men remained 'youths' beyond the biological age where that label would ordinarily be considered applicable.

In many respects this gendered dimension of the context of the disorders at Broadwater Farm is reminiscent of some of the arguments Beatrix Campbell made about later disorders in the predominantly white districts of Oxford, Cardiff and Newcastle in 1991 (Rowe, 1996). Campbell (1993) argued that the lack of employment for the young men in these areas denied them their traditional source of status within the community and left them in a state of extended 'youth', still dependent on others for their economic survival. However, the experience at Broadwater Farm also drew upon issues of racism. The black women were considered in the light of stereotypes which do not apply to white women in the same way, since white women have traditionally had more options open to them.

In concluding this discussion of the reactions to, and explanations of, the disorders at Broadwater Farm, it is worth reiterating a point made earlier. The themes identified in this analysis should not be regarded as exhaustive. Little attention has been paid to the interpretation of events offered by those directly involved or by minority voices in the media. Such an exercise would be a useful one in itself but is not the aim of this book. Instead, what is being offered is intended to give some insight into how the disorders were understood by the voices of the mainstream — those with the ability to shape directly or indirectly the public agenda by means of their established positions.

Furthermore, the division of these arguments into different categories is intended as a heuristic device and does not imply major concrete distinctions between them. The twin discourses of gendered and racialised arguments are closely related, and reinforce a central feature of the racialisation problematic, the framework delineated in Chapter One, which is that ideas about 'race' articulate with many other socially-produced concepts. Indeed, one of the key suggestions in this study is that many analyses of disorder have recognised the significance of processes of racialisation but have ignored the important formative issue of gender roles. One of the key features of the response to the disorders at Broadwater Farm was the way in which much of the debate was conducted in a form of 'code', whereby arguments about national identity during this period meant that discussions of 'race' in Britain could take place implicitly, in terms of 'community breakdown' or 'inner-city problems'.

Conclusion

Just as the various explanations, outlined in the previous sections, were not the only ones put forward after the disorder at Broadwater Farm, neither were they specific to those particular events. Many of the arguments were also employed following disorders elsewhere and the causes of the riots in Tottenham were often debated alongside the events which occurred in Handsworth, Brixton, and other localities. Ontologically, Keith (1993) may be correct in insisting that such events can only be understood as discreet isolated occurrences, but it is not possible to ignore the tendency of politicians and media pundits to aggregate them and assign post-hoc explanations. This concluding section locates this process of aggregation and explanation within the broader context of political and ideological developments in Britain during this period. In particular, it illustrates how such incidents were explained by, and subsequently contributed to, culturally-based racism. The role of this racism within the wider project of Thatcherism is also considered. These points reflect key aspects of the critical realist racialisation problematic developed in Chapter One, which suggests that racialised discourse is grounded in the specific context in which they occur and articulate with other themes and concerns.

It is generally accepted in social science analysis that the mid-1970s were a watershed in British society, when the postwar settlement was ended as the New Right emerged with an abrupt ideological radicalism (Hall and Jaques, 1983; Gamble, 1994). The prevailing cross-party political consensus had regarded low unemployment, a corporate industrial strategy, and welfarism, as central aspects of the Keynesian strategy of state intervention in the interests of broader social and political gains.

Whatever the precise moment of its demise, this status quo was undermined by the twin processes of economic recession and an ideological reassertion of neo-liberal *laissez faire* economics on the part of the ascendant Thatcherite-wing of the Conservative Party. Although the ideology of Thatcherism was not developed entirely, or even principally, by Margaret Thatcher herself, it was her election as leader of the Conservative Party in 1975, and then as Prime Minister in 1979, that sealed the triumph of this new era in British politics.

Some analyses of the period of her three governments, from her initial victory in 1979 until her resignation in 1990, have disputed the extent to which the period shared a cohesive theme necessary to warrant the label of an 'ideology' (Jessop *et al*, 1988). This view holds that the 'Thatcher years' did not represent so distinctive a break with the past as has often been suggested and that the rhetoric of the period outweighed genuine innovations in patterns of governance. Two examples can be used to illustrate this point. First, the principles of low taxation heavily espoused in Conservative political propaganda masked a reality in which overall levels of taxation became heavier.[52] Secondly, the rhetoric that government should maintain a non-interventionist stance in the economy was not rigorously applied in practice — for example, substantial subsidies were offered to Japanese-owned companies interested in establishing factories in the UK (Garrahan and Stewart, 1991).

The question of the extent to which Thatcherism represented a real 'sea-change' in British politics is disputable. That, however, is not a central concern of this text and is discussed fully elsewhere (Hall and Jacques, 1983; Jessop *et al*, 1988; Gamble, 1994). What is less contestable is that the New Right agenda relied heavily upon a re-emphasis of a certain conception of the British nation as a central object of political debate. Whereas the postwar political consensus was built around a class-based conception of society, the New Right preferred to talk of the family and the nation as the fundamental units of social life. Whereas the political consensus of the postwar period relied upon a 'social contract' to unite otherwise disparate classes, the New Right agenda sought to create unity around a particular conception of national identity. A key dimension of this identity was held to be respect for authority and, so, for the rule of law.

Many of the themes outlined in this Chapter are good exemplars of the New Racism described by Barker in 1981. This form of racism is reminiscent of the cultural racism that enjoyed currency amongst British imperialists in the late nineteenth century at a time when crude biological race thinking was increasingly discredited (Rich, 1990). What distinguished the New Right position in the 1970s was the argument that public concern about immigration, however misinformed, was a real phenomenon and so worthy of recognition by politicians. This effectively suggested that racism was a primordial instinct, based on the fear of strangers, and thereby it ignored the socially-situated dimension of racism. A similar understanding of racism has been advanced by the French *Front Nationale*, and was mentioned in the discussion of the 'race riots' of 1958–59, discussed in Chapter Four. It was this kind of logic that underpinned the Conservatives' commitment to tighten immigration during the late 1970s. The argument was that such a policy had to be pursued because of genuine public concern. The validity of these concerns remained unquestioned because they were held to be an inevitable feature of a multi-ethnic society. This conception of racism as an inherent human trait was important because it meant that politicians could adopt a coded approach whereby they could reinforce fundamentally racist attitudes, because these reflected 'public concern', whilst maintaining that they were actually neutral and not racialised.

Such coded discussions were also evident after the unrest in Tottenham in 1985. Many of the newspaper articles rarely made direct reference to the ethnicity of those involved but talked instead about youths and problems of the inner city. Effectively these kind of terms became metaphorical and were used as a code for 'black people'. Once the newspapers identified 'hundreds of West Indian youths' battling with the police, or suggested that the estate's population was 'mostly black', the debate condemning those involved could be conducted without further explicit reference to their 'race'. This tendency to invoke ideas about 'race' without direct reference to ideas about biology, genetics, or skin-colour reflects the third dimension of the critical realist racialisation problematic described in Chapter One.

The association of the disturbances at Broadwater Farm with those elsewhere also served to draw attention, albeit implicitly, to the ethnicity of the participants. Discussion of Broadwater Farm in conjunction with other areas which witnessed disorder, such as Brixton or Handsworth, is an example of Hall *et al's*, (1978: 329, emphasis in original) comment that 'the specification of certain *venues* ... reactivates earlier and subsequent associations'. Once reference had been made to these localities, the newspapers did not need to draw any further attention to the ethnicity of those they were discussing — the reader already knew that these were black people. Van Dijk (1991) made a similar point about the press coverage of minority ethnic groups when he wrote of the 'script' which underpins such articles. The concept of the 'script' stems from the fact that press stories, necessarily, do not contain every piece of information relating to an event. The story thus relies upon the reader bringing a 'baggage' of their own preconceived understandings and stereotypes of the matter in hand. In any particular instance of public disorder, the media coverage cannot be isolated as though readers had no prior exposure to images from previous coverage. The construction of racialised images in the media over many decades illustrates the second feature of the critical realist model outlined in Chapter One, which stresses the importance of historically generated ideas to understandings of 'race' in any one context. In the case of the disorders at Broadwater Farm, the press coverage and political reaction cannot be isolated from more entrenched media racism which, for years, had identified young black men as criminal and threatening (Hartmann and Husband, 1974; Searle, 1989; van Dijk, 1990).

The predominant explanations following the disorders at Broadwater Farm fitted neatly into the broader ideological project and reinforced the New Right struggle to assert its discourse over others. By blaming the black population, either implicitly or in the coded language of debates about inner cities, more difficult questions for the government, about racism, discrimination, or socio-economic problems, could be avoided. Furthermore, this process of racialisation also reaffirmed the ideological construction of British identity as peaceable, tolerant, and law abiding. In this sense, the denial of the British legacy of disorder reinforced the notion that the blame for the disturbances began and ended with the black community. There was little or nothing that was conceptually new in the debates about minority ethnic groups that followed these events, so the process of racialisation cannot be adequately explained solely in terms of the ideological or economic requirements of Thatcherism. However, the urban unrest at Tottenham in 1985 occurred at a time which created a remarkable opportunity for well-established racialised themes of national identity and public order to combine together.

The critical realist racialisation problematic thus enables a coherent analysis of the debates which followed the disorders at Broadwater Farm in October 1985. The manner in which ideas about 'race' were used to understand the events cannot be understood apart from the particular temporal and spatial circumstances of the unrest. The local reputation of Broadwater Farm was such that disorder was widely anticipated, and national debates and specific developments in other cities also contributed to this expectation.

Historically prevalent notions were also important, though. One example of this is the axiomatic view that 'multi-racial' communities were inherently problematic and difficult to police. This view was evident in the debates outlined in respect of Broadwater Farm and the other case studies reviewed in this study. The diversity of racialised discourse, another feature of the model, was evident in these debates, for example, in the different arguments which were applied to black women compared to black men. This example also illustrates something of the articulation between racialised ideas and other issues of debate, such as gender relations or urban decline.

Notes

1 For example, links were occasionally made between the television news coverage of black people fighting for political and social rights in South Africa and events on Broadwater Farm (see, for example, *Race and Class*, 1987). A similar parallel was also made by Shirley Williams, President of the Social Democratic Party, who claimed that events in Birmingham in October 1985 'brought South Africa to the streets of Handsworth' (ITN, 1985).
2 The most obvious example was the non-fatal shooting by the police of Mrs Cherry Groce, which preceded the Brixton disorders of September 1985.
3 World in Action, 14 October 1985.
4 *Observer*, 13 October, 1985; World in Action, 14 October 1985.
5 Gifford (1986: 105) records contrary accounts.
6 World in Action, 14 October 1985.
7 *Daily Telegraph*, 7 October 1985; the *Economist*, 12 October 1985.
8 *Guardian*, 7 October 1985.
9 *Daily Express*, 7 October 1985.
10 *Daily Mail*, 7 October 1985.
11 *Daily Mirror*, 7 October 1985.
12 The *Daily Mail*, for example, published a story POLICE WILL GET TOUGH: PLASTIC BULLETS AND CS GAS END SOFT LINE on 8 October 1985.
13 *Parliamentary Debates*, vol. 84, col. 30, 21 October 1985.
14 *Daily Telegraph*, 8 October 1985.
15 *Daily Mail*, 8 October 1985.
16 *Daily Telegraph*, 8 October 1985.
17 King and Brearley (1996), Waddington and Critcher (1996), Waddington, (1994), Waddington (1992) and Northam (1988) provide further analysis of changing policing strategies since the early 1980s.
18 *Daily Mail*, 8 October 1985.
19 *Daily Express*, 8 October 1985.
20 *Daily Express*, 8 October 1985.
21 Although Lord Scarman's inquiry into the Brixton disturbances of 1981 was often referred to as though it was his first investigation of such issues, it was actually his fourth report into incidents of disorder in the UK.
22 *Parliamentary Debates*, vol. 84, col. 356, 23 October 1985.
23 *Parliamentary Debates*, vol. 84, col. 355, 23 October 1985.
24 *Daily Telegraph*, 8 October 1985.
25 Gifford (1986: 23) suggests that the ethnic composition of the estate was: white – 49%, Afro-Caribbean – 42%, Indian sub-continent – 3%, Other – 6%.
26 *Daily Mail*, 8 October 1985.
27 *Parliamentary Debates*, vol. 84, col. 33, 21 October 1985.
28 *Parliamentary Debates*, vol. 84, col. 370, 23 October 1985.
29 *Parliamentary Debates*, vol. 84, col. 377, 23 October 1985.
30 *Parliamentary Debates*, vol. 84, col. 376, 23 October 1985.
31 In contrast to Newman's view, the Gifford Inquiry reported (Gifford 1986: 52) that 'we have not heard from anybody [from Broadwater Farm] who is not pro

law and order. We have not heard from anybody who does not want the police to do a job for the community'.

32 *Daily Express*, 7 October 1985.
33 *Daily Mirror*, 8 October 1985.
34 'For example, the *Wood Green and Tottenham Weekly Herald*, reported on 7 April 1978 that 'following a report in the *Weekly Herald* that ... Broadwater Farm estate is a "slum", over 300 signatures have been collected from tenants who are furious about the story'.
35 *Wood Green and Tottenham Weekly Herald*, 30 April 1976.
36 *Wood Green and Tottenham Weekly Herald*, 5 October 1977.
37 *Wood Green and Tottenham Weekly Herald*, 8 September 1983.
38 *Daily Mail*, 8 October 1985.
39 *Sun*, 9 October 1985.
40 For example, on 17 July 1991 the Sun printed a story entitled NEVER FORGET THE MURDEROUS RECORD OF WINSTON SILCOTT which again portrayed him as the criminal mastermind of Broadwater Farm and claimed that his nickname was 'Styx' – after the mythical river of the underworld – because 'cross Styx and you cross to hell'.
41 *Sun*, 28 November 1991.
42 For a discussion of policing and black women see Chigwada (1991).
43 See, for example, Stevens and Willis (1979), Norris, *et al*, (1992), Beck and Rowe (1994), Rowe (1995).
44 See Smith (1994) for a much fuller discussion of this debate than can be offeredhere.
45 *Daily Telegraph*, 7 October 1985.
46 *Daily Mail*, 9 October 1985.
47 *ibid.*
48 For more details about the activities of the Broadwater Farm Youth Association see Gifford (1986: 24-29) and *Race and Class* (1987).
49 See Gifford (1986: 60) and *Race and Class* (1987: 82).
50 During the trial of those accused of the murder of PC Blakelock, Sir Kenneth Newman argued, in a speech to the Society of Conservative Lawyers, that the high levels of unemployment the presence of a large black population at Broadwater Farm led him to wonder whether there is 'any form of social consensus in such places' (quoted in *Race and Class*, 1987: 77).
51 World in Action, 14 October 1985.
52 OECD figures indicate that tax revenue in the UK rose from 32.7 per cent of GDP in 1979 to 37.4 per cent in 1989, Mrs Thatcher's final full year as Prime Minister, Johnson (1991: 292).

6 Conclusion

Introduction

To conclude this study of the racialisation of disorder in Britain it is useful to undertake some comparative analysis of the four case studies. In drawing out various points of congruence and divergence between the events, broader and deeper insights can be gained into the ways in which public disorder has been understood in respect of 'race' and national identity in Britain. Racialised discourse has been used both to explain and marginalise the complex social dynamics which have lurked in the shadows of urban unrest. The analysis is necessarily limited to the four case studies that have been conducted. However, study of these four instances of public disorder does illustrate how certain themes have regularly appeared in the political reactions to such events and how the tendency to argue that Britain is essentially an orderly country has entailed inculpating a racialised 'other'. The racialisation of disorder has been central to the conservative explanation of public disorder, as outlined by Benyon (1987), as it involves the denial, or at least the downplaying, of social explanations of unrest. The more general points about racialisation, identified as the research themes in the Chapter One, are reconsidered in the light of the intervening discussion of the specific case studies.

Much of the discussion in this conclusion focuses on the factors shown in Table 3, which provides a framework for the arguments. It is suggested that the racialisation of disorder in the 1980s and the claim that Britain had been a traditionally orderly nation were complementary processes that both have a long history. In the Table, the lines which surround each cell should be regarded as permeable: they do not represent every facet of the debates which followed each incident of disorder and are interrelated.

Two main themes for discussion are highlighted in the Table — that of the racialisation of each incident of disorder, and those concerning law and order. These themes are highlighted for two main reasons. First, because the arguments that urban disorder was racialised in the 1980s make

Table 3: Law, Order, and the Racialisation of Urban Unrest — four cases

Themes	**Liverpool 1919**	**London 1930s**	**Nottingham and Notting Hill 1958–59**	**Broadwater Farm 1985**
Racialised discourse	naturalised social problems	traditional grievances against Jews were cause of violence	naturalised social problems	'cultural difference' explained the violence
	articulated with gendered discourse	articulated with the notion of a British culture of tolerance	articulated with gendered discourse, criminalisation, and immigration	gendered racialisation
	black people removed from the colonial city			coded discourse articulated with notions of a crisis in law and order
'Law and order' discourse	relatively minor reaction	violence seen as anathema to British social and political traditions	signifier of social malaise	issue of primary concern
	disorder was a result of unsophisticated reaction to 'real' problems	concern over emergence of 'Continental' form of politics	disorder seen as alien to tolerant British tradition	law and order crisis was symptomatic of 'multi-racial' society, and blamed on criminality of black youths
			blamed on white 'riff-raff'	

it instructive to consider the historical antecedents of this process. Whilst it is not suggested that this has occurred in an even manner from 1919 through to 1985, something is revealed about discourse of British identity by the understanding of each incident through the 'prism' of 'race thinking' (Hall, 1978b: 30). The second, related, reason for examining these themes is to challenge the denial of Britain's legacy of public disorder, which became increasingly widespread in the 1980s and relied upon the racialisation of unrest that was highlighted in the final case study in Chapter Five. By locating the genesis of the problem in the black community, perhaps because of dysfunctional families or innate criminality, the argument could be made that the problem was primarily caused by the presence of black people in the inner city. Thus it was implied that the roots of urban unrest were shallow — only extending as far back as 1948 when the disembarkation of 400 or so 'West Indian' migrants from the SS Empire Windrush began the postwar period of African Caribbean immigration into Britain.

In the final part of the Chapter it is argued that both of these factors — racialisation and the law and order discourse — can be more fully understood by drawing upon Cohen's (1988) notion of 'codes of breeding', and Miles' (1993) concept of the 'racialisation of the interior'. It is suggested that these concepts illustrate the manner in which the conservative understanding of public disorder denies any social cause of urban unrest and effectively blames individual actors.

The racialisation of disorder

The discussions of each individual case study have shown that a major theme in explaining the disorder has entailed a racialised understanding of the events. The literature review in Chapter One delineated the concept of racialisation by developing the ideas of some key thinkers (Miles, 1989; Solomos, 1993; Small, 1994). Racialisation is a complex and contradictory process whereby social relations, in this context public disorder, come to be understood by discourse which assumes that humankind can be categorised into discreet 'races', and that these categories possess some explanatory power. As was explained in Chapter One, racialised ideas are used to simplify what are, in fact, fractured and multicausal events. They are also used, on some but not every occasion, effectively to apportion blame and, thereby to exonerate, certain groups of people. The critical realist model indicated that racialised ideas evident in any particular situation are determined by the specific context in question and by prevailing historically established discourse.

Miles (1989: 80) suggested that racialised discourse offers 'a practically adequate way of understanding the world', and although the nature of the process in each case considered here has been different, racialisation performed just such a role in each of the cases of disorder studied in this book. However, although racialised discourse provides a heuristic framework for each instance of disorder, the significance of ideas about 'race' is not the same in every case. This further reflects the first aspect of the critical realist approach developed in Chapter One — which is that racialisation is contingent upon the particular context in which it occurs. The underlying ideas about 'race' in the context of 1919, for example, were relatively axiomatic and a matter of 'common sense'. In the aftermath of Broadwater Farm, by contrast, racialised explanations had become of ideological importance. They were more than just a way of understanding the events themselves — they also explicitly resonated with wider ideological developments. This point draws upon Hall's (1996: 431) interpretation of Gramsci's distinction between common sense and ideology, which is that the former is a disjointed form of traditional wisdom compared to the relative coherence of the latter.

Before these arguments are explored in greater detail, by expanding upon the points listed in the Table 3, a number of broad similarities between the racialised understanding of each event will first be highlighted. There seem to be many areas of congruence in the way in which ideas about 'race' have been used in debates about each instance of disorder, but this took a substantively different form in the case of the 1985 disturbances at Broadwater Farm. This is considered further below, and then the articulation between this discourse and other themes, most notably gender, is examined in order to demonstrate that the specific context of any incident is crucial to a thorough understanding. This reinforces the theoretical point that racialisation cannot be considered as a singular phenomenon but rather should be considered as a partial, contradictory, and differential process (Miles, 1993; Solomos, 1993; Rattansi, 1994). This feature was outlined in the third aspect of the critical realist racialisation problematic developed in Chapter One.

It seems clear that racialised ideas were used in each case of public disorder to rationalise complex social processes, which could have been explained in any number of other ways. For example, there is no reason why the disturbances in Liverpool in 1919 could not have been predominantly interpreted in terms of the socio-economic problems facing the men returning from the war. Of course, it is clear that, on one level, the disorders were primarily defined by those white people on the streets who interpreted their own situation via a racialised prism with immediate and alarming consequence. What is less clear, however, is why politicians, journalists, senior police officers, and civil servants should readily adopt this particular discourse. That there was no significant challenge to this understanding suggests that it was regarded as a matter of self-evident common sense. Even when other factors, such as unemployment, were alluded to, illustrating the way in which racialised discourse articulates with other factors — as the critical realist model indicates — the presence of a distinct racialised group was still considered to be the root cause. That black residents in Liverpool and elsewhere were 'voluntarily repatriated' to the Caribbean, regardless of their country or even continent of origin, indicates a bipolar division between the 'British' and the undifferentiated colonial 'others'.

The reason why racialised explanations were so readily grasped to interpret these disturbances cannot be found solely in terms of the material events themselves. This reflects the theoretical point that 'race' is a socially-constructed concept rather than one based in biological, environmental, or cultural reality. The context of Britain's role as a colonial power, albeit one at the beginning of a long decline, provided a ready framework (Rich, 1994; Young, 1995) in which racialised discourse could be drawn upon to provide an easy understanding of events. This demonstrates one way in which the historical generation of racialised ideas impacts upon understandings of 'race' in any specific situation, a point outlined in the critical realist model.

The analysis in Chapter Three shows that the Jewish community in the East End of London and elsewhere were, to some degree, held responsible by opinion leaders for the hostility directed against them during the mid-1930s. They became the focus of concern and their presence was held to be the problem requiring attention — just as much as those who physically threatened them. In this case, the racialised account which partly blamed the Jews for the hostility they received articulated, as the critical realist model explains, with similar arguments which suggested that other groups involved in the disturbances, both fascist and communist, were adopting 'un-English' or 'Continental' political practices. Holmes (1991: 32-4) illustrated the fallacy of the argument that hostility to Jews was alien to the national character in his brief account of the extent of establishment anti-Semitism in Britain during the first decades of the twentieth century. Indeed, his observation (1991: 33) that 'fascist anti-Semitism is relatively easy to detect, but fascism did not possess a monopoly of anti-Semitic sentiment in the 1930s', must be considered an understatement. It was often claimed that the 'indigenous' national political culture was both tolerant of Jews[1] and naturally resistant to inferior foreign methods. The argument that Britain was sympathetic towards Jewish and other minorities appears to be, on the surface at least, a liberal and open-minded position to adopt.

However, the idea that the presence of such groups necessitates such a response implied, as Goldberg (1993: 7) noted, that they were somehow 'morally repugnant' and therefore required toleration.

The disturbances in Nottingham and Notting Hill in 1958–59 were also racialised. They could have been explained principally in relation to issues such as over-crowded housing, for example, but references to immigration in debates about the disorders indicate that these social problems were understood through a racialised lens. This is especially apparent in that the debates concentrated on 'coloured' immigration, which was in fact relatively minor and so, in numerical terms, could not be sensibly held responsible for the material problems that undoubtedly existed. The 1962 Commonwealth Immigrants Act did not directly arise from these events, but instead the legislation reflected a racialised understanding of immigration which had been established for some years prior to these disturbances. The Act legalised a system of control which had been informally negotiated between Britain and the colonies, but it did not represent a qualitatively new approach to 'coloured' migration to the 'mother country'.

In 1985, racialised arguments were employed to rationalise the events which occurred in Tottenham. Whether or not a majority of the people involved were black, the disorders were racialised in that as this phenotypical factor was invested with *explanatory* power. The issue of concern became not just how to respond to the particular problem of urban unrest but the much broader and culturally-racist consideration of the status of the entire black population in British society. The disorders at Broadwater Farm were racialised by the British media, police officers, backbench MPs, and more senior Ministers, but this was nothing new as it has been a regular feature of discourse surrounding public disorder — as the other case studies in this book indicate. This reflects the importance of historically prevalent ideas to an understanding of racialisation in any particular instance, a point made in the second feature of the critical realist model.

As well as enjoining with other ideological concerns, such as those regarding law and order and the inner city, it is clear that the racialised discourse surrounding the disturbances at Broadwater Farm also articulated strongly with gendered stereotypes of the black community. Evidence of articulation between racialised ideas and other issues of concern has been provided in each of the case studies, and is an important dimension of the critical realist model employed in this study. It was shown in Chapter Five that different arguments were advanced about black men, compared to black women, although analysis of this dimension has generally been absent from discussions of the reactions to the unrest. In particular, the supposed culpability of black women was evident in statements which stereotyped them as domineering matriarchs or emphasised their status as mothers. It was implied in press and other coverage that it was the black women who failed to maintain order on the estate, and so were co-responsible for the unrest even if they did not directly participate.

The racialised discourse surrounding these disturbances became interwoven with the subject of other press concerns such as 'loony left' local authorities, and with a perceived collapse of order in inner cities. This conflation of themes has been noted in the case of other disorders and, in particular, in the way that the names of certain locations become signifiers of urban conflict (Hall *et al*, 1978; Keith, 1993). An example of this can be seen in the description of Broadwater Farm as 'north London's Brixton', an analogy which allowed for a coded discussion of racialised themes, which drew upon prevailing images of crime and disorder amongst the black community in that south London borough. This reflects the second feature of the critical realist model, which is that racialised ideas are not wholly dependent upon specific circumstances but are also influenced by already established discourse. In such a way, comments about the position of black people can be made in an implicit way behind the facade of an apparently 'colour-blind' argument about inner cities, poor relations between 'the community' — a common euphemism for minority ethnic groups — and the police, and related issues.

Once a locality has been explicitly labelled as an area of high black residence a coded account of its problems can be given, which is underpinned by assumptions about 'race'. The local press in Tottenham 'demonised' Broadwater Farm for a period of many years prior to the unrest in 1985. This did not always entail *explicitly* racialised arguments. The coded nature of the racialised debates which followed the disturbances at Broadwater Farm reflected a central feature of the 'new racism' described by Martin Barker (1981). It is a noticeable feature of this case study which was not evident in the earlier cases of disorder. The ideological articulation between these coded discussions of 'race' and themes of law and order and British national identity was a key feature of the debates following the disorders in Tottenham in 1985, and it further illustrates the critical realist model employed in this study .

A key advantage of the critical realist racialisation problematic, developed in Chapter One, and utilised throughout this exanmination of urban unrest, is that it explicitly highlights the articulation between ideas about 'race' and other socially-generated concepts. The nature of the debate about 'race' and class is discussed in Chapter One. One problem of the Marxist approach is that by emphasising the centrality of economic relations the influence of other dimensions remains relatively ignored. One aim of this study has been to illustrate the relations between racialised debates and other discourse, and this is considered further in the following paragraphs.

Gender and sexual relations were common issues in the racialised discourse which followed the unrest in Nottingham and Notting Hill in 1958–59 and at Liverpool in 1919. In both cases, racialisation was mediated through concerns about sexual relations between black men and white women. As discussed in Chapters Three and Five, this effectively inculpated both parties in the origins of the unrest whilst at the same time exonerating the white men who, in each case, appear to have initiated the actual physical attacks. This articulation between racialised and gendered accounts reflects a specific and central theme of discourse surrounding black people, which has been more or less central to the development of 'race thinking' since the emergence of scientific racism in the mid-nineteenth century.[2] The issue of miscegenation was central to the entire debate about whether black and white people were members of the same 'race'. It was suggested that if breeding between blacks and whites was possible, and subsequent generations were fertile, then this would resolve the polygenesist versus monogenesist debate in favour of the latter school (Banton, 1987: chapter 2; Rich, 1990: chapter 6). Young (1995: 9) recorded that:

> The debates about theories of race in the nineteenth century, by settling on the possibility or impossibility of hybridity, focused explicitly on the issue of sexuality and the issue of sexual unions between whites and blacks.

Young also revealed something about the contradictory nature of racialisation when he highlighted the tacit acceptance of sexual relations between white men and black women in the colonies, whilst relations between black men and white women were considered abhorrent and threatening to the colonial hierarchy (Young, 1995: chapter six). Whilst the concerns of the authorities to maintain the 'colour line' (Du Bois, 1982) in the colonies were not evident in 1958–59, since the repatriation of black men to the colonies was no longer a viable option,[3] it is apparent that what Hyam (1990: 203) terms the 'quintessential taboo' of sexual relations between black men and white women was a continuing feature of this period. Indeed, this issue remains an occasional feature of racialised debates as a brief exchange in the letters page of the *Guardian* newspaper illustrated in June 1996. Following an article by the geneticist Professor Steve Jones, correspondence made explicit reference to interbreeding in order to provide ontological justification for biologists' continued use of the term 'race'.[4]

The specificity of racialised discourse and the importance of insisting on the plurality of racisms, a key feature of the critical realist racialisation problematic, are further illustrated by the very different themes which were drawn upon in the debate concerning the position of Jews in Britain during the 1930s. Although they were effectively blamed by many for the racism which was directed against them, this was not explained in the same terms as in the events in 1919 or 1958–59. The issue of sexual relations between Jews and non-Jews was absent from the discussion of the origin of the 'natural' dislike that the latter were held to have towards the former. Instead, other complaints were made which resounded with traditional claims that Jews were manipulative in business, presented some kind of health risk, and were overly occupied with an internationalism that set them apart from 'the British'.[5] As Lebzelter (1978: 93) argued '... Jews were systematically juxtaposed against the British society at large and accused of anti-British behaviour'.

The Jews in the East End of London were effectively racialised following the disorders in the 1930s in a manner which provided a ready explanation of what happened. In this sense, the discourse was functionally similar to those about black people in 1919, 1958–59, and 1985. However, racialisation is not a singular process, it is specific to a particular context, partial and relies upon and revisits a certain historical collection of myths and stereotypes, as the critical realist model explains. Thus, the nature of the argument about Jews was different to other discourse and articulated with different issues. Whereas racialised arguments about black-white relations evolved in terms of a supposed sexual threat, those about Jews revolved around other agendas. Although there were similarities and areas of overlap between them, the multiplicity of *racisms* ought not to be overlooked.

It is clear from the analysis in this study that the racialisation of disorder in the 1980s was not a new phenomenon. The three cases from other periods of the twentieth century demonstrate this point and illustrate how the process of racialisation, whilst similar in the examples considered in this study, is nonetheless contradictory and highly specific to each particular case. The are also similarities and differences in the law and order discourse used in reactions to the four cases of disorder and these receive further comparison and examination in the paragraphs which follow.

The 'law and order' tradition

A key feature of many reactions to the disorders of the 1980s was the assertion that such behaviour was not in keeping with British traditions.

Such views were epitomised by the claim from the Commissioner of the Metropolitan Police, Sir Kenneth Newman, that the events witnessed in Tottenham in 1985 were 'alien' to British streets. The case studies provide two interesting additions to this debate. First, they further demonstrate that the claim that British history has been relatively free of public disorder is a gross simplification. It may be that certain periods have enjoyed relative public tranquillity, but British history contains many examples of serious and sustained disorder (Morton, 1938; Rudé, 1967; Thompson, 1968; Pearson, 1983). The case studies outlined here provide further details of particular incidents of urban unrest during the twentieth century. The second feature of the debate about law and order of note was the insistence, in each case, that the particular events were aberrant, foreign, or unprecedented. Newman's remarks in the mid-1980s were themselves echoes of previous claims, such as that mentioned in Chapter Three, that public disorder was an 'un-British weed', as one MP described the violence surrounding the activities of the BUF in the 1930s.[6] Just as urban unrest was not new in the 1980s, neither was the assertion that such events were unheralded in British history.

This denial was part of a broader process whereby politicians, police officers, and newspaper editors sought to distance themselves and mainstream society from the disorder. As considered further in this Chapter, the denial of the social root of disorders is a key feature of conservative explanations of unrest. Benyon (1993: 9) characterised this position in the following terms:

> The conservative perspective tends to adopt an authoritarian, tough-minded approach, which emphasises discipline, deterrence and punishment. Support for the rule of law, and for the law enforcers, is stressed and permissiveness is rejected.

In some respects there are similarities between this conservative approach and the processes of racialisation analysed in this study. Just as racialisation serves the view that public disorder can be explained by the imputed characteristics of certain groups involved, so the disorder can be marginalised and criticised by suggesting that it is inconsistent with the history and culture of the nation. Such a view offers some semblance of reassurance to the public, in that the threat comes from those who are 'outside' the community, and it also absolves politicians and the political system of responsibility for the events.

As discussed in the conclusion to Chapter Two, the disorders which occurred in Liverpool in 1919 elicited relatively little reaction from the media or politicians, compared to the later cases examined here.

Dunning *et al*, (1987) demonstrated the pervasiveness of different forms of unrest and violence during the interwar years, and this may have meant that specific incidents were regarded as commonplace, and so received little attention. However, the unrest surrounding Mosley's British Union of Fascists a decade and a half later received considerable attention, although this may be explained, in part, by the fact that he had been a significant political actor prior to the events outlined in Chapter Three. Other reasons for the lack of political or media coverage of the 1919 disorders could include technical and logistical features of the press of the time, and the 'competition' for a space that these events faced from other contemporary developments, a feature of the news agenda in any period. Of course, these factors are by no means incompatible, and it is likely that a mixture of them offers the best explanation.

What is interesting, though, is that even the relatively little attention that was paid to the 1919 disorders frequently emphasised that the violence was incompatible with British culture, and had not been witnessed before. Two features of the response to the disorders of 1919 indicated that, fundamentally, it was assumed that urban unrest was anathema to a supposedly 'civilised' British culture. First, the resort to a repatriation scheme which sought to remove the 'problem' from the scene of the conflict effectively blamed the migrant seamen for the violence. In 'repatriating' black migrants to the Caribbean colonies, a racialised conception of cultural difference was evident which suggested that the presence of the 'coloured' men in the ports was responsible for what happened. The second feature of the 'law and order' tradition that was implicit in responses to the disorders can be seen in the condemnation of the white men and women involved in the violence. Cohen's (1988) concept of 'codes of breeding' is useful in understanding this, as it draws upon the cultural imperialism of elite groups who consider those who subscribe to different norms as inferior. In Liverpool in 1919 it can be seen that the normative standards, which were held by politicians, newspaper editors, civil servants, and senior police officers, were that public disorder was deviant from British traditions. The myth of law and order held that those who engaged in civil disturbances, whether they were based in the colonies or the working-class areas of the city, existed outside of the 'imagined community' (Anderson, 1991) of the nation. The relative neglect of these disorders in terms of the amount of press coverage or political debate they generated is apparent when they are contrasted with the other events considered in this study.

The disorders which were associated with the activities of the British Union of Fascists during the mid-1930s attracted much greater concern amongst the media, the police, and politicians than those in Liverpool in 1919. Although the newspapers sometimes represented the events as exciting or even amusing, other evidence indicates that the authorities were seriously concerned about the potential threat of the fascists (Stevenson, 1975; Stevenson and Cook, 1977). The Parliamentary debates about banning political uniforms, for example, and the Home Secretary's instructions to the police to monitor all BUF meetings indicate that they were regarded as both a significant political force and a serious threat to public order.

One way in which opponents of the British Union of Fascists tried to undermine their credibility was by insisting that the violent scenes which frequently accompanied their activities showed that they were adopting un-English 'continental' doctrines. The 'folly of coloured shirts and tin trumpets' was not just that they were doomed to fail, but that they would do so because they were out of step with British respect for law and order. As noted earlier, a key feature of the debate about the presence of Jews in Britain at this time stressed that a supposed British tradition of tolerance would ensure that the anti-Semitism of the British Union of Fascists would not gain wide currency. This notion of tolerance was also cited in connection with the disorder itself, and in many respects it was the leitmotif of the whole response to the events described in Chapter Three. As in the 1980s, politicians in the 1930s frequently claimed that urban unrest was inconsistent with British culture and that, as the Home Secretary argued, the 'grand characteristic' of political life in this country was tolerance. Given this, the British Union of Fascists was distanced from the mainstream in political debate because it transgressed this grand characteristic in two key ways — first, they were anti-Semitic and, second, they adopted a form of street politics held properly to belong on the Continent. In both respects a mythical notion of national character was evident, since Britain has had a considerable history of both anti-Semitism and public disorder. As discussed in Chapter Three, the fascists and anti-fascists alike tried to portray their position as representative of the true British tradition, and some academic accounts of these political movements explain their successes and failures in terms of a national culture which was inhospitable to anti-Semitism (Geiger, 1963). What is clear from the contradictory and multi-faceted developments in the 1930s is that any explanation of complex and varied incidents of public disorder in one-dimensional terms of a national tradition is overly simplistic and misleading.

Many of the themes discussed in respect of the events of 1919 and the mid-1930s, and reactions to them, can also be identified in respect of the disturbances in Nottingham and Notting Hill in 1958–59. Not only were black people who were subjected to racist attacks to some extent blamed in both 1919 and 1958–59, but it is also clear that the involvement of white youths in the events was explained by their deviance from the 'code of breeding' which meant that their social superiors would not engage in such behaviour. The notion that culturally-transmitted social norms explained the disturbances was used to understand the involvement of both the 'West Indian' migrants and the white 'riff raff' responsible for 'nigger hunting' in the late 1950s. This is further demonstrated by the fact that many of the contemporary accounts of the disorders offered in the press and by politicians implicitly or explicitly empathised with the grievances of the white youths, whilst condemning their violent behaviour. As the critical realist model suggests, and as was apparent in 1919, a racialised understanding of the social and material problems of the late 1950s was evident on the streets of Nottingham and Notting Hill, in newspaper offices in Fleet Street, and at the Palace of Westminster. What was condemned was the manifestation of this racism in a violent form — not specifically the racism itself.

Coupled with the comparisons with 'race riots' in the United States, the concern about the engagement of the new youth cultures in urban unrest can be understood as a metaphor for the position of Britain in the postwar world. As suggested in Chapter Four, the attention that the disorders received was disproportionate to the intensity of the violence itself. Malik (1968) may have been correct in his assertion that the 'race riots' were largely a media phenomenon, as explained in Chapter Four, but they featured strongly on the political agenda at least partly because they were understood as harbingers of social change and a foretaste of problems to come. For those who were demanding strict immigration controls this social change was clearly related to the prospect of the continued and growing presence of black people in Britain. There was another aspect to this dimension, though, which bore no relation to the presence of different 'racial' groups, but instead referred to the supposed lawlessness of young people involved in the new youth cultures. The assertion that declining standards of behaviour amongst young people was an important causal factor in the 1958–59 riots also involved the denial of the history of public disorder. It may have been comforting to be reminded that the kind of violence witnessed in Nottingham or Notting Hill was only a recent development, but the notion that public order was more secure in previous eras and amongst earlier generations meant that the events could be more easily rationalised with reference to the recent immigration of black people and the emergence of urban youth cultures. The apparent ubiquity of rosy nostalgia for a more peaceful bygone age is such that Pearson (1983: 48) noted:

> The world may change, but somehow this vocabulary of complaints against declining standards and morals is immunised against change. And the 'golden age' is there once more: glimmering in the distance,

> just out of sight, back over the next hill, twenty years ago, 'before the war'.

Of the cases examined in this book, the reactions to the events at Broadwater Farm in 1985 demonstrated the closest articulation between the discourse of law and order and racialisation. The myth of law and order was reinforced by the assertion that the violence was attributable either to the presence in British cities of the black community, with inferior cultural traditions, or to the emergence of dangerous new youth subcultures which departed from the 'code of breeding' which established a British standard of proper behaviour. As shown at the beginning of this Chapter, the claim that Britain was an intrinsically orderly society could be more easily maintained if the disorder could be blamed on a racialised group of relatively recent migrants. This racialisation of law and order has also occurred in other contexts, most notably in respect of street robbery, drug dealing, and pimping,[7] but images of public disorder provide even more dramatic scenery against which these arguments can be played out.

Ideologically, the primacy of concern about law and order in the 1980s resonated with other key themes of the New Right political project. This further illustrates Pearson's (1983) point about nostalgia — it is presumably the nature of a Conservative Party to hark back to the past. Even when Thatcherism was determined to present itself as a radical transformative project it was trying to undo the experience of the postwar political and economic consensus by reverting back to an older vision of Britain, the exact period of which is hard to ascertain. The politics of nostalgia continued under John Major's premiership, never more so than when he reassured the Conservative Group for Europe in April 1993 that:

> Fifty years from now, Britain will still be the country of long shadows on county grounds, warm beer, invincible green suburbs, dog lovers and — as George Orwell said — old maids bicycling to Holy Communion through the morning mist.[8]

It is not only a return to a less crime-ridden and more orderly past that is being advocated by contemporary Conservatism. For example, it also espouses a revival of old values in education, suggesting that past methods are preferable to more recent 'politically correct' or 'trendy' teaching methods. In the mid-1980s, many of the discussions about public disorder linked events such as those at Broadwater Farm with other political concerns of the New Right. As mentioned in Chapter Five, much media attention was devoted to Bernie Grant and he was held up as an embodiment of 'loony left' local politics, a term which preceded the epithet 'politically correct' as an object of tabloid newspaper venom. Other sections of the press also understood incidents of public disorder in terms of a broader political crisis. Five years before the riots in Tottenham, for example, the *Daily Telegraph* argued that disturbances in the St Paul's district of Bristol were caused by problematic black youths who found themselves 'lost in a society itself demoralised by socialism'.[9]

Other commentators discussed the 'crisis in law and order' in terms of the wider problem of inner-city decline. Such accounts frequently relied upon implicit or explicit racialisation of particular localities. In this way, the perceived urban crisis became interwoven with the 'problem' of the black community, so that an article in the *Daily Mail*[10] warned that 'within ten years London will have totally black pockets' and argued that such a development would pose serious law and order problems. Some accounts drew a series of bipolar contrasts which held 'white' against 'black' and rural against urban, with the first two categories corresponding to the latter two — so that 'white'/rural became counterpoised with 'black'/urban. This point further reflects the importance of space and place to discourse about law and order (Waddington *et al*, 1989; Keith, 1993; Keith, 1996). Two examples highlight this point. First, it is evident in a *Daily Mirror* article of October 1985, cited in Chapter Five, which outlined the deprivation of the Broadwater Farm estate:

> Broadwater Farm ... sounds grand — the name conjures visions of some elegant, idyllic Tory land-owners sprawl in the Cotswolds. It even borders on a lengthy road called Lordship Lane. The reality is a shoddy, graffiti-adorned set of looming unattractive flats that won an architectural prize in the bustling, progressive 1960s. Most of the people who live in the flats are black or brown.[11]

The contrast at the heart of the article worked because of the underlying divergence between the images of a Cotswolds landscape, populated by wealthy white people and the urban cityscape where minority ethnic groups reside. The piece also mocked another subject of New Right criticism, the 1960s. The equation which holds that the rural is somehow more authentically English is evident in Major's 1993 speech which eulogised county cricket grounds rather than urban sprawl.[12] It was also apparent in the memoirs of Mrs Thatcher's former Home Secretary and Deputy Prime Minister, Willie Whitelaw. Whitelaw (1989: 249) recorded how, following the disorders of 1981, he had returned to his country home after a tour of the inner-city areas affected:

> When I got there I found my wife doing her best, as always, to appear encouraging and helpful at stressful moments. But I remember sitting out after supper on a beautiful hot summer evening, looking at the fields and trees of Burnham Beeches. It was a perfect, peaceful English scene. Was it really in the same vicinity as parts of London a few miles away which at that moment were full of troubles? Surely, I thought, this peaceful countryside represents more accurately the character and mood of the vast majority of the British people.

This extract encapsulates the articulation between notions of Englishness, law and order, and the rural landscape. Even the gender roles are more traditional than those discussed in respect of the people of Broadwater Farm. The idea that a particular landscape embodies the character of a people is a romantic one when considered in the context of Burnham Beeches in summer time, but is less appealing when the logic is applied to the 'shoddy, graffiti-adorned set of looming unattractive flats' referred to by the *Daily Mirror*. Goldberg (1993: 207) suggested that such characterisations have pernicious consequences:

> Racialised space positions people in public political space, just as racialised identity circumscribes social space, as they identify the included from the excluded, the (relatively) empowered from those (largely) powerless and peripheral, the enfranchised from the disenfranchised and disinherited.

As well as engaging with other key ideological themes of the New Right, the primacy of the law and order agenda in 1985 served a direct political purpose in that it effectively denied the social context and causes of public disorder. In this way, the conservative interpretation of urban unrest (Benyon, 1987: 30-32) rebuts attempts to link collective crowd behaviour with social factors such as poor housing, unemployment, or racism and disadvantage. The argument that the disorders were a result of 'some basic and ugly facts about human nature', as the Home Secretary, Douglas Hurd, claimed in 1985, was specifically advanced in refusing demands for an official inquiry into the causes of the disturbances. As Benyon (1987: 38) noted Mrs Thatcher repeatedly rejected arguments that disorder in the 1980s was linked to socio-economic disadvantage on the grounds that 'we had much higher unemployment in the 1930s, but we didn't get violence then'. Whatever judgement may be made about connections between unrest and deprivation, the events outlined in Table 1 in Chapter Three indicate that this view of the 1930s is 'a dramatic case of historical amnesia' (Benyon, 1987: 38).

This section has drawn together some of the key features of the law and order discourse that have arisen in each of the four case studies examined here. In each incident it has been shown that a key aspect of these arguments was the claim that Britain has been, on the whole, a peaceable and orderly society, and that the events themselves were considered aberrant from the national political tradition. Whilst a considerable body of literature now exists to demonstrate that public disorder has been a recurring feature of British history for many centuries, less attention has been paid to the fact that the 'historical amnesia' apparent in the 1980s has itself been evident in debates arising from the previous cases analysed in this study.

Given this repeated denial of Britain's experience of disorder it has been shown that a number of other factors have been used to explain the events outlined in previous chapters. These have included the suggestion that incidents of unrest can be attributed, at least in part, to the actions of outside agitators or conspirators who have incited others to engage in violent acts. In addition, arguments have referred to the imputed moral or cultural propensities of those individuals involved in disorder. It was shown in Chapter Four that such perspectives were used to explain the participation of black migrants and white youths in the events in Nottingham and Notting Hill in the late 1950s. Whatever else these views might have achieved in terms of resisting demands for public inquiries or justifying additional powers and resources for the police, they also denied that existing political frameworks were responsible for the disorder in question. In doing this the liberal and radical interpretations of urban unrest, outlined by Benyon (1987), which to different degrees refer to inadequate social and political structures to explain collective violence, are discredited.

A number of similarities and differences have been identified between the four cases studies and it is clear that, in each case, notions of 'race' were used to explain and simplify otherwise complex and diverse events, and that this process was closely linked with complementary arguments that urban unrest was divergent from the national tradition. However, there were also differences in the reactions to each case and this reinforces the argument that incidents of unrest are always contingent on factors that are local and specific in time and space (Keith, 1993).

A further theoretical point is evident from the continuities and differences. The historical, ideological, generation of racialised thought is itself an important determinant of how notions of 'race' will be deployed at any single moment. In this sense, the processes that were evident during the 1980s, and continue to this day, cannot be explained adequately in terms solely of Thatcherism or New Right political reformulation. The historical development of racialised thought in Britain, which is inseparable from the specific experience of the British empire (Rich 1990; Young, 1995), was what made the discourse described in Chapter Five and in this conclusion so resonant in the 1980s. The discussion of other, earlier, events in this book represents a small contribution to ongoing attempts (Solomos, 1993: chapter two; Cohen, 1994) to uncover the archaeology of racialised thought in Britain.

Both the denial or downgrading of the history of disorder in Britain and the concomitant process of racialisation of unrest are central to the conservative interpretation of riots, outlined by Benyon (1987). Both processes seek to distance society from public disorder by establishing cultural or psychological root causes for the events. Such an approach is significant for the politics of law and order in Britain.

Distant disorder?

However salient the specific characteristics of each case studied here may have been, it is clear that more general racialised discourse has offered 'practically adequate' (Miles, 1989) explanations. Ideas about 'race' were more or less common-sensical in the earlier periods, but were more ideologically significant during the 1980s. This distinction follows Hall's (1996: 431) differentiation between common sense and ideology, in that the racialised understanding of events in 1985 was more coherent and resonated more strongly with other ideological developments of the period, a process of articulation central to the racialisation problematic developed in Chapter One. In 1919, racialised ideas were axiomatic and taken-for-granted. Whilst they were pernicious and contributed to a context in which black people were violently assaulted and even killed, they lacked the ideological momentum of the racism evident in 1985. It had to be repeatedly asserted, sometimes by implication, that black people were the law and order problem to be dealt with in 1985. In earlier times, this was assumed to be self-evident, and they could be 'repatriated' to the colonial periphery. Indeed, it did not matter if they came from Sierra Leone, they could be 'repatriated' to Jamaica. By 1985, the cultural context of 'race' had changed greatly alongside Britain's place as a colonial power on the world stage, and the Commonwealth was capable of berating Britain over the government's refusal to endorse sanctions against apartheid South Africa (Young, 1993). In this climate, British 'traditions' of orderliness and toleration — and the memory of former glories — could be rekindled by their distinction from the violence and threat of the racialised black community in Britain's inner cities (Gilroy, 1987).

As well as harking back to former glories, these racialised accounts of disorder also performed another political role. When coupled with a denial of Britain's disorderly past, and the espousal of the idea of British national identity as inherently tolerant and peaceable, the racialised themes of the 1980s and 1990s underpin the conservative perspective on unrest. This view holds that the social and political arrangements in society are intrinsically adequate and functional, and thus disorder is not a result of ineffective social policies and economic distribution, but is instead explicable by the personal characteristics of the participants, the desire for excitement, or greed for loot. The Home Secretary, Douglas Hurd, made this point in 1985 when he referred to factors such as 'the excitement of forming and belonging to a mob [and] the evident excitement of violence' when he dismissed claims that socio-economic factors led to the unrest at Broadwater Farm.[13] The argument that disorder is 'alien' to the British national character and the associated racialisation of disorder both assert that the cause of public disorder is located in the realm of the personal, the cultural, the psychological, or the 'racial'. Links between urban unrest and social conditions are denied.

Cohen (1988: 63-78) provided a useful means to understand the process by which incidents of disorder are distanced from society. Cohen argued that racism developed in Britain both in relation to groups outside the national territory and within it. As Miles (1993) also indicated, the gaze of racialised thought has been both internal and external to European societies. Cohen's (1988: 63) 'codes of breeding' are applied to '... both the indigenous lower orders and ethnic minority settlers' and the same argument which was used to justify the dominion of the white Imperialists over the indigenous populations in the Empire were also used to rationalise the position of the ruling class vis-a-vis 'the masses'. Thus, the cultural inferiority of the 'lower orders' was analogous to the inferiority of the racialised populations in the Empire. Such a discourse was apparent in the response to the disorder in Liverpool, which held that the actions of the white and black people involved were explicable in terms of the cultural inferiority of both groups. The code of breeding held that whilst those in Whitehall or Westminster might share with the unemployed dockers the racialised conception of existing material problems, their superior culture fitted them with the ability to respond in 'more appropriate' manner. This reflects a key dichotomy within the code which privileges the mental over the physical, and links the former with the rational cultured behaviour of elite groups and the latter with the behaviour of the indigenous lower orders or the uncivilised 'races' in the colonies.

Where this approach corresponds with the conservative perspective of law and order, and of crime in general, is in the shared emphasis on the importance of culture. The cultural demarcation of those involved in disorders from the rest of the society is a key means by which the social and economic context of unrest is denied. Not only does this distancing process effectively inculpate those involved, it also reasserts the claim that such events are peripheral to British history, and allows political elites to disassociate themselves from any implication that they may have some responsibility for them, as a result of inadequate social and economic policies.

Finally, it is important to return to the four dimensions of the critical realist racialisation problematic identified in the Chapter One. Each of the dimensions has been evident in the case study chapters and in this conclusion. The four dimensions are:

- ideas about 'race' in any one period cannot be divorced from the specific context in question. They are always contingent and never fixed or preordained, but may be used to understand or interpret real material events;

- nonetheless, racialised debates also draw upon prevailing historical discourse which interact with the specific contexts;

- racialisation is an inconsistent, contradictory, and multi-directional process. It holds mutually incompatible beliefs at once and relies upon diverse myths and stereotypes in regard of different groups. It does not necessarily involve direct reference to genetics, biology, or culture;

- racialised discourse articulates with other themes, of which gendered debates and ideas about 'law and order' are obvious examples.

In concluding this study it is worth reiterating some of the key points about the racialisation of disorder in the 1980s. Chapter One shows that many explanations of this process (Gilroy, 1987; Hall, 1988) have linked it to the broader ideological project of Thatcherism. The long history of racialisation indicates that a full understanding of the debates surrounding disorders such as those at Broadwater Farm in 1985 cannot be gained solely in terms of the New Right project. In addition, cognisance needs to be taken of prevailing historical racialised discourse, as the critical realist model suggests. Whatever the ideological context and impact of the racialisation of events in the 1980s such a process could only be developed because of the resonance of discourse which explain public disorder in terms of inherent 'racial differences'. This point reflects the first two dimensions of the critical realist racialisation problematic and suggests an important qualification to arguments which insist that racialisation is always specific in time and place. Whilst the salience of the particular must not be overlooked, the prevalence of more general discourse about 'race' and law and order is also evident from the case studies considered here.

The interaction of particular and more general discourse is also evinced by the contradictory and varied nature of racialised debates. It has been shown how different groups have been racialised in diverse ways — with specific stereotypes being applied in each case. Not only are separate collections of racialised myths applied to different ethnic groups but contradictions and disparities exist within each circumstance. It has been shown, for example, that 'West Indian' migrants in 1958–59 were held to be a threat to the employment prospects of indigenous workers whilst, at the same time, representing a strain on the public purse as a result of unemployment benefits. This kind of evidence demonstrates the contingent, non-rational, and inconsistent nature of *racisms*. The diversity of racialised discourse and the manner in which it articulates with other issues of concern has been a feature of the discussion of each case study in this text, reflecting the third and fourth aspects of the critical realist model outlined above.

Finally, it is clear that in every case considered in this research racialised themes have articulated with other concerns and fears. This point is related to several aspects of the critical realist problematic. If a full understanding of any particular debate is to be achieved it can only occur through a detailed consideration of the rich and complex web of discourses prevalent in each case. This point, though, does not reduce everything to the particular. Another research project, for example, might consider the symbolism of gender roles in explaining urban unrest in greater detail than has been possible in this study. It is plain that the other discourse with which racialised debates interact are themselves both specifically and historically constituted. This research has begun to uncover the complex role of racialised thought in recent British history. Although this has necessarily been limited to specific debates surrounding public order some interesting themes for further investigation have been identified.

Notes

1 Notwithstanding the 1905 Aliens Act designed to prevent them migrating to Britain, (Solomos, 1993: 43-47).
2 Fryer, (1984: 165-90).
3 Partly because of the continuing need for labour (Phizacklea and Miles, 1980).
4 *Guardian*, 7, 10, and 11 June 1996.
5 An argument reiterated by Skidelsky (1975: 381).
6 *Parliamentary Debates*, vol. 317, col. 1422, 25 November 1936.
7 In July 1995, for example, Sir Paul Condon, Chief Constable of the Metropolitan Police, caused a furore when he claimed in a private letter to community groups that young black men were responsible for the majority of 'muggings'.
8 Cited in the *Guardian*, 24 April 1993.
9 *Daily Telegraph,* 7 April 1980.
10 *Daily Mail*, 9 October 1985.
11 *Daily Mirror*, 8 October 1985.
12 Bale (1994) provides further discussion of the relationship between cricket, rural images, and notions of English national culture.
13 *Parliamentary Debates*, vol. 84, col. 356, 23 October 1985.

Bibliography

Adams, J. (1992), *Tony Benn — A Biography*. London: Macmillan.

Adorno, T., Frenkel-Brunswik, E., Levinson, D. J. and Sanford, R. N. (1950), *The Authoritarian Personality*. New York: Harper and Row.

Allen, W. D. (1933), 'The Fascist Idea in Britain', in *Quarterly Review*, No. 518, October, pp223-238.

Anderson, B. (1991), *Imagined Communities — Reflections on the Origins and Spread of Nationalism*. Revised edition. London: Verso.

Anderson, G.D. (1983), *Fascists, Communists, and the National Government — Civil Liberties in Great Britain, 1931-1937*. Columbia and London: University of Missouri Press.

Bale, J. (1994), *Landscapes of Modern Sport*. Leicester: Leicester University Press.

Balibar, E. (1991), 'Class Racism' in Balibar, E. and Wallerstein, I. (eds), *Race, Nation, Class — Ambiguous Identities*, pp204-216. London: Verso.

Balibar, E. and Wallerstein, I. (eds) (1991), *Race, Nation, Class — Ambiguous Identities*. London: Verso.

Ball. W. and Solomos, J. (eds) (1990), *Race and Local Politics*. London: Macmillan.

Banton, M. (1967), *Race Relations*, New York: Basic Books.

Banton, M. (1987), *Racial Theories*. Cambridge: Cambridge University Press.

Banton, M. (1991), 'The Race Relations Problematic', in *British Journal of Sociology*, Vol. 42, No. 1, pp115-129.

Barker, M. (1981), *The New Racism*. London: Junction Books.

Barker, M. (1990), 'Biology and the New Racism', in Goldberg, D. (ed.) (1990), *Anatomy of Racism*, pp18-37. Minneapolis: University of Minnesota Press.

Bauman, Z. (1988), 'Is There a Postmodern Sociology?', in *Theory, Culture and Society*, Vol. 5, No. 2, pp217-237.

BBC TV (1994), *Forbidden Britain*, 17 November, BBC2. Bristol: Testimony Films.

Beck, A. and Rowe, M. (1994), *The Police and the People of Leicestershire — a Study of the Representation of the Population in Police Data*. Unpublished report for Leicestershire Constabulary. Leicester: Centre for the Study of Public Order.

Benewick, R. (1972), *The Fascist Movement in Britain*. London: The Penguin Press.

Benyon, J. (1987), 'Interpretations of Civil Disorder', in Benyon, J. and Solomos, J. (eds), *The Roots of Urban Unrest*. Oxford: Pergamon Press, pp23-41.

Benyon, J. (ed.) (1984), *Scarman and After — Essays Reflecting on Lord Scarman's Report, the Riots and their Aftermath*. Oxford: Pergamon Press.

Benyon, J. (1993), *Disadvantage, Politics and Disorder — Social Disintegration and Conflict in Contemporary Britain*, Occasional Paper No. 1. Leicester: Centre for the Study of Public Order.

Benyon, J. and Solomos, J. (eds) (1987), *The Roots of Urban Unrest*. Oxford: Pergamon Press.

Boyne, R. and Rattansi, A. (eds) (1990), *Postmodernism and Society*. London: Macmillan.

Brah, A. (1992), 'Difference, Diversity and Differentiation', in Donald, J. and Rattansi, A. (eds), *'Race', Culture and Difference*. London: Sage, pp126-145.

Brewer, R.M. (1993), 'Theorizing Race, Class and Gender — the New Scholarship of Black Feminist Intellectuals and Black Women's Labor', in James, S.M. and Busia, A.P.A. (eds), *Theorizing Black Feminsms — the Visonary Pragmatism of Black Women*. London: Routledge, pp13-43.

Broadwater Farm Youth Association, Broadwater Farm Residents Association, Broadwater Farm Defence Campaign (1987), *Manifesto of the Movement for Civil Rights and Justice*. London: Broadwater Farm Defence Campaign.

Butler, Lord (1971), *The Art of the Possible: the Memoirs of Lord Butler*. London: Hamish Hamilton.

Callinicos, A. (1989), *Against Postmodernism — a Marxist Critique*. Cambridge: Polity.

Campbell, B. (1993), *Goliath — Britain's Dangerous Places*. London: Methuen.

Carr, E. (1961), *What is History?*. London: Macmillan.

Carter, B., Harris, C. and Joshi, S. (1987), 'The 1951-55 Conservative Government and the Racialisation of Black Immigration', *Policy Papers in Ethnic Relations*, No. 11. University of Warwick: Centre for Research in Ethnic Relations.

Carter, T. (1986), *Shattering Illusions — West Indians in British Politics*. London: Lawrence and Wishart.

Cashmore, E. and McLaughlin, E. (eds) (1991), *Out of Order? Policing Black People*. London: Routledge.

Centre for Contemporary Cultural Studies (1982), *The Empire Strikes Back — Race and Racism in '70s Britain*. London: Hutchinson.

Chigwada, R. (1991), 'The Policing of Black Women', in Cashmore, E. and McLaughlin, E. (eds), *Out of Order? Policing Black People*, pp134-150. London: Routledge.

Coates, K. and Silburn, R. (1967), *Poverty, Deprivation and Morale in a Nottingham Community: St. Ann's*. Nottingham University: Department of Adult Education.

Cohen, P. (1988), 'The Perversions of Inheritance: Studies in the Making of Multi-Racist Britain', in Cohen, P. and Bains, H. S. (eds), *Multi-Racist Britain*, pp9-118. Basingstoke: Macmillan Education.

Cohen, P. and Bains, H. S. (eds) (1988), *Multi-Racist Britain*. Basingstoke: Macmillan Education.

Cohen, R. (1994), *Frontiers of Identity — the British and the Others*. London: Longman.

Cohen, S. (1972), *Folk Devils and Moral Panics: the Creation of the Mods and Rockers*. London: MacGibbon and Kee.

Cole, M. (1996), 'Race and Racism', in Payne, M. (ed), *The Dictionary of Cultural and Critical Theory*, pp449-453. Oxford: Blackwell Publishers.

Cole, M. and Hill, D. (1995), 'Games of Despair and Rhetorics of Resistance: Postmodernism, Education, and Reaction', in *British Journal of Sociology of Education*, Vol. 16, No. 2, pp165-182.

Collins, P. Hill (1990), *Black Feminist Thought— Knowledge, Consciousness, and the Politics of Empowerment*. Routledge: New York and London.

Commission for Racial Equality (C.R.E.) (ed) (1978), *Five Views of Multi-Racial Britain*. London: C.R.E.

Cox, O. C. (1971), *Caste, Class, and Race*. New York: Modern Reader Paperbacks.

Crook, S., Pakulski, J., and Waters, M. (1992), *Postmodernization — Change in Advanced Society*. London: Sage.

Cross, C. (1961), *The Fascists in Britain*. London: Barrie and Rockliff.

Cross, M. and Keith, M. (eds) (1993), *Racism, the City and the State*. London: Routledge.

Curtis, L. (1984), *Nothing But the Same Old Story — the Roots of Anti-Irish Racism*. London: Information on Ireland.

Daily Express.

Daily Herald.

Daily Mail.

Daily Telegraph.

Davison, R. B. (1962), *West Indian Migrants — Social and Economic Facts of Migration from the West Indies*. London: Oxford University Press (issued under the auspices of the Institute of Race Relations).

Deakin, N. (1978), 'The Vitality of a Tradition', in Holmes, C. (ed.), *Immigrants and Minorities in British Society*, pp158-174. London: George Allen and Unwin.

Donald, J. and Rattansi, A. (eds) (1992), *'Race', Culture and Difference*. London: Sage.

Dunning, E., Murphy, P., Newburn, T. and Waddington, I. (1987), 'Violent Disorder in Twentieth Century Britain', in Gaskell, G. and Benewick, R. (eds), *The Crowd in Contemporary Britain*, pp19-75. London: Sage.

Durham, M. (1989), 'Women and the British Union of Fascists, 1932-1940', in *Immigrants and Minorities*, Vol. 8, nos. 1 & 2, March, pp3-18.

During, S. (ed.) (1993), *The Cultural Studies Reader*. London: Routledge.

Encounter, December 1958. London: Encounter Ltd.

Fielding, N. (1981), *The National Front*. London: Routledge and Kegan Paul.

Foot, P. (1985), 'Rocky Ride from Fleet Street to Tottenham', in *New Statesman*, 18 October, p15.

Fraser, N. and Nicholson, L. (1988), 'Social Criticism Without Philosophy: An Encounter between Feminism and Postmodernism', in *Theory, Culture, and Society — Explorations in Critical Social Science*, Vol. 5, Nos. 2 and 3, pp373-394.

Fryer, P. (1984), *Staying Power — the History of Black People in Britain*. London: Pluto Press.

Gabriel, J. and Ben-Tovim, G. (1978), 'Marxism and the Conception of Racism', in *Economy and Society*, Vol. 7, No. 2, May, pp118-154.

Gamble, A. (1990), *Britain in Decline — Economic Policy, Political Strategy and the British State*. Third edition. London: Macmillan.

Gamble, A. (1994), *The Free Economy and the Strong State — The Politics of Thatcherism*. Second edition. London: Macmillan.

Garrahan, P. and Stewart, P. (1991), *The Nissan Enigma*. London: Cassell.

Gaskell, G. and Benewick, R. (eds), *The Crowd in Contemporary Britain*. London: Sage.

Geiger, D. M. (1963), *British Fascism as Revealed in the British Union of Fascists' Press*. New York University: Unpublished PhD Thesis.

Giddens, A. (1990), *The Consequences of Modernity*. Cambridge: Polity Press.

Gifford, Lord, (chair) (1986), *The Broadwater Farm Inquiry— Report of the Independent Inquiry into Disturbances of October 1985 at the Broadwater Farm Estate, Tottenham*. Chaired by Lord Gifford, QC. London: Broadwater Farm Inquiry.

Gilbert, N. (1993), 'Research, Theory, and Method', in Gilbert, N. (ed.), *Researching Social Life*, pp18-31. London: Sage.

Gilbert, N. (ed.) (1993), *Researching Social Life*. London: Sage.

Gill, D., Mayor, B. and Blair, M. (eds) (1992), *Racism and Education — Structures and Strategies*. London: Sage Publications.

Gillborn, D. (1995), *Racism and Anti-racism in Real Schools*. Buckingham: Open University Press.

Gilroy, P. (1987), 'The Myth of Black Criminality' in Scraton, P. (ed.), *Law, Order, and the Authoritarian State*, pp107-120. Milton Keynes: Open University Press.

Gilroy, P. (1987), *There 'Ain't No Black in the Union Jack — the Cultural Politics of Race and Nation*. London: Routledge.

Gilroy, P. (1990), 'One Nation Under a Groove: the Politics of "Race" and Racism in Britain', in Goldberg, D. (ed.), *Anatomy of Racism*, pp263-282. Minneapolis: University of Minnesota Press.

Gilroy, P. (1993), *The Black Atlantic — Modernity and Double Consciousness*. London: Verso.

Glass, R. (1960), *The Newcomers*. London: Centre for Urban Studies.

Goldberg, D. (1993), *Racist Culture — Philosophy and the Politics of Meaning*. Oxford: Blackwell Publishers.

Goldberg, D. (ed.) (1990), *Anatomy of Racism*. Minneapolis: University of Minnesota Press.

Guardian.

Hall, S. (1978), 'Racism and Reaction', in C.R.E. (ed.), *Five Views of Multi-Racial Britain*, pp23-35. London: C.R.E.

Hall, S. (1988), *The Hard Road to Renewal — Thatcherism and the Crisis of the Left*. London: Verso.

Hall, S. (1992), 'New Ethnicities' in Donald, J. and Rattansi, A. (eds), *'Race', Culture and Difference*, pp252-259. London: Sage.

Hall, S. (1996), 'Gramsci's Relevance for the Study of Race and Ethnicity', in Morley, D. and Chen, K. H. (eds), *Stuart Hall — Critical Dialogues in Cultural Studies*, pp411-440. London: Routledge.

Hall, S. and Jacques, M. (eds) (1983), *The Politics of Thatcherism*. London: Lawrence and Wishart.

Hall, S., Critcher, C., Jefferson, T., Clarke, J. and Roberts, B. (1978), *Policing the Crisis — Mugging, the State, and Law and Order*. London: Macmillan.

Hamel, J., Dufour, S. and Fortin, D. (1993), *Case Study Methods*. London: Sage.

Hammersley, M. (ed.) (1993), *Social Research — Philosophy, Politics, and Practice*. London: Sage Publications.

Hamnet, C. (1992), 'Running Housing: Housing Policy and the British Housing System', in *Running the Country*, Unit 9, D212 course material, pp3-55. Milton Keynes: The Open University.

Hansard, *Parliamentary Debates*. London: Hansard.

Hartmann, P. and Husband, C. (1974), *Racism and the Mass Media*. London: Poytner-Davis.

Heller, Z. (1991), 'The Silcott Variations', in *The Independent on Sunday*, 28 July, The Sunday Review.

Hibbert, C. (1989), *King Mob — the Story of Lord George Gordon and the Riots of 1780*. New York: Dorset Press.

Hill, H. (1959), 'A Negro in Notting Hill', in *New Statesman*, 9 May, pp635-6.

Hiro, D. (1973), *Black British, White British*. Revised edition. Harmondsworth: Penguin Books.

Holmes, C. (1979), *Anti-Semitism in British Society, 1876-1939*. London: Edward Arnold.

Holmes, C. (1991), *A Tolerant Country? Immigrants, Refugees and Minorities in Britain*. London: Faber and Faber Ltd.

Holmes, C. (ed.) (1978), *Immigrants and Minorities in British Society*. London: George Allen and Unwin.

hooks, b. (1989), *Talking Back: Thinking Feminist, Thinking Black*. Boston: South End Press.

Hyam, R. (1990), *Empire and Sexuality: the British Experience*. Manchester: Manchester University Press.

Hytner, B. (1981), *Report of the Committee of Enquiry Into the Moss Side Disturbances*. Manchester: Greater Manchester Council.

Independent Television News (1985), *News at Ten*, 9 September.

Institute of Race Relations (1989), *Racism and the Press in Thatcher's Britain*. London: Institute of Race Relations.

Interview with Mr Ernest Marke, 29 April 1994, London.

Interview with Mr Jack Shaw, 3 February 1994, London.

Jacobs, J. (1978), *Out of the Ghetto: My Youth in the East End, Communism and Fascism 1913-39*. London: Calverts North Star Press Ltd.

Jacobson, D. (1958), 'After Notting Hill', in *Encounter*, December, p3. London: Encounter Ltd.

Jenkins, R. (1994), 'Re-Thinking Ethnicity: Identity, Categorization, and Power', in *Ethnic and Racial Studies*, Vol. 17, No. 2, April, pp197-223.

Jenkinson, J. (1993), 'The 1919 Riots', in Panayi, P (ed.), *Racial Violence in Britain, 1840-1950*, pp92-111. Leicester: Leicester University Press.

Jessop, B., Bonnett, K., Bromley, S. and Ling, T. (1988), *Thatcherism — A Tale of Two Nations*. Cambridge: Polity Press.

Johnson, C. (1991), *The Economy Under Mrs Thatcher, 1979-1990*. London: Penguin.

Joshua, H. and Wallace, T. (1983), *To Ride the Storm — the 1980 Bristol Riots and the State*. London: Heinemann.

Katznelson, I. (1976), *Black Men, White Cities*. Chicago: University of Chicago Press.

Keeler, C. (1989), *Scandal!* London: Xanadu.

Keith, M. (1993), *Race, Riots, and Policing — Lore and Disorder in a Multi-racist Society*. London: UCL Press.

Keith, M. (1996), 'Old Style Racism, New Style Criminalisation: 'Racial' Subjects and Criminal Justice in the East End of London', in Waddington, D. and Critcher, C. (eds), *Policing Public Order — Theoretical and Practical Issues*. Aldershot: Avebury, pp71-82.

King, M. and Brearley, N. (1996), *Public Order Policing — Contemporary Perspectives on Strategy and Tactics*. Leicester: Perpetuity Press.

Labour Party (1958), *Racial Discrimination — Statement by the Labour Party*. 26 September. London: Labour Party.

Lather, P. (1991), *Getting Smart: Feminist Research and Pedagogy With/in the Postmodern*. New York: Routledge.

Lawrence, E. (1982), 'Just Plain Common Sense: the "Roots" of Racism', in Centre for Contemporary Cultural Studies,*The Empire Strikes Back — Race and Racism in '70s Britain*, pp47-94. London: Hutchinson.

Layton Henry, Z. (1984), *The Politics of Race in Britain*. London: Allen and Unwin.

Lebzelter, G. C. (1978), *Political Anti-Semitism in England 1918-39*. London: Macmillan.

Lewis, D. S. (1987), *Illusions of Grandeur: Mosley, Fascism and British Society, 1931-81*. Manchester: Manchester University Press.

Lloyd, C. (1994), 'Universalism and Difference: The Crisis of Anti-Racism in the UK and France', in Rattansi, A. and Westwood, S. (eds), *Racism, Modernity and Identity On the Western Front*, pp222-244. Cambridge: Polity Press.

Lovibond, S. (1990), 'Feminism and Postmodernism' in Boyne, R. and Rattansi, A. (eds), *Postmodernism and Society*, pp154-186. London: Macmillan.

Lyon, D. (1994), *Postmodernity*. Buckingham: Open University Press.

Lyotard, J.-F. (1984), *The Postmodern Condition*. Manchester: Manchester University Press.

Lyotard, J-F. (1993), 'Defining the Postmodern', in During, S. (ed.), *The Cultural Studies Reader*, pp170-173. London: Routledge.

MacInnes, C. (1959), *Absolute Beginners*. London: MacGibbon and Kee.

Macmillan, H. (1973), *At the End of the Day, 1961-1963*, London: Macmillan.

Maguire, M., Morgan, R. and Reiner, R. (eds) (1994), *The Oxford Handbook of Criminology*. Oxford: Clarendon Press.

Malik, K. (1996), *The Meaning of Race — Race, History and Culture in Western Society*. London: Macmillan.

Malik, M. A. (1968), *From Michael de Freitas to Michael X*. London: Andre Deutsch.

Mallalieu, J. P. W. (1959), 'Background to Trouble', in *New Statesman*, 11 July, pp39-40.

Marke, E. (1975), *Old Man Trouble*. London: Weidenfeld and Nicholson.

Matthews, R. and Young, J. (eds) (1992), *Issues in Realist Criminology*. London: Sage Publications.

May, R. and Cohen, R. (1974), 'The Interaction Between Race and Colonialism: a case Study of the Liverpool Race Riots of 1919' in *Race and Class*, Vol. XVI, No. 2, pp111-126.

McClintock, A. (1995), *Imperial Leather — Race, Gender, and Sexuality in the Colonial Contest*. London: Routledge.

Metropolitan Police (1936), *Report of the Commissioner of Police to the Metropolis*. Cmnd 5457, Vol. 14. London: HMSO.

Metropolitan Police (1986), *Public Order Review: Civil Disturbances, 1981-1985*. London: Metropolitan Police.

Metropolitan Police (1996), *Public Order Offences and Arrests — Statistics Provided by Performance Information Bureau*. Private Correspondence.

Miles, R. (1982), *Racism and Migrant Labour*. London: Routledge.

Miles, R. (1984a), 'Marxism Versus the Sociology of "Race Relations"?', in *Ethnic and Racial Studies*, Vol. 7, No. 2, pp217-237, April.

Miles, R. (1984b), 'The Riots of 1958: Notes on the Ideological Construction of 'Race Relations' as a Political Issue in Britain', in *Immigrants and Minorities*, Vol. 3, No. 3, November, pp252-275.

Miles, R. (1993), *Racism After 'Race Relations'*. London: Routledge.

Morley, D. and Chen, K. H. (eds) (1996), *Stuart Hall — Critical Dialogues in Cultural Studies*. London: Routledge.

Morton, A. L. (1938), *A People's History of England*. London: Gollancz.

Mosley, N. (1983), *Beyond the Pale — Sir Oswald Mosley and Family, 1933-80*. London: Secker and Warburg.

Mullin, J. (1992), 'Putting the Case for Self-Defence', in *The Guardian*, 25 April.

Mullings, M. M. (1984), *The Left and Fascism in the East End of London: 1932-1939*. London: Polytechnic of North London: Unpublished PhD Thesis.

Murdock, G. (1984), 'Reporting the Riots: Images and Impact', in Benyon, J. (ed.), *Scarman and After — Essays Reflecting on Lord Scarman's Report, the Riots and their Aftermath*, pp73-95. Oxford: Pergamon Press.

Murray, N. (1989), 'Anti-Racists and Other Demons' in Institute of Race Relations, *Racism and the Press in Thatcher's Britain*, pp1-19. London: Institute of Race Relations.

New Statesman (1959), 'Knives in Notting Hill', 23 May, p1.

Nicholls, A. J. (1981), 'Germany', in Woolf, S. J. (ed.), *Fascism in Europe*, pp65-91. London: Methuen.

Northam, G. (1988), *Shooting in the Dark — Riot Police in Britain*. London: Faber and Faber.

Norris, P., Fielding, N., Kemp, C. and Fielding, J. (1992), 'Black and Blue: an analysis of the influence of race and being stopped by the police', in *British Journal of Sociology*, vol. 43, no. 2, pp207-224.

Orwell, G. (1968), 'Anti-Semitism in Britain', in Orwell, S. and Angus, I. (eds), *The Collected Essays, Journalism and Letters of George Orwell, Volume III, As I Please, 1943-1945*, pp332-341. London: Secker and Warburg.

Orwell, G. (1982), 'England Your England' in *The Lion and the Unicorn: Socialism and the English Genius*, pp33-70. Harmondsworth: Penguin.

Panayi, P (ed.) (1993), *Racial Violence in Britain, 1840-1950*. Leicester: Leicester University Press.

Pearson, G. (1983), *Hooligan: A History of Respectable Fears*. Basingstoke: Macmillan Education.

Peele, G. and Cook C. (eds) (1975), *The Politics of Reappraisal, 1918-39*. London: The Macmillan Press.

Phizacklea, A. and Miles, R. (1980), *Labour and Racism*. London: Routledge and Kegan Paul.

Pilkington, E. (1988), *Beyond the Mother Country — West Indians and the Notting Hill White Riots*. London: I. B. Tauris & Co. Ltd.

Pilkington, E. (1996), 'Baron Baker: Obituary', in *The Guardian*, 28 August.

Platt, S. (1986), 'The Innocents of Broadwater Estate', in *New Society*, 11 October, pp48-50.

Police Review (1986a), 'Broadwater Farm: "a Planned and Organised Riot"', Vol. 95, No. 4846, 17 January, p105.

Police Review (1986b), 'Senior Officers 'Ignored Riot Warnings'', Vol. 95, No. 4847, 24 January, p165.

Police Review (1986c), 'Broadwater Farm Police Chief Was Wrong, says Met Report', Vol. 96, No. 4869, 4 July, p1382.

Popkess, A. (1960), 'The Racial Disturbances in Nottingham', in *Criminal Law Review*, October, pp673-677.

Pryce, K. (1979), *Endless Pressure — A Study of West Indian Lifestyles in Bristol*. Bristol: University of Bristol.

Public Records Office CAB 23 (15) 24 October 1919, CO 111/621 20 December 1918, 318/349 6 October 1919, 318/352 15 November 1919, 323/848 1 December 1920.

Race and Class (1987), 'Broadwater Farm: 'a Criminal Estate'? — an Interview with Dolly Kiffin', in *Race and Class*, Vol. XXIX, No. 1, Summer, pp77-85.

Ramdin, R. (1987), *The Making of the Black Working Class in Britain*. Aldershot: Gower.

Rattansi, A. and Westwood, S. (eds) (1994), *Racism, Modernity and Identity on the Western Front*. Cambridge: Polity Press.

Rex, J. (1970), *Race Relations in Sociological Theory*. London: Weidenfeld and Nicolson.

Rex, J. (1986), 'The Role of Class Analysis in the Study of Race Relations — a Weberian Perspective', in Rex and Mason (eds), *Theories of Race and Ethnic Relations*. Cambridge: Cambridge University Press.

Rex, J. and Mason, D. (eds) (1986), *Theories of Race and Ethnic Relations*. Cambridge: Cambridge University Press.

Rex, J. and Tomlinson, S. (1979), *Colonial Immigrants in a British City*. London: Routledge and Kegan Paul.

Rich, P. (1990), *Race and Empire in British Politics*. Cambridge: Cambridge University Press.

Rich, P. (1994), *Prospero's Return? Historical Essays on Race, Culture and British Society*. London: Hansib Publication.

Rosaldo, R. (1994), 'Subjectivity in Social Analysis', in Seidman, S. (ed.), *The Postmodern Turn — New Perspectives on Social Theory*. Cambridge: Cambridge University Press, pp171-183.

Rose, D. (1992), *A Climate of Fear — The Murder of PC Keith Blakelock and the Case of the Tottenham Three*. London: Bloomsbury.

Rowe, M. (1995), 'The Police and Stereotypes of Ethnic Minorities', in Shelley, L. and Vigh, J. (eds), *Social Changes, Crime, and the Police*. Reading: Harwood Academic Publishers, pp130-143.

Rowe, M. (1996), 'Urban Disorder and the Racialisation of the Interior', in Waddington, D. and Critcher, C. (eds), *Policing Public Order — Theoretical and Practical Issues*. Aldershot: Avebury, pp83-97.

Rudé, G. (1967), *The Crowd in History*. New York: Wiley.

Sayer, A. (1992), *Method in Social Science — a Realist Approach*. London: Routledge. Second Edition.

Scarman, Lord (1981), *The Brixton Disorders: 10-12 April 1981 — Report of an Inquiry by the Rt Hon Lord Scarman, OBE*. London: HMSO.

Schofield, J. W. (1993), 'Increasing the Generalizability of Qualitative Research', in Hammersley, M. (ed), *Social Research — Philosophy, Politics, and Practice*, pp200-225. London: Sage Publications.

Scraton, P. (ed.) (1987), *Law, Order, and the Authoritarian State*. Milton Keynes: Open University Press.

Searchlight (1995), *When Hate Comes To Town: Community Responses to Racism and Fascism*. London: Searchlight Educational Trust.

Searle, C. (1989), *Your Daily Dose: Racism and the Sun*. London: Campaign for Press and Broadcasting Freedom.

Seidman S. (1994), 'The End of Sociological Theory', in Seidman, S. (ed.), *The Postmodern Turn —New Perspectives on Social Theory*. Cambridge: Cambridge University Press, pp119-139.

Seidman, S. (ed.) (1994), *The Postmodern Turn —New Perspectives on Social Theory*. Cambridge: Cambridge University Press.

Sewell, T. (1985), 'Contradictions That Freeze Black Leadership' in *New Statesman*, 18 October, pp12-13.

Shelley, L. and Vigh, J. (eds) (1995), *Social Changes, Crime, and the Police*. Reading: Harwood Academic Publishers.

Silverman, J. (1986), *The Handsworth/Lozells Riots, 9-11 September 1985: Report of an Inquiry by Mr Julius Silverman*. Birmingham: Birmingham City Council.

Sivanandan, A. (1982), *A Different Hunger*. London: Pluto Press.

Skidelsky, R. (1975), *Oswald Mosley*. London: Macmillan Ltd.

Small, S. (1994), *Racialised Barriers: The Black Experience in the United States and England in the 1980s*. London: Routledge.

Smith, D. (1994), 'Race, Crime, and Criminal Justice', in Maguire, M., Morgan, R. and Reiner, R. (eds), *The Oxford Handbook of Criminology*, pp1041-1117. Oxford: Clarendon Press.

Smithies, B. and Fiddick, P. (1969), *Enoch Powell on Immigration*. London: Sphere Books.

Solomos, J. (1986), 'Varieties of Marxist Conceptions of 'Race', Class and the State: a Critical Analysis', in Rex, J. and Mason, D. (eds), *Theories of Race and Ethnic Relations*, pp84-109. Cambridge: Cambridge University Press.

Solomos, J. (1988), *Black Youth, Racism and the State — The Politics of Ideology and Policy*. Cambridge: Cambridge University Press.

Solomos, J. (1993a), *Race and Racism in Britain*. Second edition. London: Macmillan Press.

Solomos, J. (1993b), 'The Local Politics of Racial Equality: Policy Innovation and the Limits of Reform', in Cross, M. and Keith, M. (eds), *Racism, the City and the State*, pp144-156. London: Routledge.

Solomos, J. and Back, L. (1996), *Racism and Society*. London: Macmillan Press Ltd.

Solomos, J., Findlay, B., Jones, S. and Gilroy, P. (1982), 'The Organic Crisis of British Capitalism and Race: the Experience of the Seventies', in Centre for Contemporary Cultural Studies, *The Empire*

Strikes Back — Race and Racism in '70s Britain, pp9-46. London: Hutchinson.

Stevens, P. and Willis, C. F. (1979), *Race, Crime, and Arrests. Home Office Research Study No. 58*. London: Home Office.

Stevenson, J. (1975), 'The Politics of Violence', in Peele, G. and Cook C. (eds), *The Politics of Reappraisal, 1918-39*, pp146-165. London: The Macmillan Press.

Stevenson, J. and Cook, C. (1977), *The Slump*. London: Quartet Books.

Sun.

Sunday Telegraph.

The Times.

Thomas, R. (1987), 'Looking Forward: The Detroit Experience After the Riots of 1943 and 1967', in Benyon, J. and Solomos, J. (eds), *The Roots of Urban Unrest*, pp141-152. Oxford: Pergamon Press.

Thompson, E. P. (1968), *The Making of the English Working Class*. Harmondsworth: Penguin.

van Dijk, T. (1991), *Racism and the Press*. London: Routledge.

Vieux, S. (1994), 'In the Shadow of Neo-Liberal Racism', in *Race and Class*, Vol. XXXVI, No. 1, pp23-32.

Vindicator (1934), *Fascists at Olympia*. London: Victor Gollancz Ltd.

Waddington, D. (1992), *Contemporary Issues in Public Order — a Comparative and Historical Approach*. London: Routledge.

Waddington, D. and Critcher, C. (eds) (1996), *Policing Public Order — Theoretical and Practical Issues*. Aldershot: Avebury.

Waddington, D., Jones, K. and Critcher, C. (1989), *Flashpoints — Studies in Public Disorder*. London: Routledge.

Waddington, P. A. J. (1994), *Liberty and Order — Public Order Policing in a Capital City*. London: UCL Press.

Werbner, P. (1988), 'Taking and Giving: Working Women and Female Bonds in a Pakistani Immigrant Neighbourhood', in Westwood, S. and Bhachu, P. (eds), *Enterprising Women — Ethnicity, Economy, and Gender Relations*, pp17-26. London: Routledge.

West, C. (1993), 'The New Cultural Politics of Difference' in During, S. (ed.), *The Cultural Studies Reader*, pp203-217. London: Routledge.

Westwood, S. and Bhachu, P. (eds) (1988), *Enterprising Women — Ethnicity, Economy, and Gender Relations*. London: Routledge.

Whitelaw, W. (1989), *The Whitelaw Memoirs*. London: Aurum Press.

Wickenden, J. (1958), *Colour in Britain*. London: Oxford University Press.

Wood Green and Tottenham Weekly Herald.

Woolf, S. J. (ed.) (1981), *Fascism in Europe*. London: Methuen.

World in Action (1985), *The Broadwater Farm Riots*, 14 October.

Wright, N. (1985), 'And This I Saw' in *New Statesman*, 11 October, pp16-17.

Yin, R.K. (1994), *Case Study Research — Design and Methods*. Second edition. London: Sage Publications.

Young, H. (1993), *One of Us — A Biography of Margaret Thatcher*. London: Pan Books.

Young, R. J. C. (1995), *Colonial Desire — Hybridity in Theory, Culture, and Race*. London: Routledge.

Index